MOTOR FLEET

Safety Manual

3rd EDITION

MOTOR FLEET
Safety Manual

A guide to building and maintaining an effective accident control system

3rd EDITION

GREEN CROSS FOR SAFETY ®

National Safety Council

444 North Michigan Avenue
Chicago, Illinois 60611

First Edition © 1966

Second Edition © 1972

Third Edition

International Standard Book Number: 0-87912-047-9

Library of Congress Catalog Card Number: 83-63146

Printed in the United States of America

5C1290 Product No. 221.32

Contents

Appendices

Preface

Today, economic survival for motor fleets is substantially dependent upon the implementation of efficient, cost-effective safety programs. It is to this issue that the third edition of the *Motor Fleet Safety Manual* is directed.

During recent years, closely following the advent of deregulation, the entrance of a number of newly formed fleet organizations has helped to bring about an industry change to a more aggressive business climate. The increased competition and, in many cases, rising costs for labor, parts, and other vital goods and services have caused companies to take a long, hard look at their operations. Making better use of available resources by streamlining systems, extending vehicle life, raising employee productivity, and otherwise reducing expenses has been the answer for those companies able to expand their customer bases and profitability.

Motor fleets, through their safety directors, are, more than ever, concentrating their efforts towards controlling the direct and indirect costs of accidents and injuries. The reduction of these errosive drains on profits is recognized as an urgent goal:

- The losses, even temporarily, of valued employees adversely affects company profits. The costs of compensating workers for disabilities, injuries, and wage loss; hiring and training temporary help; and delays and inconveniences are expenses best estimated by you. Companies showing a genuine concern for the welfare of their employees, through the implementation of safety programs, are those most likely to receive higher degrees of productivity and loyalty in return.
- Even minor accidents result in higher insurance premiums. Sometimes the costs involved, just to protect your operation from false claims settlements, can total many thousands of dollars.
- There is no such thing as "total" insurance coverage. There are costs that must be paid directly out of company funds, or the costs show up indirectly as lowered profits. These are the uninsured (the deductible amounts on insurance policies) costs of repairing vehicles, replacement values of damaged materials and merchandise, payroll hours spent in investigating and cleaning up after an accident, losses due to the interruption of normal business, and, sometimes, the loss of customer loyalty and good will.
- Each fleet vehicle represents a large financial investment. This investment can be protected by implementing accident and injury preven-

tion programs that require high standards of performance from drivers and all other employees.

Accident cost is a controllable business expense. *Motor vehicle accidents can be prevented.* Collision causes are as identifiable as any other business or production mistakes, wastes, and errors. The safety program can do for fleet operations what a preventive maintenance program does for the vehicle; stop potential problems *before* they can cause damage and require costly reparative actions.

The Motor Transportation Division, and its sections, of the National Safety Council is internationally recognized for the development of motor fleet safety programs that do work. Members of this group, through field work and professional experience, have formulated and refined methods that effectively reduce vehicle accidents and resulting personal injuries. This manual distills and presents their collective knowledge. Their continuing support and contributions are greatly appreciated.

The National Safety Council would like to acknowledge and thank three experts in the field of motor fleet safety who offered guidance, and made contributions to this manual, each in his own area of specialty: Frank M. Williams, Fleet Administrator, Liquid Air Corporation, San Francisco, Calif.; Campbell G. Dewey, Manager of Loss Control for Fleet and Safety Services, Alliance of American Insurers, Schaumburg, Ill.; and Walter D. Weiss, Group Director of Safety, Leaseway Transportation Corp., Birmingham, Mich.

Editorial guidance was provided by Frank E. McElroy, director of technical publications of the National Safety Council. Editing and rewriting were handled by Carol North; indexing, by Jan Elliott.

While it is realized that many women are in the workforce, which includes drivers and safety personnel, for ease in reading, the male gender of pronouns is used throughout this book.

Reader comments and suggestions are welcome.

DAN L. CONSALVO, Manager
Motor Transportation Department
National Safety Council

JOSEPH M. KOEBERL, Coordinator
Commercial Vehicle Programs
National Safety Council

Chapter 1

Why Accident Prevention?

People generally agree that it is pretty much a waste of time to worry about events over which they have no control. When the risk of the event affecting them adversely is small enough, it is accepted as being "a part of life." For example, tornados and earthquakes are examples of happenings that cannot yet be prevented; nevertheless, millions of people continue to live in areas where these happenings frequently occur.

On the other hand, deaths due to motor vehicle accidents averaged about 46,000 yearly in the mid 80s. Motor vehicle accidents, far more frequent killers than tornados or earthquakes, *can* be prevented. Analysis shows that accidents always have a cause; and where there is a cause, there is also a cure. The excellent results achieved from safety efforts by participating motor fleets, over the billions of miles they drive, prove that accident prevention is possible and necessary . . . and financially rewarding for the company that works on it. Because prevention of accidents and the resulting injuries is possible, it must be pursued; it saves lives and pain and money. Any program that has these important goals should be encouraged.

Government regulation is a factor in the way every company is run. Powerful federal bureaus can put a firm out of business if it does not effectively control accidents and occupational illnesses. Agencies gain this power because laws give it to them; and these laws are passed when the public perceives a need for control, and pressures its lawmakers in Washington to pass the appropriate legislation.

Tighter regulations, the possibilities of costly litigation, pressures from the general public and labor unions, and increased attention by members of the medical profession have made occupational accident and illness control an issue of national proportions. The future is wide open for individuals entering the field of safety specialization. Companies in the forefront of the safety movement are certain to experience economic and other benefits because of their participation.

Accident prevention gives a valuable competitive edge. Almost all businesses that operate motor vehicles are in competition with other fleet operators, as well as alternate means of transportation. Reducing operating costs by reducing accident and injury costs enables a company to pass that savings on to customers; it will be able to charge less for more efficient service and capture a larger market share. Also, because a financially stable company can afford to institute and maintain satisfactory wage rates and benefit programs for its employees, it will attract and retain better employees.

Finally, but not the least important, every motor fleet has a duty to provide safe transportation for its cargo—whether it be passengers or freight. Both the people and the valuable goods have been entrusted to the carrier to be delivered quickly and *safely* to their destination. Any company that doesn't do this can be forced out of business by its safety-conscious competitors.

Because of all these reasons, plus others discussed later in this chapter, no motor vehicle fleet operator can afford to ignore having a strong accident and injury prevention program.

This book will show *how* and *why* such a program can work to reduce losses in the three main accident areas—motor vehicle accidents, employee injury accidents, and off-the-job accidents.

Employee Injury Statistics

Since 1977, the National Safety Council has ranked forty principal industries in this country according to their occupational injury and illness incidence rates. Although data and rates are available and published for other transportation groups, only the local and long distance trucking industry and local and suburban transit industry are considered and ranked by the Council as principal industries.

Among National Safety Council members who report their experience in the "Award Plan for Recognizing Good Occupational Safety Records," the trucking and transit industries rank in the lowest quartile for both incidence and severity. The on-the-job safety record of the trucking and transit industries is worse than the average for all other private sector industries.

Costs of Accidents

As mentioned earlier, the three main areas of fleet accident are those arising from (*a*) vehicle accidents, (*b*) employee injury accidents, and (*c*) off-the-job accidents.

In the case of passenger carriers, there is a fourth area, namely passenger accidents, not resulting directly from vehicle accidents.

Vehicle accident costs

In a typical fleet, vehicle accidents (especially those involving injury) will usually represent one of the largest dollar losses. Every time a company vehicle moves on or off the premises, it runs the risk of becoming involved in an accident. It matters little whether the vehicle comes from a large or small fleet, from a common or private carrier, whether the vehicle is a passenger car or a semi-trailer truck, or who is driving it. If it becomes involved in an accident, the company may be held liable—the actual cost will depend on many variables over which the company now has little control.

Although a fleet may buy insurance to cover such contingencies, the fact is that in the long run every fleet pays for its own accidents. When an insurance company pays for a vehicle accident, it does so with fleet money (from premiums paid)—and, in addition, the insurance company gets paid for overhead costs, taxes, and its profit.

Insurance, however, is not only a method of distributing accident costs over a period of years (in other words, budgeting to meet them), it is also a means of obtaining expert claims and legal service which serves as a valuable buffer between the fleet owner and claimants. Depending upon the accident experience of the fleet, the insurance premium can be modified. More accident costs mean higher premiums to pay. Therefore, the best way to reduce insurance premiums is to reduce accident experience.

In addition to the insurance premium and other direct costs of vehicle accidents, there are many indirect costs. These result from disruption of service to customers, cargo loss, downtime of damaged vehicles, supervisory time and expense involved in cleaning up after the accident, overtime, and many other expenses. Total indirect costs are often many times the direct costs (see Figure 1-1).

Employee accident costs

Injuries incurred on the job by the company's own employees are another very significant accident cost. Another form of insurance—known as workers' compensation—is designed to compensate an injured worker for *(a)* loss of wages while recovering from an injury or *(b)* any permanent bodily impairment resulting from the injury.

Here again, regardless of the type of insurance carried, the premiums over the years are about in proportion to the fleet's own employee

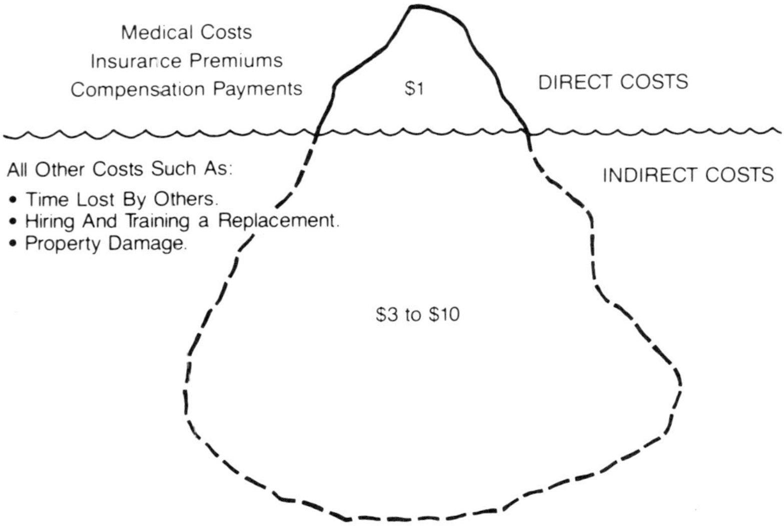

Figure 1-1. *Accident costs can be compared to an iceberg—the more hidden (indirect) costs usually add up to much more than the obvious (direct) costs.*

injury costs, and, in addition, the fleet must pay the indirect costs. Although often difficult to assess in dollars and cents, these indirect costs drain an organization's resources and efficiency.

Examples of this indirect cost drain are:

- Working time lost by other employees leaving their regular jobs to assist the injured employee
- Cost of equipment repairs
- Value of material damaged; or the cost of replacement
- Extra labor and supervisory cost to straighten out or cleanup after the accident
- Cost of investigating and reporting the accident by supervisors and management personnel
- Cost of training replacement workers while the injured person is off.

Off-the-job accidents

Injuries to employees while off the job are another fleet expense that is seldom calculated. The principal cost to the fleet of such accidents is absenteeism—lower productivity through loss of skilled and experienced workers. Another cost is wages paid for nonproductive time or for below-standard work, such as done by a person returning from an injury. If replacement workers must be hired, there are personnel department costs, medical fees, and training costs.

One thing is certain: when accidents are avoided, accident costs are also avoided.

Controllability of Vehicle Accidents

To what extent, then, are accidents controllable? Let's look at examples.

- Some fleets fail to control accidents to such a degree that their insurance rates become several times those of their competitors, or, sometimes, insurance is unobtainable through normal channels. In order to survive, such fleets must institute accident prevention programs to reduce their accident frequency rates and their premiums.
- The Bureau of Motor Carrier Safety reports many fleets allow their level of compliance with its regulations to fall so low that operating rights are in jeopardy. To forestall this, carriers must institute effective safety programs and give safety the priority required. Most fleets admit that if they had started a safety program earlier, they could have saved many dollars. Some single-fleet savings have totaled millions of dollars.
- The National Safety Council's National Fleet Safety Contest records tell the story of many individual fleet improvements. Frequency rates over the past decade have shown substantial reductions. The all-contest rate for 1932 was over 30 reportable accidents per million vehicle miles. Today, this accident rate had been reduced to less than 10.

Controllability of Employee Injuries

As numerous as vehicle accidents are, the most frequent cause of employee injury occurs outside the truck cab or driver seat. These are injuries caused by slips and falls, overexertion, the hazards of cargo handling, or related to the transportation of passengers.

Work injuries, too, can be controlled. Even rudimentary accident prevention efforts can prove successful. For instance, when the construction superintendent of a large building project became alarmed at the rise in accidents, he called his foremen and supervisors together and stated in no uncertain terms that he wanted accidents stopped. He repeated this order several times. Responsibility was placed and records were kept. This alone resulted in a 30 percent reduction in accident frequency during the remainder of the project.

Controllability of Off-the-Job Injuries

Another dimension of accident prevention, off-the-job accident losses, can also be controlled. A decade ago, off-the-job injury rates were at about 10 per million hours of exposure. Today that nationwide figure had been reduced to 6.2. See Chapter 15 for detailed information on setting up an off-the-job safety program.

Human and Social Costs of Accidents

Although cost saving provides strong motivation for management to strive for maximum accident prevention effectiveness, there are higher motivations: management's moral obligations.

- A disabling injury sustained by an employee, or a member of his family, inevitably involves loss to the employee—reduced income while away from work, as well as pain and suffering. If a permanent bodily impairment is involved, the worker must always live with it and no amount of financial compensation will actually offset the loss.
- Deaths and disabling injuries due to accidents have a social cost which affects the worker's family and the whole community. When a family loses a father and wage-earner; it loses many other things as well, including emotional security and many plans for the future.
- Management also has a civic obligation because company vehicles travel on the public streets and highways. Not only should such vehicles be operated so as not to endanger the lives of other highway users and pedestrians, but, in fact, career drivers should set an example of exemplary traffic safety.

Management Rewards

Management will find that although accident prevention techniques must be learned, the time spent in learning and applying them provides personal satisfaction as well as contributes to the welfare and profits of the company.

- Most important is pride in executive skill. Managerial skill has many components: certainly the ability to make accident prevention work and work well is one of them. Stockholders often look at a company's accident rate as an index to the overall efficiency and the skill of the manager. The good executive should be expected to be good at controlling vehicle accident and personal injury loss. As one fleet manager put it, "You can't separate management effectiveness into good and bad. If the top man is good at marketing, but loses money through a poor accident record, he's still a poor manager. A good manager is good all the way around: he includes accident prevention as one of his top responsibilities."

- One of the basic management functions is to provide leadership. For this, the safety program offers many opportunities. Through it, employees see the chief executive in the role of inspirer and persuader, reconciling the interests of the employee and that of the enterprise in an area where mutuality of interest is easy to see. Having accepted management leadership in this role, the average employee will more readily respond to the same leadership in working toward the other goals of the fleet.
- Improved supervision is another fringe benefit of the safety program. Enforcement of safety rules by the supervisor is merely a reflection of the company's interest in the personal welfare of employees. This provides the basis for improved communications between the supervisor and his subordinates whether they be drivers, mechanics, dock workers, or other employees.
- The safe company is a better place to work than the company that pays little attention to safety. A worker not only has less chance to be injured, but he finds his work easier because there is evidence of concern for his dignity and worth. The safety program thus contributes to good morale, company loyalty, and improved job performance.

Safety and Public Relations

Safety is not limited to the operations function of the fleet; it also can contribute to the marketing function. A reputation for safety is a definite asset.

The motor vehicle fleet operates in the public eye and the public expects it to be operated by drivers with high professional ability. Because of this expectation, it is news when a company vehicle has an accident. But it can also be news when the fleet wins an award for safety, or its drivers earn safety awards. (See Appendix A, "Getting Publicity from 'Safe Driver Awards.' ")

Any company would like an attractive billboard in the high-traffic areas of a city—and a well-maintained, politely driven vehicle can provide just that. (See Chapter 12.)

The fleet manager is justified in actively seeking a reputation for excellence in traffic safety, since this is a definite public relations asset for his company and for the industry. It should not be forgotten, however, that in the long run, the public judges a company for what it is rather than what it pretends to be.

Any bid for public recognition for safe operation should be based on sincere effort and on achievement by all members of the fleet.

Chapter 2

Elements of a Fleet Safety Program

What is a fleet safety program? What are its main elements? What and whom does it involve? How is it done, anyway?

The fleet safety program encompasses all that the fleet does systematically to prevent accidents—all accidents: vehicle accidents, work injury accidents, and off-the-job accidents. This chapter touches on the four main elements of a fleet safety program:

1. The setting of standards and policies by management;
2. The selection, training, and supervision of employees;
3. The recording of accidents and injuries, and the progress of the fleet safety program;
4. The encouraging and rewarding of improved performance through awards, recognition, and other interest-sustaining activities.

Later chapters will discuss in greater detail the parts of the program, and its application to fleets.

Management Standards for Leadership

The cornerstone of any company activity— and especially of a safety program—is management. The success of the fleet safety program depends largely upon what the top manager knows about safety, what he thinks and feels about safety, what he expects from the safety program, and how much money, people, and personal participation he will invest in it.

The fleet manager must be convinced that accident prevention is a good investment. A good manager should also know the basics of accident prevention and should know when the fleet is doing well and when it is falling short. He should be willing to provide leadership through face-to-face talks with other top management, supervisors, and employees, and through policy statements and safety policy. He should radiate enthusiasm and determination for safety and, above all, he should set a good example. He should work well with his safety director.

The manager's interest in accident prevention should be sincere because employees can sense this attitude. If it is insincere, it can harm the entire program. A former chief of staff of the United States Army once said, "The leader must be everything that he desires his subordinates to become. Men think as their leaders think, and know unerringly how their leaders think."

Perhaps fleet management has not placed sufficient emphasis on accident and injury prevention because accident problems are not clearly understood. To help clarify this, here is a summary of steps that must be taken by the manager when starting a program:

• Arrange for reports that truly reflect the total costs of accidents and, therefore, the entire scope of the problem. Such reports should reflect not only the direct costs of accidents—such as workers' compensation, fleet insurance, and medical costs—but also reflect at least an estimate of the indirect costs (responsible studies show these average three to ten times the amount of the direct costs). (See Figure 1-1.)

• Publish a clear, easily understood company safety policy. One of the classic policy statements is that of the former Bell Telephone System:

> No job is so important and no service is so urgent—that we cannot take time to perform our work safely.

• A large fleet should give serious consideration to hiring a trained and experienced safety specialist to set up and administer its program. In other cases, a person already in the employ of the company can be designated to take responsibility for the safety program. If he is not already a professional safety specialist, the company employee still can be trained to administer the safety program. There are many opportunities for a person to be trained in accident prevention techniques (discussed later in this chapter). If at all possible, the position of safety director should be full-time employment.

• Make it clear to all levels of supervisory management that (*a*) they have responsibility for preventing vehicle accidents and employee injuries, and (*b*) the safety specialist works with and through them.

• Budget sufficient funds to provide all necessary safety

equipment—for employees, vehicles, and garages and terminals. Supplies such as eye, face, head, and body protective equipment, and all necessary respiratory equipment should be included.

- Budget sufficient funds for training foremen, supervisors, superintendents and nonsupervisory employees in safety practices.
- Budget sufficient funds to cover the cost of holding safety committee meetings, and at least one or two general employee safety meetings annually, the latter to be scheduled for the presentation of safety record awards such as safety cards or certificates or plaques, or for other reasons.
- Budget sufficient resources to permit a reasonable investigation of each accident. Nondisabling injuries may require only a little extra time of a foreman or supervisor. Serious injuries will require an investigation. This is not a responsibility that can be shifted through to an insurance company.
- Budget sufficient funds to permit a periodic safety inspection of the facility, tools, and equipment. The hours spent on such activities are usually considered as "nonproductive time," when it should be called productive time. A realistic cost comparison of the total of all injury prevention costs *vs.* uncontrolled injury costs will show the value of safety programs.
- Provide personal leadership for the program. Plan to personally attend, as often as practical, safety meetings and safety committee meetings to show personal interest in these activities, and to compliment outstanding safety records achieved by departments, divisions, sections, or the company as a whole. Reemphasize management's sincere concern for the personal safety of each and every employee; express personal concern over accidents and injuries by requesting information on causes and corrective actions taken. Encourage group pride in what has been accomplished, and establish increased safety goals.

This list can be adjusted to fit the size of and to cope with the accident experience of each fleet.

The Safety Policy

Management's attitude toward safety should be carefully phrased in the form of a written safety policy made known to all employees, supervisors, and top management. A written policy serves as a checkpoint whenever a conflict arises between safety and expediency, and is useful in enforcement of safety rules by the supervisors. The precise form of the written policy is not important, so long as it is a clear and forceful statement of management's desires.

• A large fleet expressed its belief in safety in a policy manual for all employees:

> Why do we have an accident prevention program? Because we know that money spent to pay for property damage or for personal injuries resulting from accidents is a direct loss to our company—a direct charge against our profits. Accidents can be prevented. Through such prevention, these costs are reduced with a resulting increase in profits. It makes no difference whether the cost is in the form of insurance premiums or direct payment by our company through any of several forms of self-insurance, since in either case it is our money that is spent. Accordingly, it is the policy of the company that every effort be made to prevent accidents. It is the responsibility of all personnel—from top management, through all ranks of employees—to comply with this policy.

• One of the first policy statements on safety was issued in 1906 by Judge Elbert Gary, President of the United States Steel Corporation. It has now become an historic safety document.

> The United States Steel Corporation expects its subsidiary companies to make every effort practicable to prevent injury to its employees. Expenditures necessary for such purposes will be authorized. Nothing which will add to the protection of the workmen should be neglected.

• Sometimes the safety policy can be expressed in a very short form, almost in the nature of a motto. An example is the policy of the former Bell Telephone System, cited earlier, which reads "No job is so important and no service is so urgent—that we cannot take time to perform our work safely." This policy was shown on dashboard decals, desk mottos, posters, and in so many other places throughout the company, that is probable that any former Bell employee could repeat it verbatim if asked.

Assigning Safety Responsibility

Top management has the ultimate responsibility for the safety performance of the fleet, but this responsibility must be extended, as authority is delegated, in a direct line through the operating departments to the drivers and other employees. Management must see to it that this responsibility is fully accepted, and then—in turn—hold supervisors and foremen accountable for the safety performance of their respective departments.

Safety direction

Every supervisor in the organization has a responsibility for accident prevention, but a specific person should be assigned responsibility for directing the accident prevention effort through line management. The job title of this person may be "safety director," "safety manager," or "safety counselor." Whatever the title, it is important that the position be one of responsibility, authority, and respect.

In larger fleets, safety direction will be a full-time assignment. Often additional personnel are needed to carry on departmental and specialized functions. In smaller fleets, safety direction may be a part-time responsibility, carried on in addition to an employee's other duties. Where such an arrangement is necessary, the safety duty portion of the job should be carefully spelled out to make certain that sufficient time is alloted for accident prevention work. The press of other duties should not interfere with necessary accident prevention work. In a very small fleet, the owner or manager can direct the activity. The important point is that one person in the organization should assume this special responsibility.

Duties

The safety director's duties shall be to organize and administer an effective safety program through line management, along the lines described in this manual. He must study all hazards existing in any part of the fleet operation and formulate practical plans for their elimination, control, or for protection against them. His recommendations in this regard are submitted to management for approval, after which they become the official directives of management. (This is why management interest is essential to success.) The safety director should keep records of the fleet's safety performance (see Chapter 4 for details) and keep management informed as to the degree of success of the program.

Considering the amount of money that can be saved through a carefully planned and administered safety program, the selection of a qualified person to direct the program is as important as the selection of a good sales manager, or superintendent of transportation or maintenance. The person selected should—in addition to being knowledgeable and sincerely interested in safety—be a good administrator, a sound technician, and one who can sell ideas equally well to the newest driver or to the boss.

More details are given in the next chapter.

Part-time

When the fleet must assign safety as a part-time job, the person must be capable of learning the basic techniques. There are, unfortunately, few schools or colleges that provide complete courses in fleet safety engineering. The National Committee for Fleet Supervisor Training conducts training programs at locations throughout the country. Their address is 70 Kellogg Center, Michigan State University, East Lansing, Mich. 48824-1022. State trucking associations and private truck groups sometimes conduct their own courses.

More information on these courses may be obtained by writing to:

Motor Transportation Department
National Safety Council
444 North Michigan Avenue
Chicago, Ill. 60611

These courses can provide a new safety director with the fundamentals of the job. He will have to increase his knowledge of accident prevention by reading manuals such as this one, by participating in regional and national motor vehicle safety conferences, and by keeping posted on current information from safety periodicals and trade magazines.

Accident Reports

Every accident prevention program must include (*a*) careful gathering of information about the fleet's accidents and (*b*) the application of this information towards the prevention of future accidents. The accident reporting system also plays an important role in the handling of claims. A good system with good accident reporting discipline is absolutely necessary. More details are given in Chapters 4 and 5.

Program Elements

The purpose of a fleet safety program is to protect employees, prevent and control accidents, increase the effectiveness and reduce the costs of operations. Elements that are vital to a program are described next.

Driver selection

When a new employee is added to the payroll, the selection procedure should be designed to properly evaluate—in terms of safety and loss prevention—the employee's past experience and his potential.

Safety experts generally agree that proper driver selection is so important that it alone can account for at least half of the good results received from a fleet safety program. New drivers are, in general, experienced when hired and, thus, have ingrained (and possibly, bad) driving habits. An unsafe driver if hired may remain to haunt the company for a long time.

It is the responsibility of the safety director to guide employment personnel in determining, insofar as possible, the ability of each prospect to work and drive safely. More details are given in Chapter 8, "Driver Selection and Hiring."

Driver training

Every organization conducts a certain amount of training for new employees: company policy, work rules and conditions, and job essentials. In some cases, this is accomplished by assigning the worker to an experienced employee; in other cases, the supervisor does the training. In larger fleets, training the new employee may involve formalized training. One of the primary functions of the safety program is to make sure that the training program teaches the new employee not only what to do, but how to do it safely. Details in Chapter 9.

Vehicle safety

The safety director should be consulted in the specification, selection, painting, purchase, and maintenance of vehicles. The selection of color or color combinations should be determined with safety in mind. Vehicles must be kept in a safe condition and provided with all needed safety and emergency equipment. Adequate pretrip inspections, en route reporting of difficulties, and procedures for reporting and correcting mechanical defects should be instituted. Details in Chapter 12.

Employee safety

The fleet safety program is not complete unless it concerns itself with the prevention of work injuries to all employees. Drivers, clerical staff, dock help, maintenance employees, outside sales force, and all others should be included in the overall safety programing.

Buildings, grounds, and all other physical facilities should be planned to control accidents. Interiors should be well lighted, heated, and ventilated. The selection of attractive color schemes for interiors not only makes pleasanter places in which to work, but aids safety. Poor housekeeping, especially at garages and terminals, should not be tolerated. Safety thrives in an environment that has the "look of safety," that says "management cares about safety." Not surprisingly, efficiency does too.

The employee safety program should include good injury reporting with corrective follow-up to assure that a repetition of the accident cannot occur. Hazardous job operations should be carefully studied and safe practices devised to safeguard against the hazards. Machine guards and protective clothing should be provided and used wherever needed. All workers must then be trained to follow the safe procedures.

There should also be good supportive communication with injured workers in order to encourage a quick recovery and return to the job.

Off-the-job-safety

The safety program should also include activities designed to encourage workers to practice safety while off the job. In this area there are a number of effective things management can do. A safety program animated with the spirit of "Safety Everywhere—All the Time" reinforces all safety work in the three areas—safe driving, safe work practices, safety off the job. Details in Chapter 15.

Safety supervision

The most important person in any safety program is the *worker's immediate supervisor.* Only this person can truly motivate the employee and carry out an effective program. If, the supervisor isn't motivated or, worse still, belittles the program in front of the workers, the safety effort will fail.

Supervision has two aspects: positive and negative. The first is concerned with motivating workers to a high quality and quantity of output; the negative, with finding and correcting substandard performance.

There is also a safety aspect of supervision: safety standards are to be met in every job. The supervisor's positive task is to inspire total compliance with safety rules (policies) and encourage high safety performance among drivers. Negatively, unsafe acts and conditions must be corrected.

Good safety supervision is animated by top management support. It also depends upon the safety training of supervisors. They must be taught that safety is *a part of* every job, not *apart from* any job. See Chapter 10 for details.

Interest-sustaining activities

Every successful safety program includes activities aimed at arousing employee interest in safety and keeping it at a fairly high pitch. The inexperienced safety director is likely to think that a safety program is solely concerned with this objective. This, of course, is not true. Interest-sustaining activities, while important, cannot have any great impact unless they are actively coordinated with all the other elements that make up a sound safety program.

It is sometimes difficult to separate interest-sustaining activities from some of the other elements such as training, but they can be classified as being of three main types.

- *Informative activities* cover such things as safety meetings, special emphasis campaigns, posters, dash cards, driver letters, bulletins, and magazines. Their function is to provide information as well as to remind and inspire. Their effect is cumulative.
- *Competitive activities* include various contests and awards based on group and individual safety performance. These appeal to the competitive spirit.

"Safe driver" and "safe worker" awards recognize continuing accident- and injury-free performance and also appeal to the pride of the driver or worker.

- *Expressions of management interest.* These include award presentation ceremonies, safety banquets, rallies, carnivals, and special events attended by management for the purpose of expressing personal appreciation for successful group and individual safety efforts. The scale of such events, the care with which they are planned, and the sincerity of management's participation will be regarded by employees as the company's true feeling of the importance of safety.

The objective of all three types of interest-sustaining activities is to keep alive the employee's interest in safety, maintain the desire to achieve a good safety performance record, and still keep an element of fun in the whole thing. See "Maintain interest in accident prevention" in Chapter 7.

Integrating Safety With the Job

Is safety something that is superimposed over the daily functions of the fleet? Or should it be an integral part of the job?

Certainly, every job has an objective, whether it be grinding a valve or driving a vehicle through an intersection. Think of safety as those necessary precautions integral to the job, and which make certain the job objective is achieved without accident or harm.

In the training of employees and supervisors, it might be helpful to separate the safety content of the job from the functional aspect. But in actual performance, any distinction between the two should disappear: safety should blend in with the functional part of doing the job; because the safe way is usually the most efficient.

This integration of safety should apply to the whole safety program. As time goes on, the safety program becomes less and less obtrusive. It is accepted and becomes part of the day-to-day activities of the fleet.

It is to this fundamental objective that this entire Manual is dedicated.

Chapter 3

Safety Direction

Regardless of who administers the fleet loss-control program—whether the boss or a highly skilled specialist—the program must include certain elements that are, to a degree, unique to that company.

When fleet operation is the sole concern of a business (such as a for-hire common carrier), it is often easier to organize the loss-control program. Nevertheless, the fleet operation of any business or agency must contain these basic elements of control if it is to be efficient and successful.

As a guide to organizing the work of safety direction, this chapter explains the elements involved in developing and administering a fleet safety program.

Background Required

It has often been said that a safety director must be a "jack-of-all-trades." In many respects this is so. There are, unfortunately, no jack-of-all-trades finishing schools. Fleet safety directors are often persons of varied backgrounds and education—much of which was not intended to prepare them for the task.

Although the past several decades have produced much information on how to build a workable safety program, unfortunately there are still relatively few academic courses. Perhaps, some day fleet management will endow schools of higher learning to investigate and prepare a thorough academic approach to fleet loss-control management. For the most part, such training now consists of short courses presented by industry safety directors guided through the work of the National Committee for Fleet Supervisor Training at Michigan State University. A few colleges and universities offer degree instruction in elements of loss prevention. Some state trucking associations offer fleet safety courses.

A background that includes either education or work experience in business administration, human relations, traffic, or law enforcement has proved valuable to present-day safety directors. The most successful directors have supplemented this type of background with short courses in management, safety engineering, writing, speaking, and other valuable subjects.

One characteristic that separates *fleet safety* from general safety is the emphasis on the human element; since direct control and supervision is impossible, workers must be influenced and motivated to do their jobs safely. Training or practical experience in human relations will prove invaluable for success.

Typical Job Descriptions

The following two examples of typical job descriptions provide some insight into the many, varied talents needed for effective management of loss-prevention programs.

Job description—I

Position Described: Director of Safety and Personnel

DEPARTMENT: "Operations" (division of)
REPORTS TO: Vice President of Operations
SCOPE: Entire system
FUNCTION: Initiate general and specific safety programming, and oversee operation for compliance with management's safety policies. Provide management and supervision with information and techniques for the prevention of motor vehicle accidents, personal injuries, and fires. Supervise inspections of all locations for potential accident situations including buildings, grounds, vehicles, tools, and work areas. Maintain liaison with outside agencies to bring new knowledge back to improve our present program.

Specific Duties

A. Reports and Recording

- Properly report all accidents to company officers, and state and federal agencies.
- Keep individual accident and injury reports on all employees.
- Analyze this information to recommend corrective action.

• Receive driver violation reports and/or arrest notifications and forward to proper supervisor for action.

• Prepare monthly recap for each terminal, listing persons who had accidents during the month. Classify all reports as to "preventability."* Keep the information up-to-date on terminal bulletin boards.

• Maintain individual safety award (safe driving and no work injury) records. Procure and present awards.

• Prepare required Bureau of Motor Carrier Safety (BMCS) reports of accidents and fires. Also certain reports of same to state agencies. Keep detailed BMCS Accident Register up to date.

• Process any BMCS driver equipment compliance reports arising out of BMCS road inspections.

• Check on trailer interchange policies and techniques to make certain they are in compliance with BMCS Regulations.

• Maintain perpetual inventory of all fire extinguishers and other safety equipment in terminals and in vehicles, and make certain that maintenance schedules are followed and servicing is done.

B. Investigations

• Investigate serious accidents, injuries, and fires. Direct investigations by local supervision of others.

• Investigate all instances of rough handling or reported abuse of equipment.

• Make recommendations to responsible parties of solutions to the problems found.

• Follow up on recommendations, and report any difficulties to management.

C. Personnel Practices

• Personally interview all prospective or new employees after initial screening by the local terminal manager. This is done prior to the individual's being employed or before the 30-day probationary period has expired.

• Review all references returned from previous employers, public agencies, and other sources. Check information and review against original application for accuracy.

• Make decision from this information and notify the manager concerning the desirability of hiring or retaining applicant.

• Periodically check employee files in various terminal locations to review information being retained.

---

*Explained in Chapter 9 under "Defensive driving."

• Personally interview employees to compliment them for unusual or outstanding conduct or service.

• Attend and occasionally chair meetings of local supervisors to determine disciplinary action to be taken.

• Process all physical examination reports.

• Maintain master personnel file in general office.

D. Services

• Prepare and distribute information pertaining to new or revised company safety rules or personnel policies.

• Prepare and distribute information about new or revised laws that relate to drivers or their activities.

• Distribute bulletins and literature furnished by the National Safety Council, American Trucking Associations, and insurance companies.

• Follow up with drivers and supervisors concerning the regular use of safety belts by all drivers.

• Follow up by seeing that drivers and dispatchers fulfill their required hours of service, and that drivers get sufficient rest.

• Order safety equipment.

• Maintain a tickler file and provide notification to terminal personnel to keep drivers' BMCS physical examinations up to date.

• Make available current issues of BMCS Regulations to all interested personnel along with information on handling and transport of dangerous articles.

• Conduct safety meetings with drivers, supervisors, and other employees.

• Counsel employees through personal interviews.

Job description—II

The following job description shows the complex responsibilities required of the position as safety director of a large utility fleet that also operates a community transit fleet.

Position described: Staff safety specialist in prevention of employee injuries

In the motor fleet activity, a staff safety specialist has as his primary responsibility the prevention of mishaps to motor vehicles, passengers, merchandise, and the general public. This is as it should be, for it is in this area that sizeable savings can be made.

If the staff safety specialist must also set up and administer a productive employee injury-prevention program, he will probably do the following:

- Keep informed about employee accident-prevention techniques, including industrial health hazards and their control.
- Teach accident prevention to both employees and supervisors. This will require some classroom instruction and the use of visual aids.
- Help foremen, supervisors, and superintendents set up effective safety programming within their jurisdictions.
- Provide continuous help to foremen, supervisors, superintendents, and safety committee chairmen so that they can direct such activities effectively.
- Encourage the attendance of foremen, supervisors, superintendents, and safety committee chairmen at the annual National Safety Congress, and at regional, state, and local safety conferences and safety equipment exhibitions. This will help to keep them apprised of the latest techniques and safety aids.

If there are other key company personnel who would benefit from attending these safety meetings, the staff safety specialist should arrange for them to attend specific meetings. In conjunction with this, he could include coordinating transportation, hotel reservations, and preconference registrations; preparing a list of suggested conference sessions; and encouraging a daily critique of what was learned that could be put to use. Upon return from safety conferences, he should be prepared to coordinate or file an activity report.

- Develop a schedule of mutually agreeable meeting dates for safety committee meetings in departments, divisions, sections, shops, stations, or garages.
- Attend all company safety committee meetings—in the role of counselor or advisor.
- Attend general safety meetings. At such meetings, the safety specialist will:

  a. Give a brief summary of the safety record of the company. Include any outstanding record of employee hours worked without a disabling injury or extended fleet records.

  b. Assist members of management and others in the presentation of safety awards. Prepare fact sheets to assist in the preparation of remarks to be made by management.

  c. Report the facts concerning an employee injury or motor vehicle accident that is of particular interest and to be discussed at the meeting.

  d. Exhibit and demonstrate new items of safety equipment.

  e. Introduce safety films and provide background information.
- Coordinate use and purchase of safety posters for the safety department, and foremen, supervisors, or safety committee chairmen. Assign responsibility for changing posters no less than semi-monthly.
- Procure safety training materials used, such as motion pictures, video tapes, filmstrips, slides, Safetygraphs, and exhibits.

• Maintain an up-to-date library of safety reference publications, such as the National Safety Council's *Accident Prevention Manual for Industrial Operations,* pertinent selected lists of "Industrial Safety Data Sheets," and other fleet safety resource materials.

• Advocate membership in the National Safety Council. Include purchase of suitable administrative units for key personnel.

• Keep management informed of progress—or lack of it—made in preventing accidents.

• Prepare suggestions to determine hazardous conditions, and/or unsafe acts related to employee injuries or motor vehicle accidents.

• Prepare a guide for the safety inspection of plant and equipment.

• Encourage setting up an effective employee safety suggestion system.

• Prepare articles for publication in a company magazine or newspaper relative to off-the-job accidents. If no company magazine is published, safety information can be prepared in bulletin or memorandum form for distribution to all concerned.

• Prepare publicity concerning safety awards. The articles should emphasize the number of times such awards have been earned, their significance in terms of injuries avoided, and the safety-minded teamwork that was required to earn the awards.

• Prepare material suitable for the company's annual report. Such material could include a photographic reproduction of any safety achievement awards received during the preceding calendar year, and a brief summary of the company's safety record—both motor vehicle and employee.

• Arrange for suitable "Safe Driver" and "Safe Worker" recognition, including certificates and emblems. Provide rules governing the awarding of such forms of recognition.

• Apply for, on behalf of eligible employees, membership in the Wise Owl Club of America (eyesight saved), and the Golden Shoe Club (foot injuries avoided), and other safety award programs.

• Counsel employees on personal accident prevention problems. For example: arrange for the purchase of safety glasses made to the individual's prescription.

• Represent the company with the National Safety Council, state and local safety councils, the American Society of Safety Engineers, industry associations, and other groups.

• Work with the company's casualty insurance carrier.

• Cooperate with the company medical office.

• Coordinate safety matters between the safety department and the training department.

• Provide safety liaison between the safety department and all other departments of the company.

• Assist in selection of first aid equipment. Assist in setting up a replacement material control program to make sure first aid kits are correctly stocked.

- Coordinate the selection of adequate firefighting equipment.
- Supervise and direct the work of safety subordinates.
- Prepare the annual budget for expenses of the safety department and approve such expenditures.
- Stimulate interest in accident prevention work throughout the company. Stimulate pride in group safety achievements at all levels. The safety specialist should handle the paper work necessary to apply for such awards. He will maintain an up-to-date record of employee-hours worked safely by the company and by each subordinate group. He will arrange to display awards, plaques and trophies in a prominent location and to get maximum publicity concerning them.

Participate as much as possible in community safety work. Provide outside leadership as an authority on accident prevention.

From these two job descriptions, we see that safety direction, contrary to popular opinion, is not hit-or-miss. The techniques of loss prevention are sound and are as demanding of academic preparation as any of the other arts, sciences, or professions.

For maximum effectiveness, the techniques of loss prevention must be channeled through line supervision to every element of a business. The time-worn but erroneous statement, "That's the safety director's responsibility," has merely been buck-passing by poorly qualified line supervisors. If accidents occur, the supervisor has failed in his safety responsibilities. Remember the safety of the worker can only be achieved through the actions of his immediate supervisor. To the extent that higher levels of line supervision fail to make the supervisor do this job, they are also responsible for the resulting accidents.

Seven Steps to Safety Direction

To sum up, the job of safety direction includes seven factors. These will shift in importance at various stages in the creation or maintenance of an accident loss-prevention program.

Preparation

The safety director's preparation or qualifying period will consist of formal education, special safety training, and prior pertinent work experience.

Preparation, just as in many professions, is a continuing endeavor. All available means of keeping up-to-date must be used by the safety director. These include the use of professional journals and trade publications, attendance at conferences and seminars, and participation in the activities of various safety organizations.

Preparation may even consist of going back to school to study special subjects required by peculiar conditions or problems.

Preparation will be a continuing consideration of the safety director that will allow him to keep up with changing science, new products and procedures, and new federal and state regulations.

Investigation

In every safety program, new or old, there is a time when the safety director must dig for facts. Whether establishing a new program or revitalizing an on-going program, such investigative work should be thorough. Time spent in checking out a problem is well invested.

Investigation may involve many facets. Most likely it will start by a thorough examination of accident records. Analysis of past accidents (for several years, when available) should indicate high-frequency types, locations, causes, and other factors.

Quite often, accident reports will not reveal all pertinent information. It may be necessary to interview the involved parties and personally examine the evidence.

Plant, building, dock, and similar facilities should be visited, and work methods, job instruction, and routine supervision should be examined.

It is extremely important that key information be logged for future reexamination. (This preliminary work is known as "fact finding.")

Planning

Once armed with information from accident investigation, inspections, and personal interviews, the safety director can analyze the pieces and assemble a suggested plan of action. This may require changing procedures, work habits, supervision, and even a reordering of the plant facilities. The plan is the blueprint to obtain management consent for action, therefore suggestions must be complete, understandable, and practical. The more carefully prepared the plan, the better the prospects for success.

Plans must also be flexible. Not only must they include alternate courses of action, they should be designed to allow revision. Frequently, changes are dictated by new experience, procedures or practices.

At this point, it would pay to verify conclusions by sampling opinions or seeking the advice of other experts. Veterans in the business (within, or outside of the organization if necessary) can help avoid costly mistakes.

Selling

Once convinced that the most effective action has been planned, the safety director must sell management on embarking on such a program. Whether the safety administrator reports to the chief executive of the organization or not, the chief executive must be apprised of the program and concur in the recommendations.

Management can best be sold on supporting a safety program when the case is presented in a factual and businesslike manner. Too often, a safety program is expected to be bought because it's the "right thing or moral obligation" of management to do so. Actually, this is a weak reason for management to support any business function. Any manager worthy of the job will examine any proposal on the basis of its anticipated cost and its relative value to the organization, decide whether to go ahead, then leave the work to subordinates.

The cost of the safety program, or any part of the program, together with the possible dollar return in savings, should therefore be first examined by the safety director and included with proposals presented to management.

Training

In most companies the safety specialist advises top management, executive staff, and line supervision. As an advisor, he must institute training plans, either directly for the classroom or as a guide for management.

Training for accident prevention starts with line supervision. All too often the first-line supervisor is the "forgotten person" in the training effort. As the vital link between management and the employee, the supervisor must be carefully trained if there is to be any measure of success with the employees.

Supervision must be given a chance to examine all new safety procedures and plans. Supervision also must be allowed ample time to question these and to become thoroughly familiar with them. "Sell the supervisor and you sell the employees" is an axiom of successful safety programming.

Not only must the supervisor be kept informed of all programs, but also should be instructed how to best present accident prevention information to his employees, and how to coordinate it with other training the employee may receive.

No matter who does safety training—the line supervisor or a training specialist—it must be checked by the safety administrator. In fact, from a practical viewpoint, such training will probably originate with the safety group.

All job training, job specifications, and work methods should be reviewed by the safety director to make sure no opportunity is lost in incorporating safe methods in the employee instructions.

Indoctrination training is usually done by the training specialist. Sometimes the safety director handles it. The training of drivers, including those employees whose driving is incidental to their regular employment, must be adequately planned and outlined in training procedures.

Follow-up

A safety program, once set into motion, requires periodic follow-up. Such follow-up can be simple or extensive.

- For example, a monthly memo report of accident absentees can be obtained from payroll records to make certain injury or vehicular accident reports are being submitted.
- Safety inspection by committees on a regular schedule will determine how well supervisors comply in such matters as housekeeping, personal protective equipment usage, and vehicle upkeep.

Incomplete accident reports should be returned for additional information. When remedial action is indicated, check for compliance after a reasonable time.

An important part of follow-up is the continuing analysis of accident and injury records in order to make sure that the program is getting results. If it is not, the reasons should be learned as quickly as possible so the program can be modified.

Reporting

Report to management and to all employees at regular intervals. Management reports should be informative and business-like, and prepared using accepted accounting methods. To be accepted and respected, it is very important that reports to management use the formats and organizational divisions familiar to company executives.

Employee reports should emphasize the object lesson. It is not as important, for instance, that employee Bill Smith was involved in an intersection collision as it is that the accident resulted from Smith's failure to approach the intersection carefully.

Reports must be fair and accurate, but they should not soft-pedal individual mistakes. Mistakes can cause accidents; and reading about them is a lot more pleasant than having them. Also, people don't like having their mistakes become known. Some will fear this exposure and work safely even though the threat of traditional discipline would not bother them.

The 'How To' of Safety Direction

So far we have merely indicated the highlights of the job of safety direction. Suggested plans, reports, and procedures that illustrate the principles discussed are included, in this chapter and others, to show the elements of safety direction in action.

The following example of a safety program proposal uses costs figures fairly typical of those for a large over-the-road carrier company operating in the mid 1980s.

Proposal To Start a Safety Program

A. Problem

- Average of 1,500 work days lost through disabling injuries during each of the last three years: Salary loss equivalent to about $180,000 a year (figured at $15.00 an hour).
- Five permanent disabilities in current year, four in previous year, and three in year before that. (Describe these, such as lost eye, finger amputation, 30 percent loss of use of left arm.)
- Two employees killed in motor vehicle accidents. (Tell where and how.)
- Liability insurance premium $6,000 per vehicle, compared with rate of $5,000 per comparable vehicle in competitive operations.
- Workers' compensation premium $11.00 per hundred dollars of payroll, compared with industry rate of $7.00 per hundred.
- Estimated excess costs of accidents compared to industry average—

Liability insurance (100 vehicles @ $1,000 each):	$100,000
Workers' compensation (100 drivers @ $4 per $100 of payroll):	124,800
• Direct Costs	$224,800
• Estimated indirect costs (experts indicate a 10 to 1 ratio, but to be conservative, use a 3 to 1 ratio):	$674,400
TOTAL EXCESS COSTS:	$899,200

B. Cause

- Lack of a system to select, train and supervise workers and drivers.
  EXAMPLE: Selection system does not include check of previous driving experience or examination of driving ability.
- Drivers put to work without indoctrination training.
- Supervisors lack accident prevention know-how.

C. Solution

- Reorganize selection system. Provide one additional

clerk to check references, state vehicle department, and license revocation records. This person will also process and analyze accident reports and records. Salary approximately:	$15,000
• Employ full-time safety specialist to organize and develop loss control program, including training of drivers and key supervisory personnel. Salary approximately:	35,000
• Secretary-clerk in safety department. Salary:	16,000
• Provide facilities for safety department and training program (furniture, office supplies, etc.) Annual charges:	4,000
• Staff time (average 20 hours at $15 an hour per employee for first year:	30,000
• Provide transportation for safety specialist (car purchase or lease and expenses):	10,000
• Outside services, memberships, material:	5,000
TOTAL COSTS OF SAFETY PROGRAM:	$115,000
• Estimated direct dollar reduction in accident losses annually:	224,800
	$109,800
• Estimated savings in indirect losses (same ratio as costs—3 to 1):	674,400
ANTICIPATED NET ANNUAL SAVINGS:	$784,200

NOTE: The above is based on the premise of reaching an industry average within 1 to 2 years. It should be explained that better-than-average results could be obtained over a longer period.

In actual practice, this proposal would be more detailed and would include a step-by-step description of the program including suggested training materials, training schedules, and other details. Also, the cost figures used will vary widely in different types of operations.

Safety Budgeting

Progressive fleet organizations have established budget costs relating to accidents. They hold the departmental or divisional manager just as responsible for excesses in this budget as they would for other items (such as salary, production costs, and maintenance). When accident losses are an integral part of a supervisor's or manager's operating efficiency (on which he is rated for salary increases and promotion), it is more difficult to shift the responsibility to a safety director or other "scapegoat."

Do not overlook any costs

In order to provide accurate records for management's use and guidance, it is necessary to set up cost controls that provide sufficient information to make valid comparisons. It is very easy to overlook pertinent items or to purposely omit costs that might be disguised in some other element of operating cost.

Many costs are revealed in a superficial examination of the records. Among these are salaries and wages lost to accident absenteeism. Doctor, hospital and other fees are also easily identified. The not-so-easy-to-see costs can be considerable, however, and often involve judgment and "guesstimates."

For example, when a capable employee is replaced by a novice (even temporarily), there is usually an appreciable difference in work output attributed to the accident as a loss. Lost time due to other employees stopping to help, watch, or discuss an accident is a factor difficult to measure.

For the injured worker, fringe benefits, such as family medical insurance or coverage, paid holidays, vacation, and pension contributions, will probably continue while he is off. This can be a sizeable expense to the employer.

All supervisory time spent in reporting and investigating an accident, as well as time spent in cleanup, and in ordering and obtaining replacement or repair of machinery, equipment, or vehicles, should be charged against the accident that triggered the series of events in the first place.

It is rare, however, that an organization will examine every accident (vehicular or occupational) in terms of its absolute cost. To do so would require an elaborate and costly investigative setup. It is easier to spot check periodically to determine fluctuations in the total costs of typical incidents. These costs, including hidden costs, can then be applied (by ratio) to the complete accident record.

Accident Prevention

Whether it be fleet loss control or any other managerial program, observing certain fundamentals will ensure success.

Set standards

Regardless of the activity—driving, production, service, or whatever—management must establish performance standards. Production standards must include work behavior as well as quality control. The most common standard used to judge professional driving performance is the ability to avoid *preventable* accidents (as defined in Chapter 5 under "The Post-accident interview," and in Chapter 9 under "Defensive driving.") Other standards can be used.

The standard, once adopted, must be thoroughly explained to the employee. It must be upheld and administered both strictly and fairly. (Also see discussion in Chapter 10, "Driver Supervision.")

Train employees

Once the standard has been announced, every effort must be made to train the employee to achieve it. Remember that a standard, by itself, cannot prevent accidents—it is but a goal to achieve through constant training and supervision. Training must be adequate.

In the training effort, there should be safeguards to prevent preachment of rules as a substitute for job instruction. Rules as they exist must be obeyed out of respect and understanding. Principles must be given for guidance. Good driving is an art. It requires intelligence, not blind obedience.

Supervise and check

A regular system of checking driving performance includes adequate and factual accident reporting. Without such a system, it is difficult and often impossible to ascertain training effectiveness and compliance to the standard. However, all drivers must be checked occasionally without waiting for accidents to show up the hazardous employee.

Although the driver is often considered to be a company's most "unsupervised" employee, it is not impossible to check his performance. Usually only those drivers who are known to stretch the rules are checked extensively. Follow-up remedial and rehabilitation efforts should be extensive at the outset until there is evidence of satisfactory performance.

Spot checks for all drivers are occasionally needed to disclose "soft spots" in their performance, and to help in training and retraining.

Motivate

Because he cannot be personally supervised every minute, the professional driver must be motivated to police his own driving. This means that he must understand what is correct performance. Many drivers learned from a friend and may not know the correct way to drive safely. Once they are trained in technique, drivers can then be motivated through pride of workmanship, skill, or other factors, to do a superior job.

To avoid any possible feelings, by the employee, of harassment or discrimination it is important that motivational methods and disciplinary actions be in accordance with established and *published* company policies.

The driver with a long accident-free record frequently is lulled into a false sense of security and may develop careless safety habits. Help to overcome this problem through the use of incentive programs, periodic retraining, and consistent demonstrations of the importance of safety by the fleet's specialist. These shall be discussed later.

Chapter 4

Organizing Motor Vehicle Fleet Accident Data

Accidents are caused. This is the first axiom of accident prevention. *Accidents can be prevented,* then, by removing or controlling their causes. A large part of a fleet safety director's job is (*a*) identifying accident causes and (*b*) recommending ways to remove them or to guard against them by protecting the employee.

Many facts about accident causes are found in published motor vehicle accident statistics, in summaries and reports of the Bureau of Motor Carrier Safety, in records of highway and roadway agencies, and in special studies released by insurance companies, trade associations, and the National Safety Council. Use these as background when planning a safety program and accident-reporting system.

However valuable these reports may be, they can never reveal the exact distribution of accident causes in any one particular fleet. General reports cannot pinpoint specific accident causes or tell their relative importance. To get this information about accident causes—essential to any effective accident prevention program—a system of accident reporting, recording, and analysis must be carefully planned and intelligently used. This chapter analyzes accident causes, then tells how to organize accident-causing factors, and operate a system that will pinpoint causes and provide effective follow-up.

How Accidents Are Caused

When a vehicle collides with a person, another vehicle, or any other object, this event is caused. Moreover, the accident usually results from several factors working together: the result of a chain of causal events.

This is illustrated in the following example.

Bill Jones was dispatched to transport a load of freight to a distant city. He recognized that his tractor was hooked up to a trailer that was different from those he usually pulled. Bill noticed that this particular trailer had an unusually high center of gravity. The entire capacity of the trailer—from front to rear and from bottom to top—was loaded with knocked-down cardboard cartons. This elevated the center of gravity still further.

A rookie driver was assigned to Bill for the trip.

Seeking to impress this new driver, Bill negotiated a right turn faster than he should. To make matters worse, the road was crowned. The combination of speed, load, crown of road, and centrifugal force worked together to create an accident situation. The accident was triggered by Bill's desire to "show off a little."

If this accident must be attributed to one factor, "Speed too fast for conditions" is usually recorded. Unfortunately, "speed too fast for conditions" by itself would not be a good subject on which to base corrective action unless the complete story were told. The company's analysis of Bill's accident could trigger many changes, other than reducing speed. Some of these might be:

- Use of a low center of gravity trailer for the type of material hauled.
- Rerouting to avoid the section of high-crowned road.
- Establish a company rule to lower speeds at right or left turns.
- Refresher training of driver who breaks in new drivers.
- Vehicle or trailer design modification.

Organizing an Accident Record System

Accident prevention lists the factors that could cause an accident and then compensates for them by planning ahead. Although accidents usually result from several contributing factors, accident prevention activity is based on the premise that removal of one or more factors, in any accident situation, may have prevented the accident. Therefore, the primary purpose of an accident reporting, recording, and analysis system is to determine *all* the factors contributing to the accident, in order to eliminate as many of these causes as possible.

The organization and operation of such a system must include: (*a*) gathering accident data; (*b*) analyzing the data; (*c*) using the data to develop countermeasures; and (*d*) using the data in the administration of an accident prevention program.

Gathering Accident Data

A carefully planned system for gathering all pertinent information about fleet accidents is essential not only for the determination and elimination of accident causes, but also for these additional reasons:

- *Court action.* There is always the possibility that the employee-operator of the vehicle will be cited to traffic court or indicted in a criminal action as a result of an accident. The thoroughness with which accident data has been gathered is, in many cases, the balance upon which any traffic court or criminal court action may hinge. Complete data is the first line of defense in a civil court action. Many cases have been won because of the thoroughness with which a company obtained the facts about the particular accident.
- *Places responsibility where it rightfully belongs.* When gathering information, never be concerned with "white-washing" the actions of the company driver. Any attempt at this nullifies the whole value of the process. Only by knowing the full facts, whether favorable or unfavorable to the company, can the necessary corrective action be taken.
- *Labor relations.* The vehicle operator involved in an accident should know that his safety record, as well as his security of employment, will be treated fairly. Where discharge is indicated, labor unions will concur in such action only upon the presentation of factual evidence.

The accident report form

The basic tool of an accident data gathering system—the accident report form—blueprints the information-gathering process. It lists the types of facts to be gathered for every accident in order to be available later for the analysis of the accident. Because it serves as a checklist for the person completing the form to assure that all the essential information is obtained, it should provide for accurate recording of important information about the accident, yet it should be as easy as possible to complete and to analyze. The person reading the report should be able to visualize exactly how the accident happened.

The National Safety Council's Form Vehicle 1 "Motor Transportation Driver's Accident Report" is suggested as a guide to an adequate report form. Various insurance company report forms may also prove adequate for company accident prevention administration. Accidents reported to local or federal authorities will probably require the use of specific governmental forms. Most companies have special forms too. Any form may be modified to meet the needs of a particular organiza-

(*Text continues on page 42.*)

National Safety Council
Form Vehicle 1

MOTOR TRANSPORTATION
DRIVER'S ACCIDENT REPORT

READ CAREFULLY - FILL OUT COMPLETELY

(For office use)
FILE NO. ....
☐ PREVENTABLE
☐ NOT PREVENTABLE
☐ REPORTABLE
☐ NOT REPORTABLE

COMPANY ....

DIVISION .... ADDRESS ....

TIME

Date of Accident .... ,19 .... Day of Week .... Hour .... a.m. p.m.

LOCATION

☐ CITY
☐ SUBURBAN
☐ RURAL

PLACE WHERE ACCIDENT OCCURRED:
County .... City, town or township ....

If accident was outside city limits indicate distance from nearest town. Use two distances and two directions if necessary.

.... miles .... *north - south* / .... miles .... *east - west* of ☐ limits of / ☐ center of .... *City or Town*

ROAD ON WHICH ACCIDENT OCCURRED: ....
Give name of street or highway number (U.S. or State)

☐ AT ITS INTERSECTION WITH: ....
Name of intersecting street or highway number

OR

☐ NOT AT INTERSECTION .... feet .... *north - south* / .... feet .... *east - west* of ....
(Check and complete one)
Show nearest intersecting street or highway, house number, curve, bridge, railroad crossing, alley, driveway, culvert, milepost, underpass, numbered telephone pole, or other identifying landmark. Show exact distance, using two directions and two distances if necessary.

ACCIDENT INVOLVED

MOVING
☐ Another com'l vehicle
☐ Passenger car
☐ Pedestrian
☐ .... *(Specify other)*

FIXED
☐ Building or fixture
☐ Parked vehicle
☐ .... *(Specify other)*

TYPE

☐ HEAD ON ☐ REAR END ☐ FRONT END ☐ NON COLLISION (Describe)
☐ SIDESWIPE ☐ OTHER (Describe) ....
☐ RIGHT ANGLE

DRIV

COMPANY VEHICLE NO 1		VEHICLE NO 2
....	← Driver's Name →	....
....	← Address →	....
☐ Chauffeur	← City And State →	.... ☐ Chauffeur
☐ Operator	← Driver's License →	.... ☐ Operator
☐ Beginner Age .... Sex	Driving experience .... yrs	Age .... Sex .... ☐ Beginner

ERS

Date employed .... month .... day .... year

Hours on duty since last period of 8 consecutive hours off duty ....

Actual hours of driving since last period of 8 consecutive hours off duty ....

Condition of Driver ....

(If vehicle driven by other than owner)

Owner's name ....

Address ....

City and State ....

VEHICLES

COMPANY VEHICLE NO 1		VEHICLE NO 2
....	← Type of Vehicle →	....
Make .... Year .... No.		Make .... Year .... No. ....
State .... No.	← License →	State .... No. ....
....	← Vehicle Damage →	....
....	← Other Damage → (cargo loss etc.)	....

INJURED

	Name	Address	Age	Sex	Describe Injuries
Driver vehicle 1					
Driver vehicle 2					
Passenger veh. ...					
Passenger veh.					
Pedestrian					
Pedestrian					
Others					

WITNESSES

Name	Address	Remarks
Company representative		
Insurance representative		
Police	Badge no	Station

Figure 4-1a. *"Motor Transportation Driver's Accident Report," Council Form Vehicle 1—front page.*

MOVEMENT

VEHICLES 1	2	
☐	☐	Going straight ahead
☐	☐	Passing
☐	☐	Being passed
☐	☐	Turning
☐	☐	Pulling from curb or loading zone
☐	☐	Pulling into curb or loading zone
☐	☐	Backing
☐	☐	Stopped in traffic lane
☐	☐	______ (Specify other)

PEDESTRIAN

- ☐ Walking with traffic
- ☐ Walking against traffic
- ☐ Coming from behind parked vehicle
- ☐ Crossing at intersection
- ☐ Crossing not at intersection
- ☐ Alighting from a vehicle
- ☐ Working in roadway
- ☐ Playing in roadway
- ☐ ______ (Specify other)

PASSENGER

- ☐ Boarding vehicle
- ☐ Alighting from vehicle
- ☐ Caught in doors
- ☐ Seated
- ☐ In motion in vehicle
- ☐ Other (describe)

______

______

______

CONDITIONS

DRIVERS AND PEDESTRIAN

1	2	Ped	
☐	☐	☐	Influenced by alcohol
☐	☐	☐	Had not been drinking
☐	☐	☐	Asleep or fatigued
☐	☐	☐	Sick
☐	☐	☐	Physical defects
☐	☐	☐	Not known
☐	☐	☐	No defects

VEHICLES

1	2	
☐	☐	Defective brakes
☐	☐	Defective steering
☐	☐	Defective lights
☐	☐	Defective tires
☐	☐	No defects
☐	☐	______ (Specify other)

WEATHER

- ☐ Clear
- ☐ Raining
- ☐ Snowing
- ☐ Sleeting
- ☐ Fog
- ☐ ______ (Specify other)

ROADWAY

- ☐ Under repair
- ☐ Holes or ruts
- ☐ Slippery
- ☐ Muddy
- ☐ Icy or snowy
- ☐ No defects

CONTRIBUTING FACTORS

VEHICLES

1	2		1	2	
☐	☐	Did not have right-of-way	☐	☐	Improper backing
☐	☐	Following too closely	☐	☐	Improper traffic lane
☐	☐	Failure to signal intentions	☐	☐	Improper parking
☐	☐	Speed too fast for conditions	☐	☐	No improper driving
☐	☐	Disregarded traffic signs or signals	☐		______
☐	☐	Improper passing		☐	______ (Specify other)
☐	☐	Improper turning			

SPEED

VEHICLES

1	2	
☐	☐	Exceeding legal limit
☐	☐	Too fast for conditions
___ MPH	___ MPH	Safe speed
___ MPH	___ MPH	Estimated speed when danger noticed
___ MPH	___ MPH	Estimated speed at moment of impact

INDICATE ON THIS DIAGRAM WHAT HAPPENED

Use one of these outlines to sketch the scene of your accident, writing in street or highway names or numbers.

1. Number each vehicle and show direction of travel by arrow: ——[1]⟩⟨[2]——

3. Show pedestrian by: ————○

4. Show railroad by: +++++++++

5. Show distance and direction to

INDICATE NORTH BY ARROW ○

At what distance was danger first noticed? ____ feet

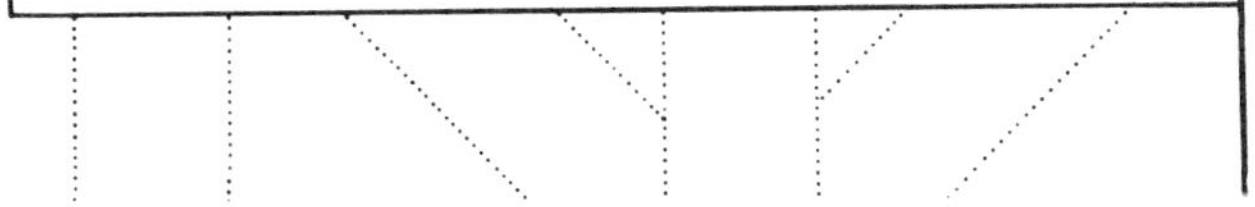

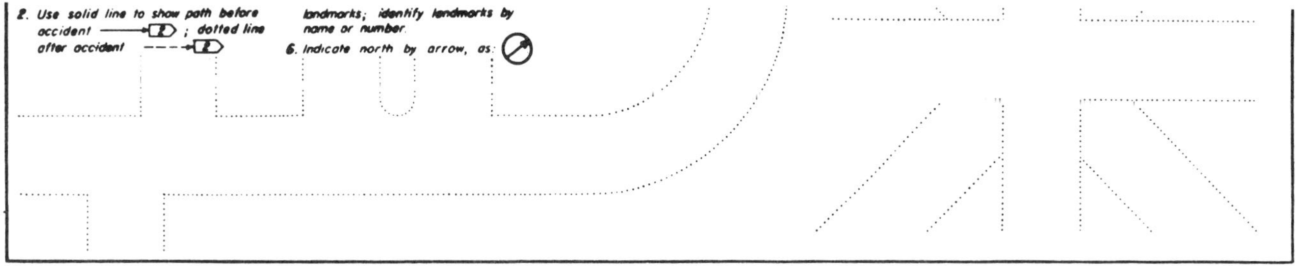

DRIVER'S ACCOUNT OF ACCIDENT ....

(Refer to vehicles by number)

Use this space for listing additional injured persons. Also explain questions not fully answered by checking in the boxes provided.

If more space is needed use another form or a sheet of paper the same size.

....

Suggestions for PREVENTING future accidents of this type: ....

....

★ **SIGNATURE** ....

Signature of person submitting report is required — Address — Date of report

☐ Driver
☐ Investigator
☐ Supervisor

Figure 4-1b. *Page 2 of "Motor Transportation Driver's Accident Report," Form Vehicle 1.*

tion. The person starting a safety program may want to look over report forms used by similar organizations and operations and incorporate their ideas.

Form Vehicle 1 is shown in Figure 4-1.

Accident reporting rules

The driver should be instructed how to complete an accident report on the designated report form for every incident coming under the following definition:

> Any incident in which a company vehicle is involved (whether in motion, temporarily stopped, parked, or being unloaded or loaded) that results in personal injury and/or property damage, regardless of who was hurt, what property was damaged, or who was responsible.

Most companies require that drivers also report any claims that they were involved in an accident, even if they were not. The company also may require drivers to report complaints, the witnessing of an accident, the rendering of aid, or any other unusual incident arising from the operation of their vehicles.

It is often company policy that failure to report an accident will be considered a cause for dismissal. The enforcement of this rule requires continuous attention. When strict compliance is obtained, the company is said to have "good accident reporting discipline." This is also a very good index to overall safety discipline.

Good accident reporting discipline requires not only the reporting of every incident, but also the submission of complete and well-written accident reports. To accomplish this, supervisors should be required to submit complete accident reports and to train their drivers how to conduct themselves at the accident scene, with emphasis on their data-gathering responsibilities. Incomplete reports should be returned to the supervisor if necessary to obtain complete reporting. Failure to report an accident or alleged accident means no investigation can be made by supervisors or the insurance company. This can result in the imposition of a claim for damages by default.

It is very important that every company supervisor understands what has to be reported, and makes sure it is done. If complete and uniform reporting is not carried out by everyone, the lax supervisor wins safety contests only because he reports fewer accidents. Thorough reporting must be automatic before incentives can be given for better records.

Devote sufficient time to development of accident reporting discipline during the driver and supervisor training sessions. Drivers who submit substandard reports should be made to correct them.

Recording Accident Data

All accident data should be recorded and preserved in such a manner that the data can be of the greatest possible value in the accident prevention program. Accident data should be transferred to permanent accident record forms; this is essential for efficient accident control.

The 'accident register'

Most fleets maintain an "accident register," such as the Council's Form Vehicle 8 (see Figure 4-2), that provides a journal of ready information on all accidents in chronological order. As a checklist for follow-up, it assures that the fleet operator will have a single record of all accidents.

The accident register provides considerable analytical information.

In large fleets, the register may be kept at the office that has direct supervision over the driver involved and that is also responsible for initially receiving the driver's report of the accident. In small fleets, records are usually kept by the person responsible for loss control. Information from accident reports should be transcribed to the register and kept up-to-date as follows:

- *Accident date:* This is the date the accident occurred, not the date the accident was reported. File chronologically.
- *Accident number:* In this column, enter the number that has been assigned to the accident file. This serves as an excellent cross-reference to the file itself.
- *Driver's name:* This is another excellent cross-reference to the master file in that it will identify the accident and refer back to the number of the master file.
- *Driver's home terminal:* When a control register is maintained at the company's general office, this column helps to locate accidents by terminal and provides a quick résumé of the accidents that occur.
- *Vehicle number:* The vehicle number assists the maintenance, operations, and safety departments. Whenever practical, the numbering system should give an indication as to the type of vehicle.
- *Accident type:* This is the first major breakdown with regard to type. This breakdown should include head-on, sideswipe, right angle, front end (your vehicle), rear end (your vehicle), overturn, other.

(*Text continues on page 46.*)

National Safety Council

MOTOR TRANSPORTATION

ACCIDENT REGISTER

PERIOD COVERED ________ TO ________

ACCIDENT NUMBER ________ TO ________

COMPANY ____________________

LOCATION ____________________

NATIONAL FLEET SAFETY CONTEST

KEY CODE NO. ____

DIVISION OF CONTEST ________

	ACCIDENT DATE	ACCIDENT NUMBER	DRIVER'S NAME	DRIVER'S HOME TERMINAL	VEHICLE NUMBER	ACCIDENT TYPE	SHOW NEAREST CITY & STATE
1							
2							
3							
4							
5							
6							
7							
8							
9							
10							

Figure 4-2a. *"Motor Transportation Accident Register," Council Form 8, upper half of first page.*

FOLD

THIS FORM CAN BE CONVENIENTLY FILED IN A THREE RING BINDER. TEAR OFF THIS FLAP AND FOLD AS INDICATED AND THE PAGE IDENTIFICATION WILL WILL BE UNCOVERED FOR REFERENCE.

TEAR OFF HERE

ACCIDENT LOCATION			OBJECTS, PERSONS OR VEHICLES INVOLVED	ESTIMATED COST INFORMATION					USASI D-15		REPORTS FURNISHED				
				COMPANY		OTHER PARTY									
URBAN	SUBURBAN	RURAL		PERSONAL INJURY	PROPERTY DAMAGE	PERSONAL INJURY	PROPERTY DAMAGE	TOTAL	REPORTABLE	NOT REPORTABLE	CO. HDQTS.	INS. CO.	POLICE	BMCS	
															1
															2
															3
															4
															5
															6
															7
															8
															9
															10

Figure 4-2b. *"Motor Transportation Accident Register," upper half of second page.*

• *Accident location:* This section will furnish location data of a general nature that can be used later for analytical purposes. These data can indicate where the preponderance of accidents are taking place and where special emphasis must be laid.

• *Objects, persons, or vehicles involved:* Here, as in the section above, descriptive information should be recorded that can be analyzed by categories; such as truck and car, bus and pedestrian, taxi and utility pole.

• *Estimated cost information:* The importance of this area cannot be overemphasized. A company must know what accidents are costing or might be going to cost. Accurate estimates furnish the data for making realistic financial projections.

• *"Reportable" or "not reportable":* To be compared on an equal basis, all fleets must use the same standard of accident reportability. The National Safety Council's National Fleet Safety Contest uses American National Standard *Method of Recording and Measuring Motor Vehicle Fleet Accident Experience and Passenger Accident Experience,* D15.1-1976, as do other national contests.

• *Reports furnished:* In some cases, specific reports must be furnished to company headquarters, the insurance company, the police, and the DOT's Bureau of Motor Carrier Safety. This area furnishes a handy reference check to make sure that such reports have been made.

The 'award and accident record' card

The safety record of each driver is important to the evaluation of his overall job performance. A special Council form, Form Vehicle 6, "Award and Accident Record," illustrated in Figure 4-3, lists dates of all accidents and summarizes the essential facts about each. The card also records commendations for good performance and dates of safety awards earned. The cards may be kept in a special file or included with other personnel records of the driver.

The driver's accident record may be kept with those of all other drivers in a visual index file, or even be placed in the computer as part of the personnel or payroll master file, where it can be displayed or printed out on demand.

Analyzing Accident Data

Although an accident often results from several contributing factors or multiple causes, it usually could have been prevented by the removal of one or more of these factors.

Accident analysis—a means of studying accident data to determine what actions will result in the greatest improvement—requires breaking down every accident into its component parts, and tallying the information so that it can be viewed objectively. Accident-causing factors must be isolated so an attempt can be made to eliminate them.

Purpose of an accident analysis

Accident investigation reports are of little use if they are merely placed in the files and forgotten. They must be properly evaluated. Accident analysis—by evaluating the causes—pinpoints bad situations and suggests remedies. Should it indicate that defective equipment is a contributing factor, it would reveal that the maintenance program has shortcomings. Should it show that a large number of accidents occur at intersections, then the safety director could conclude that drivers need additional education and training.

Accident analysis can reveal significant causes. If defective brakes, for example, are a contributing factor, then the mechanic who is responsible for inspecting and maintaining brakes should be called to account. If a large number of drivers are shown to be accident repeaters, then the person who is responsible for driver selection may not be using adequate selection techniques. Analysis may point out discrepancies between a problem and any action taken to remedy the problem. It may further indicate ways of taking the necessary corrective action.

If a truck operator received inside information that robbers planned to highjack a valuable cargo, he certainly would take the necessary corrective action to prevent it. Similarly, accident analysis provides fleet operators with "inside information" of what accident experience is likely to be. Because it relates the times, places, conditions, causes, and other factors that most often contribute to accidents, it indicates which action should be taken to prevent the accident or to reduce the accident frequency.

How often should an analysis be made?

An analysis should be made as often as the number of accidents indicates a trend or reveals a need for any change in accident prevention activities. This would indicate that the intervals between accident analysis reports would depend upon the size of the fleet operation. A ten-vehicle operation that has very few accidents may not warrant an accident analysis summary more than once a year (or possibly every two years), unless accidents increase. In a much larger fleet, a summary may be warranted once a month.

JAN	FEB	MAR	APR	MAY	JUN	JUL	AUG	SEP	OCT	NOV	DEC

MOTOR TRANSPORTATION AWARD AND ACCIDENT RECORD

National Safety Council
Form Vehicle 6

Company ....

Address ....
Number *Street*

Name ....
Last *First* *Middle*

Location ....

Badge Number .... Date Employed .... Age ....
Month *Day* *Year* *At Emp.*

SAFE DRIVER AWARD RECORD

Earned .... Year N. S. C. Award during period
from .... to .... with
Company ....
Certified by ....

DRIVING TESTS

Date	*Score*	*Remarks*

Award earned	*Certificate Number*	*Date Award earned*	*Preventable Accidents*		*Non-Driving Time*	
			File No	*Date*	*From*	*To*

REMARKS: ....

Figure 4-3a. *"Motor Transportation Award and Accident Record," Council Form Vehicle 6.* *(See p. 50 for list of factors.)*

ACCIDENT RECORD

Accident File No.	Date of Accident	Co. Veh Number	Type of Company Vehicle	Type of Accident	Location	Preventable or Not-Preventable	Violation

Figure 4-3b. *Reverse side of award and accident record. Card is 5 1/8 by 8 inches.*

Mechanics of an accident analysis

Analysis is the process of taking a thing apart. In the analysis of a group of accidents, the separate factors in each accident are isolated and counted. This is largely a mechanical process; once the analysis system has been designed, it can easily be programmed into a small computer that will store and count the factors. In order to establish this system, the safety director must decide (*a*) what accident facts to analyze, and (*b*) what subcategories to use for each factor to show either its presence or absence or its relative effect.

Selecting factors to be studied

Because an accident can be highly complex, it is very difficult to record for study all the factors that may have brought it about. Therefore, there must be some guidelines to follow in selecting factors:

- *Availability of the information.* What information is available and how easily can it be obtained? Because analysis is usually confined to those items on the "Driver's Accident Report," all the items that are to be analyzed should be filled in.
- *Suspected importance of the factor.* There are many factors surrounding an accident that may or may not be associated with its causes; to study them all would complicate the analysis and make it too costly. For example, operator's height, weight, and hair color are quite unlikely to be associated with accident causes and, even if they were, probably nothing could be done about them. The safety director should limit his analysis to those factors that are related in such a way that they are subject to some control if found to be accident-producing factors. (Suggested factors are listed a little further on.
- *Mechanical limitations of the system.* Because sorting is mechanical (either done by hand or by machine), the amount of data that can be placed in a record is limited. This, in turn, limits the number of factors that can be studied, but should not, however, preclude the safety director from making special studies occasionally of unusual factors that are suspected of being related to accident causes. Such studies will be set up independently of the regular analysis system.
- *Selecting the factors.* The following are some of the accident factors usually selected for accident analysis:

Date of accident	Weather condition
Date reported	Light condition
Name of driver	Road condition
Age of driver	Type of accident

Length of service of driver
Hours on duty
Driver's home terminal
Vehicle type
Vehicle number
Time of day of accident
Accident location
Direction traveling
Traffic violation
Other vehicle type
Pedestrian
Property
Vehicle or object struck
By whom?
Responsibility for accident
Any failure by company driver
Cost of accident

Constructing the classification

Once you have decided what factors to analyze, construct a classification by categorizing each factor. For example, to study the pedestrian factor requires only two categories: "Pedestrian" and "No Pedestrian." More detailed information about pedestrians can be obtained by constructing a classification composed of the categories: "Male (age)" and "Female (age)."

Because the value of a classification depends entirely on how useful it is to the safety director, the following considerations should help in constructing them:

- The categories should be *mutually exclusive*—that is, a certain weather condition should be classifiable into only one category. Categories must also be *collectively exhaustive*—that is, there should be an appropriate category for every type of weather condition. A system of categories is known as a *classification.* A classification whose categories are not mutually exclusive and collectively exhaustive is defective and can introduce many errors into the analysis.
- The classification should be sufficiently detailed to provide as much specific information as needed. If categories are too general, they become worthless. For example, a classification by time of day into "A.M." and "P.M." categories is too general to be meaningful. A better classification would be into categories made up of 24 one-hour time brackets, 12 two-hour brackets, or 6 four-hour brackets.
- However, a classification should not be too detailed. This is the other extreme. Because the analysis seeks to arrive at a useful generalization about the fleet's accident experience, it is searching for a trend or a constellation of factors. This will not show up if the classification is excessively detailed.

One classification useful in guiding the training program is classification by type of accident. When well constructed, such a classification provides a certain amount of built-in analysis, and a fairly ready-made answer to the questions: "What are we doing wrong?" and "What must we do to correct it?"

The simplest and most widely used classification by type of accident is composed of the following categories:

Head-on	Rear end (Your vehicle)
Sideswipe	Backing
Right angle	Overturn
Front end (Your vehicle)	Other
	Noncollision

Other classifications may be by the movement of each vehicle (straight ahead, turning, or changing lanes, for example) or by the incorrect act of the driver when the accident has been judged as being preventable.

Using Accident Data

After painstakingly gathering the facts about all fleet accidents and carefully analyzing them, the safety manager now knows the "what," "when," "where," "who"—and to a large extent, the "how" and "why"—of the fleet's accident experience. He is now prepared to put these facts to work for the prevention of future accidents.

Every accident, even if not severe, must be treated as a matter of real importance. Management cannot afford to shrug off or dismiss any accident as being "a necessary part of doing business," "bad luck that could happen to anybody," or "regrettable, but just one of those things." *Any display of indifference on the part of the management or the supervisory force will lead the driver to feel that safety is not important and this will inevitably breed slack safety performance.*

Although this attitude must be forcefully impressed upon every driver who had an accident, management cannot go to extremes and fire a driver simply because he may have needlessly cost the company a great deal of money. He will only have to be replaced, and his replacement will have to be trained. This replacement may prove to be an even worse driver than the one discharged.

How management handles a driver who has had a motor vehicle accident can be a turning point that will determine whether the driver learns anything from it and is helped to improve his performance, or whether the incident, by being ignored, will actually confirm a bad driving practice.

Experience reports for management

Reports should be made to management monthly. These should show the actual number of accidents and the accident rate for the separate terminals, divisions, or company locations, as well as company-wide totals.

So that management can have some basis for comparison, figures for the previous calendar year-to-date should be shown. The information should be prefaced by a brief written summary that points out the most noteworthy facts in the report.

Other information that might be included in monthly and annual accident experience reports to management is:

Accident rate by type of equipment and type of accident
High-accident locations
Accidents by seniority groups
Miles operated per accident
Accident costs per mile

If the monthly reports are ranked to show which company divisions or locations have the best accident rates, and then copies are distributed to all locations, a powerful competitive safety tool will result. The record of each location is visible to the others and a judgment is made on its management results. Because company officials see this report, it would be a short-sighted supervisor who didn't try to better his standing on the next report by working harder with his team.

Carrying this effort even further, the results on the monthly summary can be tied to each supervisor's incentive programs. Actual or average accident costs can be shown. The company average and the goal for the year can be drawn in, thus separating the "above average" from the "poorer than average" standings, and showing the relationship of results to goal.

Other Benefits

Additional benefits that accrue are explained here:

Driver selection

The safety performance of the drivers hired should be checked. If some drivers do poorly and leave the company or have to be discharged, this information should be reviewed to improve the ability to select better drivers.

The driver training program

The training program for new drivers as they join the company is designed to train them how to drive safely. Accident records may indicate that the fleet drivers were not given enough instruction in some specific area, for example, how to avoid backing accidents. As a result, the training program should be altered to correct this deficiency. The training program should constantly be reevaluated to cope with the type of accident problems encountered.

Safety meetings

If regular safety meetings are a part of the safety program, the content of such meetings should be based on accident data. Accident prevention effort should always be aimed at the biggest and most remunerative target. If accident records indicate that a certain location, weather condition, or type of accident accounts for most accidents, safety meetings should be geared to showing drivers how to avoid these. Appendix B gives details.

Awards and incentives

Accurate accident records serve a very positive function as the basis for fleet contests, driver awards, and incentive systems. The operation of award and incentive plans is discussed in Chapter 10 under "Encourage High Performance."

Reports to management

Management interest and support of the safety effort will be high only if all management (middle management and supervisors as well as top management) is kept informed as to the progress of safety achievement within the company.

One of the most important measurements of accident experience is the accident rate. The rate for motor vehicle accidents is based on the number of reportable accidents per million vehicle miles driven. The American National Standards Institute D15.1, *Method of Recording and Measuring Motor Vehicle Fleet Accident Experience and Passenger Accident Experience,* * should be used to compute rates.

---

*Available from American National Standards Institute, 1430 Broadway, New York, N.Y. 10018.

Chapter 5

Accident Investigation

Accident investigation is more than filling out the proper forms, as important as they are. It is a system of collecting and documenting factual evidence.

The accident investigation itself is prefaced by the training of drivers in the correct conduct to assume at the scene of an accident, and the following procedures: notifying the authorities and the company, obtaining witness statements, marking the accident site, protecting the vehicle and its cargo, and, yes, doing the necessary paperwork.

For the safety specialist, accident investigation is all this, and more: accurate field investigation; evidence gathering; witness statement recording; site and vehicle diagraming; and training, interviewing, and retraining drivers.

This chapter gives a comprehensive overview of the accident investigation system.

Driver Conduct at the Scene of an Accident

If involved in an accident, the driver must do a number of things immediately, because he is usually the only representative of his company there at the time.

Because this is so important, all drivers should be trained in the correct procedure to follow in the event of an accident.

National Safety Council Form Vehicle 2, Accident Report Packet, shown in Figure 5-1, lists on its envelope the things to be done in the order of their importance. (Similar envelopes are available from many insurance carriers.)

(Text continues on page 58.)

National Safety Council

Form Vehicle 2 Rep. 03 Stock No. 229.32

ACCIDENT REPORT PACKET

KEEP THIS ENVELOPE IN YOUR VEHICLE

OPEN ONLY IN CASE OF ACCIDENT

FIRST —

Stop Immediately and determine damage. Avoid obstructing traffic if possible.

Place emergency reflectors, flares, lanterns or flags.

Aid the injured and see to it that they receive medical attention as soon as possible.

Report accident to local police and your company.

SECOND —

Get witnesses to sign courtesy cards.

Record information on reverse side of this envelope at scene of accident, and give this envelope to an authorized representative of your company.

IMPORTANT —

Make no statement to anyone except:

A. An officer of the law.

B. Your company's representative.

C. Your insurance company's representative. Make no settlements. Do not argue about the accident.

If the accident involves an unattended vehicle or fixed object, take reasonable steps to locate and notify the owner. If the owner cannot be found, leave a notice in a conspicuous place on the vehicle or object, listing your name and address, the company name, and a brief description of the accident, with date and time. Whenever possible get a witness signed statement.

TURN ENVELOPE—FILL IN INFORMATION

Figure 5-1a. *Accident Report Packet.*

ACCIDENT MEMORANDUM

Date of Accident .... 19.... Day of Week .... Hour ...... a.m. p.m.

☐ CITY
☐ SUBURBAN
☐ RURAL

PLACE WHERE ACCIDENT OCCURRED

County .... City, town or township ....

If accident was outside city limits indicate distance from nearest town. Use two distances and two directions if necessary.
{ .... miles .... north-south / .... miles .... east-west } of { ☐ limits of / ☐ center of } .... City or Town

ROAD ON WHICH ACCIDENT OCCURRED .... Give name of street or highway number (U.S. or State)

☐ AT ITS INTERSECTION WITH .... Name of intersecting street or highway number

OR

☐ NOT AT INTERSECTION { ... feet .... north-south / ... feet .... east-west } of .... Show nearest intersecting street or highway, house number, curve, bridge, rail crossing, alley, driveway, culvert, milepost, underpass, numbered telephone pole, or other identifying landmark. Show exact distance, using two directions and two distances if necessary.

(Check and complete one)

OTHER DRIVER'S NAME

ADDRESS

CITY STATE DRIVER'S LICENSE No.

OTHER VEHICLE OWNER'S NAME

ADDRESS

CITY STATE VEHICLE LICENSE No.

TYPE VEHICLE MAKE YEAR No.

DAMAGE TO OTHER VEHICLE AND/OR PROPERTY

INJURED PERSONS	Age	Sex	Injuries
Name			
Address			
Name			
Address			
Name			
Address			

POLICE Name Badge No.

BE SURE WITNESS CARDS ARE COLLECTED PLACE THEM IN THIS FOLDER

INDICATE ON THIS DIAGRAM WHAT HAPPENED

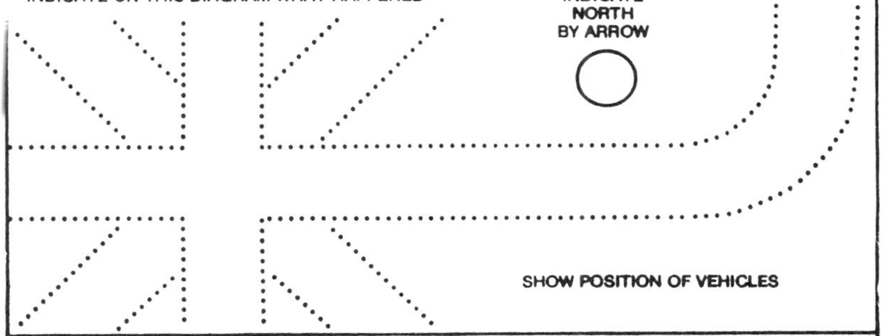

DRIVER'S SIGNATURE

Figure 5-1b. *Other side of envelope is for recording accident memoranda.*

WILL YOU KINDLY FAVOR THIS DRIVER BY FILLING IN THIS COURTESY CARD?

ACCIDENT AT ____
(show street name and no. or intersection)

DAY AND DATE ______________________ Time ____________ ☐ A.M. ☐ P.M.

DID YOU SEE THE ACCIDENT HAPPEN? ☐ YES ☐ NO

DID YOU SEE ANYONE HURT? ☐ YES ☐ NO

WERE YOU RIDING IN A VEHICLE INVOLVED? ☐ YES ☐ NO

IN YOUR OPINION WHO WAS RESPONSIBLE?

☐ THIS DRIVER ☐ OTHER DRIVER ☐ PASSENGER ☐ PEDESTRIAN

☐ OTHER

(Indicate)

NAME ____

HOME ADDRESS ____

CITY, STATE & ZIP ______________________ TELEPHONE ______________

National Safety Council
Rev. 20 M-127199 Stock No. 229.38
Form Vehicle 12

THANK YOU

Figure 5-2. *Be sure courtesy cards are distributed, filled in, and collected. They help determine who saw the accident in case witnesses are needed later.*

Courtesy cards, shown in Figure 5-2, can be used to get names and addresses of witnesses without frightening them away. A card can also be used to obtain an exonerating statement from the responsible motorist while he is still apologetic and wants to make amends.

Steps to follow

1. The first step—protect the scene of the accident. The driver should try to keep the effects of the accident from becoming worse. He should immediately place warning signals and devices to permit, as nearly as possible, the uninterrupted normal flow of vehicular traffic.

2. Second—the driver should protect the injured. If possible, he should request medical assistance from authorized sources (police, fire, hospital, etc.)

3. Report the accident. Depending upon your local reporting requirements, call the local police and state police, and notify the designated company representative. A procedure should be established whereby the driver, telephoning a report of the accident, can talk to the person who will be responsible for the accident investigation. A previously prepared telephone checklist is invaluable in recording the information reported by a driver (see Figure 5-3). With the information

DRIVING SUPERVISORS CHECK SHEET FOR PHONE CALLS ON ACCIDENTS

Driver's Name ____________________ Can you talk freely on phone? ______

1. Where are you? ____________________

   Where can you be reached by phone? ____________________

2. Are you hurt? ____________________ (nature of injury) Other people hurt? ____________________

   ____________________ Help on the way? ______

3. Have police been called? ______ Where? ____________________

4. Time of accident ______ Where? ____________________ (give exact location)

   ____

5. What happened? ____________________

   ____

6. How bad is the damage to the other vehicle? ____________________

   ____

7. How bad is our equipment damage? ____________________ (get both tractor and trailer unit numbers)

   ____

   ____

8. Do you have witness names? ______ Exoneration card used? ______

   ____

9. What equipment will be needed to bring our unit and cargo in? ____________________

   ____________________ (consider wrecker, wreckage of trailer, etc.)

10. What does cargo consist of? ____________________

    Out of: ____________________ To: ____________________

11. Is the unit safe in its present spot until a supervisor can get there? ______
    DO NOT MOVE THE UNIT UNLESS ABSOLUTELY NECESSARY

12. Have you information on other driver, car license, address of owner, insurance carrier, operator's license number, etc? ____________________

    ____

13. Where will you be when the supervisor gets there? ____________________

14. Instructions given driver by you: ____________________

    ____

TIME OF CALL: ______ DATE: ______ RECEIVED BY: ______

TWX: Safety Dept. on fatal accidents.
Dispatch Dept. on extensive loss or delay to explosives, hazardous and radioactive shipments.

PHONE: Call Insurance Adjuster.

Figure 5-3. *A simple checklist should be kept where phone calls about accidents are made or received. This helps organize the information and assures the driver and supervisor cover everything necessary.*

obtained from the telephone checklist, the company can decide whether to dispatch additional equipment, another driver, a mechanic, or additional manpower to the scene of the accident. Arrangements for whatever additional help will be needed can thus be made with a minimum of delay and confusion. Place a prominent notice somewhere on the dashboard of the vehicle to indicate who should be notified in the event the driver is incapacitated because of the accident.

4. **Obtain information.** To assist the driver in gathering information at the scene of the accident, he should be supplied beforehand with an accident report packet (shown in Figure 5-1). Outside are printed instructions and inside an accident memorandum on which the driver should record the details. In addition to the accident memorandum, the packet should contain a sharp pencil, paper, courtesy cards, a lumber crayon, coins or a phone credit card for phone calls, and other materials as needed. The driver should review the steps mentioned on the outside of his accident packet and follow the instructions. He should take "courtesy cards" (shown in Figure 5-2) from the packet and pass them out. Whether or not a person actually saw the accident occur, he should be asked to fill out the card. Use of the cards will help determine who actually saw the accident, and a statement that the individual did not see the incident might also prove to be valuable. Although these cards are often referred to as "witness cards," it is known that people do not like to be "witnesses." Therefore these should always be called "courtesy cards" to remove the stigma connected with the word "witness." Every person who was in the area at the time of the accident should be asked to fill out one of these cards and return it to the driver.

Filling out accident memorandum

At this point, the operator is in a position to fill out the Accident Memorandum (on the back of the Form Vehicle 2 envelope, Figure 5-1b). When properly filled out, this will assure getting information that may not be available later, and will provide the necessary information for the driver to report the accident to his company.

A few things need to be emphasized about filling out the accident report:

- It should be filled out completely and legibly, because it may ultimately serve as evidence in court.
- Facts should be definite and specific.
- There should be no question as to the accuracy.
- This report should identify all vehicles involved.
- The report should supply names of persons involved correctly and fully, so as to identify the specific person(s) intended.

• Addresses of all persons involved in the accident should be included.

• Date, day of week, and exact time of day should be recorded.

• The location of the accident should be designated so specifically that someone else could take this memo at a later date and go to the exact spot where the accident occurred.

• The diagram of the accident should indicate direction of travel, and show the exact location of the vehicles on the street or roadway, obstacles, traffic signs, signals, and other pertinent objects. The diagram should show exactly what happened and where it happened.

• The accident memorandum, courtesy cards, and other pertinent data should be carefully secured and preserved.

This memorandum report of an accident is usually all of the information that a company can expect its drivers to obtain at the scene of an accident. Some companies require their drivers to fill out a Driver's Accident Report, a much more detailed accident investigation report. Other companies prefer that this report be filled out later, under the supervision of a company official. (Typical report—Form Vehicle 1—was shown in Figure 4-1.)

The Accident Investigator

Because financial liability could be high, and accident prevention must be effective, every company should have available a trained accident investigator who can be dispatched to the scene of an accident, take charge of the company's interests, direct the activities of the driver, and gather additional data concerning the accident which will supplement the data gathered by the driver.

Frequently, in a city operation or in a small company, there will be no supervisor conveniently free who can make an investigation. *Company officials should make it perfectly clear that accident investigation is a job for the highest local supervisor to perform and that it takes precedence over sales or other operations responsibilities. It is not to be delegated to noncompany personnel, such as adjusters, mechanics, or tow truck operators.*

The availability of a trained accident investigator is essential. If the company driver involved was killed or disabled in the accident, a responsible company representative must show up promptly to take charge. Even if the driver is not disabled, the company should not rely solely on the driver's account of what happened. Also, a good driver has an accident so infrequently that he does not have the opportunity to acquire experience in dealing with an accident situation. The accident investigator who has presided over the cleanup of a number of accidents should have the skill and poise necessary to deal with such situations effectively.

Aside from gathering useful accident prevention information, the trained accident investigator can:

- *Keep costs at a minimum.* If the investigator arrives promptly at the scene of the accident, by his presence, he can prevent further damage from occurring and can protect company property and prevent looting.
- *Expedite the movement of traffic* by capable handling at the scene of the accident.
- *Prevent excess costs.* His efficient investigation and handling of an accident provides management control and reduction of the opportunity for fraud.
- *Preserve vital information.* Complete investigation of the situation is necessary for claims protection. Keeping a consistent record of each accident provides a comparison base for future analysis.

Accident Investigation

The accident investigator needs to be trained in the specifics of conducting a detailed investigation. He needs to use the Drivers Accident Report (Form Vehicle 1), or a similar form, as a checklist to determine if he has obtained all the necessary data during the course of his investigation to not only protect the company, but to help complete the required accident reports, the Bureau of Motor Carrier Safety report, and any other records that may be required.

Because each accident situation is unique, it may not be practical for the investigator to follow the checklist item by item. The particular situation may necessitate entering data as it presents itself. However, as many items as possible should be completed before the investigator leaves the accident scene.

An accident investigation is a search for facts. The investigator should have an open mind and an unbiased attitude. It is his responsibility to determine the factors which may have contributed to the accident, as opposed to merely filling out an accident report. The accident investigator's job is not complete until he has determined:

- All of the factors that contributed to the accident
- How the accident occurred
- All the physical evidence that might have a bearing on the case
- Sufficient information, details, and data to record and preserve so that he can reconstruct the entire accident at any subsequent time.

What To Investigate

Ideally, all accidents involving vehicles operated by the motor carrier should be investigated to determine the basic causes behind them. In practice, limitations of time and manpower, the scope of the company's operations, or other factors may preclude the complete investigation of every accident. However, an investigation should be made of every accident sufficiently serious to require a report to the Bureau of Motor Carrier Safety and/or state regulatory authorities.

Accidents involving the following should be thoroughly investigated:

- Fatalities and/or personal injuries
- Extensive property damage
- Transportation of explosives and other hazardous materials, particularly where the nature of the cargo might have contributed to the seriousness of the accident
- Vehicles or loads of abnormal dimensions and/or weight
- Unusual circumstances.

A series of accidents involving common factors or circumstances that indicate a pattern should also be investigated. Such a pattern would include but not be limited to those involving:

- A single driver, particularly in a relatively short period of time or under recurrent circumstances
- A particular locality
- Special types of cargo
- Certain types or makes of vehicles (or combinations of same)
- Factors in common, such as a particular type of accident.

Tools for Investigation

A complete field equipment kit is essential to accurate accident investigation. Factual evidence surrounding an accident site doesn't stay put for long, and the safety specialist needs to be prepared to quickly and accurately document the evidence. An initial investment in investigation tools can pay for itself many times over by clearly documenting accident damages and sites for insurance claims.

The equipment you purchase should be reliable and durable. A well-outfitted equipment kit would include the following:

- *Recording device.* A cassette tape or other recording device is needed for recording driver and witness statements.
- *Photographic equipment.* Your camera kit should include a

35mm single-lens reflex (SLR) camera, a 50mm or 55mm lens, a wide-angle 24mm or 28mm lens, an electronic flash unit, spare batteries and film, and a carrying case large enough to store all the equipment.

• *Measuring equipment.* A measuring wheel with a 6-inch or larger wheel (the greater the diameter, the more accurate the measurement), a 100-foot glass fiber or steel tape, 12- and 25-foot "wide body" measuring tapes, a tire tread gage, and tire pressure gages are desirable.

• *Accident investigation report kit.* Reporting forms and checklists, paper, pens and pencils, clipboard, courtesy cards (see Figure 5-2), business cards, coins or a telephone credit card number for phone calls, lumber crayons, chalk and chalk line, and masking and sealing tapes are among the important items to be put in the kit.

• *Auxiliary lighting equipment.* Be prepared for after-dark investigations by having floodlights and flashlights with spare batteries.

• *Emergency equipment.* The minimum in emergency equipment could consist of a multipurpose dry chemical agent fire extinguisher, a first aid kit, blankets, and a tow rope.

• *Warning devices.* Begin with flares, flags, fusees, reflectors, strobe lights, and add other approved warning devices as necessary.

• *Basic tool kit.* In addition to the basics, such as a hammer and pliers, include nails, spikes (to hold the far end of your measuring tape), a plumb bob, broom, and shovel.

• *Equipment case.* Use a sturdy, compartmentalized case large enough to protect all your equipment from damage, weather, and loss. A well-organized equipment case speeds the investigation process and cuts down on equipment loss.

Clothing for accident investigating

Many accidents occur during inclement weather. For this reason, the fleet safety specialist should consider the purchase of specific items of clothing. The following items stress comfort, manueverability, safety, and visibility:

• *Safety vest.* A flourescent orange safety vest can help prevent the fleet accident investigator from becoming the cause or victim of a second accident.

• *Rain gear.* Coat, boots, and hat in a flourescent orange or other highly visible color, and a covered clipboard with water-resistant ink pens.

• *Cold weather gear.* Parkas and insulated pants in flourescent orange are available from sports shops. Insulated boots are a necessity.

• *Gloves.* Insulated gloves should be flexible enough to allow use of tools and writing materials. Ordinary work gloves can be worn during warmer or dry weather.

Post-investigation reporting aids

The field investigation data needs to be organized into an accurate, concise report. To do this, the fleet safety specialist will need:

- An accident diagraming template.
- A calculator
- Architectural scales. Straight-edge rulers.

Investigation Procedure

Frequently, the investigator will coordinate his efforts so other experts can help him with his job. He may, therefore, go to the scene with the insurance adjuster who will be preserving evidence and getting statements from the participants. If there is a local company maintenance supervisor, he should be called on to help resolve mechanical questions and get the damaged equipment ready to be brought in. Other drivers or loaders might be needed on the scene and they may contribute valuable insight into the causes of the accident.

The following detailed procedure assumes that the investigator will be doing the entire job by himself and that the accident is serious enough that a great deal of investigative time is warranted. The basic procedure can be scaled down for more modest accidents or those where other experts will perform some of the work.

At the accident scene

Upon arriving at the scene, the investigator should park his car where it will not obstruct traffic or contribute to another accident. If it is nighttime, he may want to park so that his headlights illuminate the scene but do not blind oncoming motorists. He should make sure the accident scene will not contribute to additional accidents, and that flags, flares, fusees, or other approved warning devices have been placed in accordance with regulations and in such a manner as to ensure maximum protection. To ensure his own safety, he should be wearing a safety vest or other outer garment in a highly visible color. He should then:

- Identify himself to the police at the scene, or when they arrive, and give them his full cooperation.
- If necessary, assist in the protection of the injured until medical aid arrives. (Here he should use a good deal of caution and judgment—lest he inadvertently aggravate an injury.)
- Check the bystanders for possible witnesses and volunteer helpers.
- Ensure that steps are taken to protect company property from theft or damage.

• Examine the area carefully for any possible hazards, such as spilled gasoline, flammables, or broken electrical cabling.

• Look for any evidence that may be associated with the accident and have it guarded until it can be properly examined.

• Locate the driver of the company vehicle, properly identify himself, and assume charge of the situation. The investigator should then take possession of all reports, data, and any information the driver may have.

Filling in the details

Pursuing a step-by-step accident investigation (such as shown on the driver's Accident Report (pages 38 to 41) requires the investigator to bear in mind the following:

1. **Time.** Record the exact date, day of the week, and hour of the day. If the vehicle is equipped with a tachograph, the chart would show these. If not, every effort should be made to determine the exact time the accident occurred.

2. **Accident location.** Should be specific enough so that a complete stranger could take the report at any time subsequent to the accident and go directly to the scene where the accident occurred. In most cases, it isn't enough to say "accident occurred in the county of Fulton, ten miles north of Atlanta on U.S. Route 29." Add more specific information such as "355 feet south of the utility pole No. 647328" or "550 feet north of the north end of a bridge abutment where U.S. Highway 29 crosses Rising Creek." The diagram should reference these specific points. (Data should agree with that of the Accident Memorandum, previously filled out.)

3. **Accident involved.** The investigator should tell exactly what was involved in the accident. If there was another vehicle, a determination should be made as to (*a*) its type, and (*b*) whether the vehicle itself (as contrasted with the action of the operator) contributed anything to the accident, by virtue of its type or color, or other characteristic. The investigator should indicate when one or more pedestrians are involved and indicate the contribution made by each to the accident. If there is a fixed object involved, a detailed description of it is necessary; include the location, size, shape, marks, and any other pertinent data.

4. **Type of accident.** The accident (see Driver's Accident Report form) should be determined and recorded in the accident report. Any information with regard to type, not covered specifically in the accident

report, should be described completely so as to avoid doubt or indecision.

5. Drivers. The driver of each vehicle must be definitely identified by complete name, exact address, operator's or chauffeur's license number, and any other information necessary.

6. Vehicles. All vehicles involved in the accident must be definitely identified by type, make, year model, company number (if any), and state and number of the license. A description of the damage to the vehicles and the damage to cargo or other property should be noted. Any estimates should be as accurate as possible.

7. Injured. List the exact name and the address, age, and sex of every injured person. However, do not antagonize an injured person by persistent questioning in public. Wait until a better time presents itself, such as at the hospital, or at the person's home. Describe the injuries as completely as possible. Then, upon the investigator's visit to the doctor's office or hospital where the injured were taken, the injuries can be verified and any necessary changes made in the notes. It is important to specify whether the injured persons were drivers of vehicles, or were passengers or pedestrians. Their relationship to the accident must be given.

8. Witnesses. Seek out witnesses as soon as possible. They are not obligated to remain at the scene and may leave before you have a chance to question them. Accordingly, first record the license number of the cars parked at the accident area. Through the license numbers, other possible witnesses may be contacted at a later date if needed. Also, frequently witnesses may be found talking to a driver, discussing the accident among themselves, or examining the damage caused by the accident. The investigator should check the courtesy cards which were turned over to him by the driver. The exact spelling, and the complete name and address of any witness is important. In addition to the address, the investigator should make a notation as to how these persons might be contacted at their office, place of business or employment, or any other place where they might be temporarily. Any interest the witness may have in the accident should be indicated—whether as investigating police officer, bystander, passenger in a company vehicle, passenger in the other vehicle involved, or any other designation. Many times the driver of a vehicle that has escaped damage may have been involved in the situation leading to the accident. The investigator should get statements from such persons.

All passengers involved should be interviewed, especially in serious accidents. *While questioning passenger(s),* it may be helpful to establish the relationship of the passenger to the driver to detect a possible reason for bias in his statements. In addition, establish the position of the passenger in the vehicle to determine if the passenger could actually have seen the accident occur, as well as what the passenger was doing at the time of the accident. *When interviewing witness(es),* make sure that a witness actually saw the accident happen. The investigator should note only *facts* and not the opinions of witnesses. In addition, it is wise to determine exactly what the witness is saying. For instance, if the witness says that a vehicle was traveling "fast" determine what he or she considers as "fast." Similarly, if the witness says "a long distance" determine approximately how "long" is long.

The *reliability* of witness testimony will be enhanced if the investigator observes the following:

- If your insurance adjuster is available, have him question the witnesses; usually, adjusters are experts at this.
- Each witness should be shown courtesy and consideration at all times.
- Each witness should be interviewed separately with no other witnesses present, whenever practical.
- The investigator should get the *full* story of one witness before he asks any questions about or cites any contrary or conflicting statements made by other witnesses.
- If it serves a useful purpose, the statement obtained from one witness may be quoted to another, but the names of other witnesses should never be used.
- The investigator should make no attempt to coerce witnesses who refuse to make a statement.
- The investigator should not engage in any controversies with witnesses.
- There should be no retaliation against hostile witnesses.

9. Movement.

a. An indication should be made as to the exact movement of each *vehicle* at the time of the accident. In many cases more than one box should be checked for each vehicle involved.

b. Pedestrian. Indicate in this section exactly what any pedestrian was doing. Then in the diagram, make an effort to show exactly where any pedestrian was in relation to the accident.

c. Passenger. Identify any passengers who were involved in the accident. It makes no difference whether or not the passengers were injured—we are concerned because they were involved.

10. Conditions.

a. Drivers and pedestrian(s). Use this section of the report to indicate completely the condition of any person involved in the accident. Check all appropriate boxes in an effort to show more completely the condition of each person involved, use additional space in an effort to properly describe the conditions, if necessary. The investigator should make an effort to determine any evidence of intoxication or physical defects. In attempting to determine the driver's condition prior to the accidents, take into account such items as prior delays, coffee stops, arguments, fatigue, schedules, or other factors. Get original of driver data logs or tachograph charts that will help show these facts. Such information helps to establish the driver's mental alertness and disposition just prior to the accident and may suggest future remedies for the particular type of accident. In addition, it may be helpful to establish the amount of sleep the driver had one to four days prior to the accident.

Upon returning to the office, the following information, as it pertains to the driver, should be secured from the fleet's personnel files:

- Length of employment
- Training
- Overall driving experience, and experience in driving the particular type of vehicle involved in the accident
- Attitude toward job
- Record of physical examinations
- Illnesses and personal problems
- Accident record
- Record of traffic violations
- Commendations or disciplinary actions

b. Vehicles. Investigation should be made to determine the extent to which the mechanical condition of each vehicle involved may have been a contributing factor in the accident. The thoroughness of the check at the accident scene should be governed by the extent of damage to the vehicle. If possible, a road test should be made to determine brake performance, including a test of the braking system for leakage or inoperative parts. In addition, the steering mechanism, noticeable damage to wheel alignment, engine performance, and any other mechanisms affecting the safe operation of the vehicle should be thoroughly checked to determine if they may have been factors. Company maintenance supervisors should assist in making this evaluation. If, as a result of the accident, the condition of the vehicle does not permit a road check at the accident scene, a thorough investigation should be made of the vehicle upon its return to the storage or repair location. *Extreme care should be used when attempting to determine whether a vehicle part or system was inoperative before the accident or as a result of the accident.* In very serious accidents where lawsuits can be expected, it would pay to have this evaluation made by a reputable independent expert who can later testify about it.

c. Weather. Weather conditions at the time of the accident should be noted. In addition, indicate whether any previous weather condition may have contributed to the accident. Weather conditions may reduce visibility. For instance, sun glare can blind a driver and affect his viewing of signals, pedestrians, and other vehicles.

d. Roadway. The roadway itself contributes to a number of accidents, yet in many cases this is not noted. The proper indication should be made on the accident report; then a more detailed description should be recorded on extra paper so as to give a complete description of the roadway.

11. Contributing factors. At this point, the investigator should be aware that there are usually several factors that contribute to any accident. This means that in most cases more than one box should be checked for each vehicle involved.

a. Speed. Speed is a contributing factor to many accidents; speed, therefore, is considered of sufficient importance to warrant special consideration. Every effort should be made to fill out this section of the report carefully and the speed of each vehicle involved should be as accurately estimated as possible. Here again, if the report does not have sufficient space to properly describe the existing situation, the description should be made on extra paper.

b. The trip. The origin, destination, and related distances of the trip on which the accident occurred should be investigated. If the total trip extends over more than one day, the point at which driving began should be noted, as well as the origin and destination of the entire trip. In addition, the distance from the point of origin to the accident scene should be noted. List stops en route, time spent at each, and determine the activities of the driver at each stop. *Retrace the driver's activities* for at least 24 hours prior to the accident, showing time spent on and off duty. Investigation of the driver's activities over a longer period of time preceding the accident should be conducted when it appears desirable. The original of the driver's log record for the same period should be made a part of the company's accident file. If the vehicle was equipped with an operations recorder, the chart should be examined with special attention given to speed and stops en route, and the chart should be compared with the driver's log. The original of this chart should be a permanent part of the accident file. Insofar as possible, the activities of other drivers, or persons involved, should be reconstructed in the effort to determine the extent to which their actions or physical and mental conditions may have contributed to the accident. Such investigation should also cover at least 24 hours prior to the accident, and a longer period, if useful. Information relative to the activities of other persons will generally have to be developed through direct inquiry. Their answers might have to be verified.

12. Accident diagram. The accident diagram should be sufficiently comprehensive to show at a glance exactly what happened. Graph paper might be used to enhance the accuracy of the diagram. The use of a plotting device, such as the Northwestern University* investigator's traffic template, will help diagram the accident site. In drawing the accident scene, various factors should be recorded.

a. Primary factors. The following primary factors should be available from actual measurements taken at the accident site:

- Width of roadway, including condition and type of pavement. Indicate whether new, slippery from oil deposits, or covered with deposits of sand, gravel, stones, or full of holes, or ruts.
- Width and number of traffic lanes, with numbers assigned to each lane.
- Width and condition of shoulder (berm) of road, including the measurement of any drop-off from the pavement edge to the shoulder. Depth and running length of this "lip" should be accurately identified.
- Point of impact as indicated by physical evidence and what the physical evidence was.
- Dimensions of any intersecting street, roadway, alley, or driveway.
- Location and direction of travel of each vehicle prior to impact, at impact, and after impact.
- Pinpointing the exact location of the accident in order that its site can be definitely relocated at a later time. This may be done by identifying a number on an adjacent utility pole such as "three feet east of cen-

*The Traffic Institute, Northwestern University, Evanston, Ill. 60201.

ter line, 50 feet northeast of utility pole number 16847," or it may be done by designating any permanent object such as: "three feet east of center line, 300 feet north of the north side of Cain Creek Bridge, Highway 41, six miles north of Citizenville, Ill."

b. Secondary factors. The following secondary factors should be available from actual measurements.

- Length of skid mark for *each* wheel.
- Exact position and physical description (for example, size and height) of any objects which might have obstructed the vision of any driver, such as buildings, trees, embankments, billboards.
- Exact location of debris, spilled liquids, marks, scratches, or gouges in the pavement made by any of the vehicles involved. The location of liquid spills and stains, and other temporary debris can be marked with a lumber crayon. This should be done after taking the photo for the accident report.
- Exact location of any traffic sign, signal, or other traffic control device. Indicate whether or not devices were working at the time of the accident. If view of device was obstructed by foliage or other object, or defaced by markings, or obliterated by road film, note this on the diagram (and report).
- Location of fixed objects near the accident scene or debris that appear in the photographs, as well as any measurements related to these objects.
- Exact positions of points from which photographs were taken. Two diagrams may be necessary if a large number of the above items must be noted.

c. What should be measured. Measurements usually are needed of:

- Skid marks.
- Sight distances.
- Location and position of point of impact and final resting position of the vehicle(s).
- Location of dead or injured.
- Point at which vehicle ran off the road.
- Distance to fixed objects from which photographs were taken.

d. How to make measurements. To increase accuracy, all measurements should be made with a measuring tape or measuring wheel. The investigator should have witnesses who, if called on, can verify the accuracy of these measurements.

TRIANGULATION. In locating objects in the accident diagrams, such as spilled liquids, debris at the point of impact, or injured persons, one

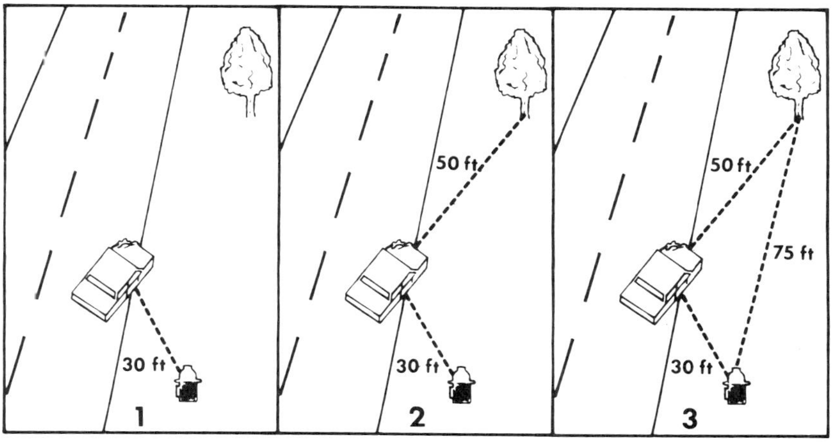

Figure 5-4. *Three steps in triangulation.* **1.** *Measure from debris to a fixed object (in this illustration, a fire hydrant).* **2.** *Measure the distance to another fixed object (a tree).* **3.** *Measure the distance between the fixed objects.*

method of measurement used is "triangulation." It is done by simply locating two fixed points, such as a utility pole or tree, and a manhole cover on or near the road. Then, measure from the object to be located to each of these points. To finish the triangle, measure the distance between the fixed points (see Figure 5-4). To relocate the exact spot at which the accident occured, use the distances measured and swing two arcs from the fixed points. Clearly identify all fixed reference points so that anyone returning to the accident scene could determine the exact points referenced in the accident diagram.

COORDINATES. The "coordinates" method of location measurement uses two reference lines, usually at right angles to each other. The two lines are chosen from the natural features of the accident site; roadway edges, berms, center lanes, and railroad tracks are possible choices.

Located at the intersection of the two reference lines is the "reference point." Measurements are taken along the reference lines, from the reference point to the spot nearest the vehicle or object. Then a *right angle measurement* is made from the reference line to the object (see Figure 5-5).

Detailed explanations of both the triangulation and coordinates systems of measurement can be found in the *Traffic Accident Investigation Manual,* by J. Stannard Baker (see Appendix E).

13. Driver's account of accident. This section of the investiga-

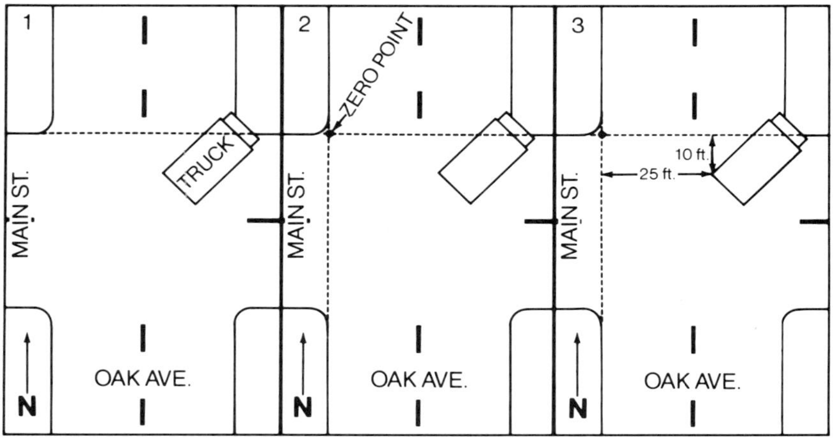

Figure 5-5. *Three steps in "coordinates" method of identifying locations.* **1.** *Locate and trace reference line A as part of some easy-to-identify feature of the accident.* **2.** *Locate reference line B (it does not have to be at right angles to A, however).* **3.** *Measure the shortest distance at right angles to each of the two reference lines.*

tion requires the driver's own statement as to how the accident occurred. The investigator should carefully interview the company driver to obtain the driver's detailed account of the accident. This should be done while the facts are still fresh in the mind of the driver. Find out how the driver attempted to avoid involvement in the events leading to the accident. Establish whether or not the driver could have possibly avoided the accident. Obtain his observations and a statement of his actions leading up to the accident. Through tachographs, logs, and schedules, establish the driver's approximate operating speed prior to the time the accident situation developed. Learn when and how the accident situation was first noticed.

14. Suggestions. This portion of the report asks for the driver's opinion as to how he should be able to prevent future accidents of this type.

15. Photographs. Photography is an excellent way to record facts and preserve evidence that may be needed in the future. It can also record things you may fail to notice. Photographs should be made of the accident scene as soon as possible in order to: (*a*) record the position of the vehicles before they are moved; (*b*) record debris, such as broken glass, oil stains, hubcaps, before they are moved or obliterated; and (*c*) record skid marks.

Here are some suggestions.

- Take several photographs of the accident scene: (*a*) in each direction *from* the point of impact; (*b*) from each approach to the point of impact, showing the view each driver had approaching the key point of the accident, as well as road alignment; (*c*) a close-up of the scene, showing the point of impact; and (*d*) an overall view of the scene.
- For each vehicle, show the extent of damage. Try to establish the angle of collision and the movement of each while in contact.
- Photograph debris, skid marks, or any other physical evidence of vehicular movement prior to and after impact.
- Photograph any broken vehicle parts. Try to establish whether the accident caused the damage or whether the damage preceded the accident.
- Take any other photographs that will preserve data such as road defects, improper signage, obstructions, foliage which blocks the view, or other physical conditions that may have been a factor in the accident. Identify each photograph as to time and date taken, direction in which taken, and location from which taken—use measurements to pinpoint the location.

Follow-up

The next step in the accident investigation involves clearing the accident scene. This should be done as quickly and completely as possible, even to the extent of sweeping the roadway to remove all debris.

Follow-up also involves removing damaged cargo to a place where it can be salvaged or recoupéd; transporting undamaged cargo to its destination (in the case of a bus accident, this would be passengers, baggage, and any express); and making arrangements for disabled vehicles to be removed to the proper repair agency for detailed estimates of damage and ultimate repair or wrecking.

A copy of the investigating police agency report should be obtained and made a part of the accident file. This report should provide all factual information determined by the investigating police officer, as well as list of any citations or summons given. In some states, this report will not reveal an opinion of the investigating officer; but this is not too important because such opinions are of little value: they are not admissible as evidence in court. If the case goes to court and the investigating officer is summoned, he can testify only to the factual information recorded in his report.

The physician who attended the injured person(s) should be contacted to obtain detailed information about the nature and extent of injuries. If the injured have been admitted to a hospital, hospital authorities should also be contacted. Whether or not the accident investigator should visit any injured persons while they are in the hospital is a moot question and each case has to be decided on its own merits in conformity with company policy and the wishes of the insurance adjuster.

The Post-Accident Interview

As soon as possible after an accident, the driver should be interviewed by his supervisor and/or the terminal manager. The safety director can give advice, but supervisory personnel must run the interview, otherwise authority is diluted.

The objectives of the post-accident interview are to:

1. Impress upon the driver the importance of driving safely.
2. Determine whether the accident in question was preventable or nonpreventable, in accordance with company standards of safe driving practice.
3. Help the driver learn from this accident how to prevent similar accidents.

The supervisor should prepare for the interview by studying the entire past safety record of the driver. For example, the driver's record may show he had three years' driving experience with tractors and semi-trailers before the date of his employment, and, in the 29 months since coming to the company, he has driven the same type of equipment. The card shows one other accident while driving for the company, 11 months prior to the date of the present accident, and also one summons for failing to stop at a stop sign.

The current accident occured at dusk, four-hours driving time away from the terminal. The truck was sideswiped as the driver was pulling away from the curb after a temporary stop. According to the accident report, the driver was attempting to maneuver into the center lane in order to make a left turn at an intersection and had signaled, but not soon enough to warn the car behind.

In the previous accident which occurred shortly after sundown, after about four hours driving, the company vehicle was struck from the rear while turning out to pass another vehicle that had slowed down abruptly. The accident report showed that, although a quick turn out was necessary to avoid striking the vehicle ahead, the company driver had been following too close at a speed too fast for the conditions of visibility, and had not allowed sufficient time to signal the vehicle following.

Noting the factors common to the accidents—that they both occurred at twilight after a period of steady driving, that both involved failure to watch out for vehicles behind when entering a different traffic lane, and that both involved improper signaling—the supervisor will plan the interview to emphasize these points.

In the preparation phase, the supervisor should also note all nonpreventable accidents the driver has had. An informal tabulation can be made showing the driver's accident frequency preventable or nonpreventable—in comparison with the group average of the fleet. He may also tabulate the cost of the accidents the driver has had and project these costs over the years remaining before the driver's retirement. The purpose of this information is to make the driver aware of the fact that the accidents he is having reflect on his driving ability as well as cost the company money. The safety director can be of real service here.

The supervisor should also study all materials available on the current accident and arrive at a tentative decision as to whether the accident was preventable or nonpreventable.

The post-accident interview should be conducted in a place where the supervisor and driver can have complete privacy and as much time as needed should be allotted. While it is important that the interview should be conducted with an air of objectivity, it must also be in a spirit of friendly helpfulness.

Even though the severity of the accident may be minor, the driver should be impressed that the important thing is to discover whether any faulty driving habits caused the accident. It should be pointed out that even though the severity of the present accident may be minor, the faulty driving habit that caused it could cause a much more severe accident in the future if allowed to persist.

After impressing the driver with the importance of safe driving, comparing his rating with that of other drivers, and projecting the cost of accidents that could be expected in the future, the supervisor should then turn to a discussion of the present accident. The supervisor already has studied all available information about the accident and the driver in order to be thoroughly familiar with the details. The purpose of the interview is to "think through together" the details of the accident: what was—or was not—done, what might—or might not—have been done, what should—or should not—have been done. In this part of the interview, the driver does most of the talking and the supervisor guides the discussion by means of a question or observation now and then.

After the accident has been thoroughly discussed, the supervisor should ask the driver whether he could have prevented it by displaying a higher degree of defensive driving. If the driver says "No," the supervisor should then say, *Does this mean that if you are permitted to continue to drive, and that every time this situation occurs, you will be involved in an accident?"* To answer this key question, the driver is forced to view the accident more objectively in terms of its *preventability.* This is therefore an important question.

At the conclusion of the interview, the supervisor should sum up the accident details, announce the decision as to preventability, spell out what that decision is and why, and tell the driver what he can do to prevent a recurrence. If he has made a sound decision and conducted the interview properly, the driver will agree with and accept this decision with good grace. The driver will leave the interview feeling that it has been a fair hearing with a reasonable decision, that he has learned something about safe driving and has a heightened respect for safe driving.

In the event the driver does not agree with the supervisor's decision as to preventability, some companies provide for a review of the accident and a decision by an accident review committee. In the event the driver is still not satisfied (or perhaps the company itself is not sure how the accident should be classified), the accident facts can be submitted to the Motor Transportation Department of the National Safety Council for decision.

The decision should be made by the immediate supervisor wherever possible, or at least by some authorized person at the location where the driver works. Decisions made at a distant headquarters tend to lack force. The decision should be made as soon after the accident as possible. Time tends to forgive an accident. Drivers will learn more from the interview and accept a preventable decision with better grace when the accident is fresh in their minds. It is most important that the supervisor sell his decision *as his own* and not behind phrases like, "The company treats *all* accidents as preventable," or "I could never get the main office to accept this as being nonpreventable."

It should also be pointed out that sound decisions on preventability can be made by a supervisor regardless of his driving experience. The old saying "You don't have to be a hen to know that an egg is rotten" applies here. Supervisors may not have had as much road experience as some of the veteran drivers, but they should at least have made a careful study of the concept of accident preventability and, through the experience of having reviewed and discussed numerous accidents with different drivers, have acquired an authoritative grasp of the essentials.

Dealing with accident repeaters

One of the most important functions of an accident record system is to quickly spot accident repeaters in order to bring them to the attention of management and the safety department for remedial training. Fleets seem to differ in their definition of an accident repeater, but usually it means having a second accident within a period of six months, nine months, or a year. This time period depends upon whether the driver drives in city or inter-city operations, with the city drivers permitted a shorter period of time between accidents due to the greater hazards of city operations. The real key is the average preventable accident frequency per driver of the group as a whole. Performance that is obviously poorer than average points to an accident repeater.

Drivers having their second accident are given the post-accident interview in accordance with the regular procedure. In addition, they may receive additional attention:

1. They are sent a warning letter, with a copy to the union if the driver is represented by one.

2. A driver trainer or supervisor is assigned to ride with the driver to report on his driving habits.

3. Special safety meetings or training courses are scheduled periodically for all accident repeaters. New approaches to learning, new films, and techniques can be used to keep the meetings from being "old hat" and from seeming more like a penalty than a learning experience.

There are a number of other corrective procedures that are sometimes used. These include special physical examinations and special counseling. When in spite of such efforts, a driver continues to have accidents, the company has no other recourse but to reassign him to a nondriving job or discharge him. Having good accident records is vital if the discharge is taken to arbitration.

Chapter 6

Organizing the Employee Injury-Prevention Program

The objective of an occupational injury reporting and investigation program is to eliminate from everyday work all unsafe acts and unsafe conditions that could cause personal injury, property damage, or fire. If these are removed, then employee injuries can be controlled. In spite of safe conditions, however, accidental injuries may still occur. And when they do, efforts should be made to learn as much about their cause as possible in order to prevent repetition. This is up to the employee's immediate supervisor, with help from the company safety department. In serious accidents, an injury investigation committee may be used.

Through time, various reasons have been given as to why some persons get hurt and others don't. Some reasons have been valid, such as "lack of experience" or "lack of attention." Many of them blame "fate": "he was just careless" or, "he was just plain stupid."

Only a valid reason points the way to proper corrective or preventive action. Also, there is little reason to seek out the basic cause or causes of a personal injury if there is not first a *determination* to set up practical measures for the prevention of a similar accidental injury. Why investigate if you know no action will be taken?

The most important responsibility of an injury investigation committee is to gather all the facts, then to evaluate them to determine the cause or causes of the injury, and finally to propose ways and means for preventing or at least reducing the number of such injuries in the future. Each will be discussed in turn.

Since 1962, American National Standards Institute (ANSI) Standard Z16.2 has afforded a way to analyze industrial injuries so that causes can be examined. It is titled, *Method of Recording Basic Facts Relating to Nature and Occurrence of Work Injuries.* It has been subdivided into the following categories:

- Nature of injury
- Part of body affected
- Source of injury
- Accident type
- Hazardous conditions
- Agency of accident
- Unsafe act

ANSI Z16.2 provides accident investigation committees with a checklist of the answers they should seek to determine how and why the accident happened.

Causes of Injuries

Because safety and accident investigation committees cannot be expected to memorize all of the provisions of the revised Z16.2 Standard, the accompanying "Guide for Determining the Hazardous Conditions and/or Unsafe Acts Related to an Employee Injury" is for reference.

Guide for Determining the Hazardous Conditions And/or Unsafe Acts Related to an Employee Injury

(Based on American National Standard Z16.2 as revised in 1962)

HAZARDOUS CONDITIONS

Defective, inferior or unsuitable tools, machinery, equipment, or materials

Broken	Loose	Improperly designed
Cracked	Slippery	Improperly assembled
Corroded	Dull	Improperly constructed
Decayed	Rough	Improperly compounded
Frayed	Sharp-edged	Improperly maintained
Worn	Defective insulation	Improperly lubricated

Dress or apparel hazards

Improperly clothed; inadequate clothing; loose clothing; loose jewelry
No shoes; shoes defective or unsuitable
No goggles, face shields, eye shields, or safety glasses; unsuitable eye protection
No respirators; respirators unsuitable or defective
No gloves; gloves unsuitable or defective
No head protection; safety hats or caps unsuitable or defective
No body protection; aprons, jackets, etc. unsuitable or defective

Environment hazards *(Not elsewhere classified)*

Congested working space; inadequate aisle space, inadequate clearance
Improper illumination; general illumination inadequate; insufficient light at point-of-operation; poor lighting due to glare, shadows, dirty fixtures, etc.
Improper ventilation; lack of a ventilating system; ventilating system of wrong type, insufficient capacity, improperly installed; poorly maintained

Hazardous methods or conditions

Improper assignment of personnel; inadequate help for heavy lifting, etc.
Use of inherently hazardous methods or procedures
Use of inherently hazardous (not defective) materials or equipment

Placement hazards

Unsafely piled materials (overloaded; unbalanced; not crosstied)
Inadequately secured against undesired motion (not unstable piling)

Inadequately guarded

Unguarded mechanical or physical hazards
Inadequately guarded; poorly guarded power transmission equipment; poorly guarded at point-of-operation
Uninsulated or ungrounded (electrical)
Unshielded or inadequately shielded (radiation)
Unlabeled or inadequately labeled materials

Hazards of outside work environments *(Not public hazards)*

Defective premises of others; defective materials or equipment of others
Natural hazards; wild animals; poisonous plants or insects; exposure to the elements; hazards of irregular or unstable terrain

Public hazards *(Encountered away from employer's premises)*

UNSAFE ACTS

Cleaning, oiling, adjusting or repairing equipment that is moving, electrically energized, or pressurized

Failure to use available personal protective equipment

Goggles	Gloves	Aprons
Safety glasses	Hats	Shoes
Hoods	Caps	Lifelines

Failure to wear safe personal attire

Loose clothing	Neckties	Loose hair
Long sleeves	Jewelry	High heels

Failure to secure or warn

Failure to place warning signs, signals, tags, etc.
Starting or stopping vehicles or equipment without giving adequate warning
Releasing or moving loads, etc., without giving adequate warning
Failure to lock, block or secure vehicles, switches, valves, or other equipment

Improper use of equipment

Using material or equipment in a manner for which it was not intended
Overloading

Improper use of hands or other body parts

Using hands instead of hand tools to feed, clean, adjust, repair, etc.
Gripping objects insecurely. Inattention to footing or surroundings

Making safety devices inoperative

Disconnecting, blocking, plugging, tying, or misadjusting safety devices

Operating or working at unsafe speeds

Feeding or supplying too rapidly. Throwing material instead of carrying or passing. Jumping from elevations (vehicles, elevators, platforms, etc.)
Running

Taking unsafe position or posture

Unnecessary exposure to suspended or swinging loads
Unnecessary exposure to moving materials or equipment
Entering tanks, bins or other enclosed spaces without proper supervisory clearance
Riding in unsafe position: on platforms, forks of lift trucks, etc.

Unsafe placing, mixing, combining, etc.

Creating a tripping, slipping or bumping hazard
Pouring water into acid

Using tools or equipment that are known to be unsafe

Driving errors *(By a vehicle operator on public roadways)*

Horseplay *(Distracting, teasing, abusing, practical joking, showing off)*

Not in revised code *(Failure to follow instructions or a proper job procedure)*

To determine the basic cause or causes of an industrial accident, it is recommended that the accident investigation committee, after hearing all the known facts surrounding the accident, come to a conclusion as to whether it was due primarily to a "mechanical cause," a "personal cause," or a combination of both. Personal causes are of three principal types:

- *Bodily defects* such as defective eyesight, defective hearing, muscular weakness, organic weakness. A safety committee will probably phrase its findings in terms of "Probable . . ."
- *Lack of knowledge or skill* such as being unpracticed or unskilled, or being unaware of the safe practice. These result in some "unsafe acts."
- *Temporary lack of safety mindedness at the time of the injury* due, possibly, to distraction, confusion, mental worry, fatigue, inattention, etc., and resulting in some "unsafe acts."

Once an organization reaches the point in its injury prevention work that it readily accepts the understanding that *accidents are caused,* then it can ferret out the individual causes with ever increasing skill, and it will buckle down to the task of preventing future accidents.

Occupational Injury Reporting And Record System

Records of occupational injuries are essential to efficient and successful safety work just as records of production, costs, sales, and profits and losses are essential to efficient and successful operations of any business.

The Occupational Safety and Health Administration (OSHA) requires that nonexempt, and some regularly exempt, employers prepare and file records of their employees' injuries and illnesses. The OSHA recordkeeping and reporting requirements are different and separate from any state's workers' compensation recording and filing procedures *(*See pages *92–93).* Information on the OSHA requirements can be obtained from the U.S. Department of Labor, Bureau of Labor Statistics, Washington, D.C. 20212.

Information on voluntary filing for contests and awards is contained in American National Standards: Z16.1, *Method of Recording and Measuring Work Injury Experience,* and Z16.2, *Method of Recording Basic Facts Relating to the Nature and Occurrence of Work Injuries.*

When kept in accordance with the standard method, work accident records provide a safety director and management with an objective evaluation of their safety program. They identify high injury fleets, terminals, or departments, and they give the safety director the information he needs to work hardest on the accident causes that contribute most to high rates.

More specifically, standardized work accident records are used to:

• *Create interest in safety* among supervisors by furnishing them with information about the injury experience of their particular company units, whether a division, terminal, department, or other subdivision.

• *Determine the principal injury sources* so that efforts may be made to reduce them.

• *Provide supervisors and safety committees with information* about the most frequent unsafe practices and unsafe conditions so that these persons can use their time and efforts to the greatest advantage.

• *Judge the effectiveness of the safety program* by showing whether the accident experience is getting better or worse and by allowing comparison with the experience of organizations doing similar work.

Note that although ANSI standard was once used as the principal method of keeping statistics, today it is only used to compare accident rates in varying states regardless of differences in workers' compensation rates. But, because of possible variations in interpretations, *use it only as a guide to, and not as the actual, employee injury status.*

The medical and first aid program is intimately tied in with the system of accident records and reports.

Medical Treatment and First Aid

Because employees may be injured at any time, smoothly operating first aid and medical procedures should be established to ensure prompt, adequate treatment.

Every fleet location should have a qualified physician to provide essential emergency medical care for all employees. Arrangements can be for on-call or consulting services. Drivers away from home should be trained in what to do in the event of accident or illness.

In addition to providing emergency medical care, the physician can also conduct preplacement physical examinations, periodic physical examinations, and, sometimes, exit examinations for those employees who quit or are discharged. This is covered more completely in the *Accident Prevention Manual for Industrial Operations, Administration and Programs* volume, published by the National Safety Council.

In many fleets or in outlying fleet operations, it is neither practical

Form IS-6

Case No.__________ Date__________

First Aid Report

Name__________ Department __________

Male ☐ Female ☐ Occupation __________ Foreman __________

Date of Occurrence______ Time____ a.m. p.m. Date of First Treatment______ Time____ a.m. p.m.

Nature of Occurrence__________

Sent: Back to Work ☐ Doctor ☐ Home ☐ Hospital ☐

Estimated Disability____ days

Employee's Description of Occurrence__________

Signed__________
First Aid

Issued by National Safety Council Inc., 444 N. Michigan, Chicago, Ill. 60611

Figure 6-1. *First aid report (4 by 6-inch card) is prepared by the first aid attendant at the time of treatment. A report should be prepared for each case, whether minor or serious.*

nor justifiable to employ full-time professional medical personnel to treat minor injuries. In such cases, the best arrangement is to provide a suitable first aid kit or a station administered by a trained first aid attendant who follows procedures and treatments outlined by the company's medical advisor. A physician should be on call or available for referral to take care of emergencies.

A first aid program should include the following:

- Properly trained and designated first aiders on every shift and at every company location.
- A first aid unit and supplies, or first aid kit.
- A first aid manual.
- Posted instructions for calling a physician and notifying the hospital that the patient is en route.
- Posted instructions for transporting ill or injured employees and instructions for calling an ambulance or rescue squad.
- An adequate injury record system.

First aid report

Some companies may require that a report be made for any first aid treatment (see Figure 6-1). Most transportation concerns do not need so

ACCIDENT INVESTIGATION REPORT

CASE NUMBER

COMPANY ______________________ ADDRESS ______________________

DEPARTMENT ______________________ LOCATION (if different from mailing address) ______________________

1. NAME of INJURED	2. SOCIAL SECURITY NUMBER	3. SEX ☐ M ☐ F	4. AGE	5. DATE of ACCIDENT
6. HOME ADDRESS	7. EMPLOYEE'S USUAL OCCUPATION		8. OCCUPATION at TIME of ACCIDENT	
11. EMPLOYMENT CATEGORY ☐ Regular, full-time ☐ Temporary ☐ Nonemployee ☐ Regular, part-time ☐ Seasonal	9. LENGTH of EMPLOYMENT ☐ Less than 1 mo. ☐ 6 mos. to 5 yrs. ☐ 1-5 mos. ☐ More than 5 yrs.		10. TIME in OCCUP. at TIME of ACCIDENT ☐ Less than 1 mo. ☐ 6 mos. to 5 yrs. ☐ 1-5 mos. ☐ More than 5 yrs.	
13. NATURE of INJURY and PART of BODY	12. CASE NUMBERS and NAMES of OTHERS INJURED in SAME ACCIDENT			
14. NAME and ADDRESS of PHYSICIAN	16. TIME of INJURY A. ______ A.M. P.M. B. Time within shift C. Type of shift		17. SEVERITY of INJURY ☐ Fatality ☐ Lost workdays—days away from work ☐ Lost workdays—days of restricted activity ☐ Medical treatment ☐ First aid ☐ Other, specify ______	
15. NAME and ADDRESS of HOSPITAL				
18. SPECIFIC LOCATION of ACCIDENT ON EMPLOYER'S PREMISES? ☐ Yes ☐ No	19. PHASE OF EMPLOYEE's WORKDAY at TIME of INJURY ☐ During rest period ☐ During meal period ☐ Working overtime ☐ Entering or leaving plant ☐ Performing work duties ☐ Other ______			

20. DESCRIBE HOW the ACCIDENT OCCURRED

____

21. ACCIDENT SEQUENCE. Describe in reverse order of occurrence events preceding the injury and accident. Starting with the injury and moving backward in time, reconstruct the sequence of events that led to the injury.

A. Injury Event ______________________

B. Accident Event ______________________

C. Preceding Event #1 ______________________

D. Preceding Event #2, #3, etc. ______________________

***Figure 6-2a** Supervisor's accident report aids investigation.*

elaborate a system, but it can increase the data used to analyze injury experience.

Employer's first report of injury

Every state requires a report of any occupational injury where there is medical treatment beyond first aid, and/or time is lost from work beyond the current shift. State forms vary and are usually available from

22. TASK and ACTIVITY at TIME of ACCIDENT

A. General type of task ____________________

B. Specific activity ____________________

C. Employee was working

☐ Alone ☐ With crew or fellow worker ☐ Other, specify ____________________

23. POSTURE of EMPLOYEE

____

24. SUPERVISION at TIME of ACCIDENT

☐ Directly supervised ☐ Not supervised

☐ Indirectly supervised ☐ Supervision not feasible

25. CAUSAL FACTORS. Events and conditions that contributed to the accident. Include those identified by use of the Guide for Identifying Causal Factors and Corrective Actions.

____

26. CORRECTIVE ACTIONS. Those that have been, or will be, taken to prevent recurrence. Include those indentified by use of the Guide for Identifying Causal Factors and Corrective Actions.

____

PREPARED BY ____________________

TITLE ____________________

DEPARTMENT ____________________ DATE ____________

Developed by the National Safety Council

APPROVED ____________________

TITLE ____________________ DATE ____________

APPROVED ____________________

TITLE ____________________ DATE ____________

Figure 6-2b. *Reverse side of report.*

the company's insurance carrier. Since this form must be made up, it is usually considered the principal injury form and other records are designed to complement it.

Employee's report of injury

It is important to get a firsthand account of how the employee thinks the injury occurred. Frequently, supervisors will color their accounts of the injury for fear of exposing some of their own shortcomings. If investigation is hurried, the facts may not be available, and wrong assumptions may be frozen into the supervisor's report. The employee is usually the best source of information about what happened, and his story should be obtained as soon as possible.

Obviously, a badly injured employee cannot be forced to make out a report immediately, but the report can usually be secured within a few days. Generally the worker welcomes the chance to "tell it like it is."

Copies of the employee's report must be furnished to him and to the company insurance carrier or department. This form should be acceptable to company labor relations experts and to the insurance carrier. They will have suggestions for a usable format.

Supervisor's report of injury

Since the state injury report form really does not analyze the injury, and the employee may not want or be able to give the full facts, it is valuable to have the immediate supervisor's version on file. This form does not go to a public agency, so the supervisor is more likely to discuss the case fully. (See Figure 6-2.)

Employee Injury Record

To maintain a record of the injury experience of each employee, information about all injuries, first aid cases, and disabling injuries is entered in a log or folder. A special form, "injury record of employee," can be used. (See Figure 6-3.)

Because supervisors cannot be expected to remember the experience of individual employees over time, a periodic study of the injury record forms may reveal that some employees are having far more accidents than others. This may be a signal for individual corrective action such as counseling, retraining, or reassignment to a less hazardous job. Many companies even issue warning letters or take other disciplinary action where the records show consistent disregard for the employee's own welfare and that of other employees.

Counting Injuries and Figuring Rates

The fleet manager and the fleet safety director need some method for measuring how well the employee safety program is doing and whether it is succeeding in cutting down injuries.

Safety performance is relative. Only when a fleet compares its in-

INJURY AND ILLNESS RECORD OF EMPLOYEE

______________________________ (Name) ______________________________ (Employee Number)

Occupation ____________ Department ____________ Date Employed ____________

Case Number	Injury or Illness	Date of Occurrence	Z16 Type (Fatal, Permanent, Temporary, Non-disabling)	Z16 Days Charged	Comp. and Other Costs	OSHA Type (Fatal, Lost Workday, Non-Lost Workday)	OSHA Lost Workdays

(Reverse side may be used for remarks)

Issued by NATIONAL SAFETY COUNCIL, 444 N. Michigan Ave., Chicago, Ill. 60611

Figure 6-3. *Injury and illness record of employee, a 4 by 6 inch card for recording injuries.*

jury experience with its own previous experience or with that of similar fleets, can it obtain a meaningful evaluation of its achievement.

A useful yardstick for this is the American National Standard Z16.1 method for determining injury frequency rate. This is the number of disabling injuries* per million employee hours worked, computed according to the following formula:

$$\text{Frequency Rate} = \frac{\text{Number of disabling injuries} \times 1{,}000{,}000}{\text{Employee-hours of exposure}}$$

For example, if the total employee hours of exposure in a given year are 2,000,000 and there are 25 disabling injuries during that period, the frequency rate is 12.5 disabling injuries per million employee hours worked.

---

*A disabling injury is one that renders the injured person unable to perform regular duties on one or more full calendar days after the day of the injury.

While the injury rate can be a valuable yardstick, it is generally not too reliable a measurement of safety success in exposures of less than one million work hours: it would take a fleet of 500 employees approximately one year to compile this exposure. Most transportation fleets are much smaller than that. Even so, the rates should be computed monthly and annually. Cumulative rates will provide meaningful information and trend indications for comparative purposes.

Using Injury Information Effectively

Three statistics should be brought to management's attention: (*a*) The injury frequency rate of the company and then of some particular department or work group, (*b*) the date of the last lost-time injury, and (*c*) the number of hours worked since the last lost-time injury.

At year's end, it is recommended that each company furnish the National Safety Council with a summary of its accidental injury experience. (The Council will furnish the reporting forms.) More and more companies are showing such facts in their annual report to stockholders, particularly when outstanding safety records have been achieved. Once a good record is established, it seems to breed a still better one.

OSHA and Injury Records

The Occupational Safety and Health Act of 1970 (OSHAct) added a new dimension to safety and health in its creation of OSHA, the Occupational Safety and Health Administration. While the impact of the act can not be reviewed here, there are important parts that must be considered in every company safety program.

• Every company location must maintain a yearly log of occupational injuries, on a form provided by OSHA. In the motor carrier industry this has been interpreted to mean a separate log for each terminal. A separate shop building, with office, would probably need to keep its own log separate from the terminal.

• At year's end, the columns of the log are summarized. On February first of the following year, the summary sheet (actually the right side of the log) must be posted where all employees can review it. At the end of the month, the posting may be removed and filed with prior year logs.

• OSHA inspectors may call on the terminal to make an inspection. In most cases, they can be denied admission until a warrant is obtained, but generally it is better to welcome them in. Although there always will be the isolated bad case, safety directors usually have found OSHA inspectors to be fair and well-qualified to do their jobs. If they find a genuine interest in the safety and health program and an attempt to provide a safe and healthy place to work, they will be helpful. They will, of course, require that unsafe and unhealthful work situations be corrected.

• Each state obtains data on company locations from sources such as occupational injury reports, and may send a survey form requesting work-hour figures and number of injuries and occupational illnesses.

• OSHA inspections can be brought about through complaints lodged by employees, by the occurrence of a serious injury, or by reported injury experience poorer than the industry average. A few are done randomly as the inspector goes on his rounds.

OSHAct has had a strong impact on safety and health, especially in eliminating unsafe and unhealthful working conditions and requiring personal protective gear. It has been less successful at correcting the unsafe acts of workers, since there are no penalties directed at the worker. OSHA takes the position that performance of the worker is the responsibility of the employer. As a result, knowledgeable employees can use OSHA regulations as a means of harrassment, to achieve ends related to labor conflict rather than safety. The perfect defense to these actions is to conduct a strong safety and health program and make it obvious every reasonable step has been taken to protect the worker.

Chapter 7

The Employee Injury-Prevention Program

We have seen in Chapters 4 and 6 that employee accidental injuries in a motor vehicle fleet can occur frequently and that these injuries are costly; fortunately, they can be prevented and the cost of their prevention is less than the cost of allowing them to occur. The conditions and procedures for the control of these accidental injuries comprise the driver and terminal employee safety program—the subject of this chapter.*

What is the difference between a fleet that has an employee safety program and one that does not?

An employee safety program requires studying every job operation in the fleet in order to know the hazards connected with each, and then—for those hazards that cannot be engineered out of the operation, or isolated, or otherwise mitigated—devising safe work procedures to control these hazards. Every employee is trained in the safety procedures connected with his job. Each supervisor checks for compliance with these safety procedures, and all those in management vigorously and continuously support the employee safety program to make it an important part of their successful fleet operation.

Contrast this with the fleet that does not have an employee safety program—hazards are not studied, safety procedures are not a recognized part of operations, safety is a hit-or-miss affair depending upon the prior safety knowledge that each individual happens to bring to his job.

---

*Under the Occupational Safety and Health Act (OSHAct), which became effective on April 28, 1971, most employers must render their establishments as free from potential safety and health hazards as possible.

How To Start a Safety Program

To start an employee safety program, the safety director must make certain that management knows the basic theories of accident prevention and how they will be put into practice. The National Safety Council's *Supervisors Safety Manual* contains details on setting up and administrating an occupational hazard control program (see Appendix E). To develop both management and employee conviction that accident prevention works, these topics should be covered early in supervisor and employee training courses:

- Accidents can happen anywhere at any time. It cannot be assumed, therefore, that any department, job, or facility is safe. Everything must be studied to eliminate hazards.
- Accidents are not the result of chance, but are caused either by specific unsafe acts or specific unsafe conditions. Accidents can be prevented by learning what these specific acts and conditions are and then substituting safe acts and safe conditions.
- Unless unsafe acts and unsafe conditions are corrected, an accident will eventually result. If corrective action is still not taken, accidents will be repeated.
- Everyone in the organization must assume personal responsibility for safety: management, each department head, each supervisor, and each individual worker and driver.

It is the purpose of the safety program to disseminate information about hazards and provide the stimulus for sustained safety effort. The training program should first be presented to all supervisors. They, in turn, should help present the material to their employees.

Make a Safety Check First

As soon as management knows what is to be accomplished, the safety director should see that management sets broad policies. If the company is quite large, a management safety committee can be formed.

After they are trained in what to look for, management or the management committee should make a system-wide safety inspection to bring all facilities up to current safety standards. The composition of any committee will depend upon the size of the fleet, but should include those who have the maximum knowledge of methods, practices, and conditions of the type the committee will encounter.

More than one type committee can be formed: company-wide or inter-terminal, terminal, department, supervisory, worker, joint labor-management, inspection, and "get-it-done" committees. Enlightened management should make policies and give moral and financial support to its committees.

Every building and every yard or facility of the company should be inspected according to the housekeeping and maintenance checklists shown later in this chapter. When making inspection of separate shops or terminals, the local managers, if not already on the committee, should join it for the local inspection.

Initial inspection

The safety director should use an initial safety inspection by a management committee to bring facilities up to date and, equally important, to train management itself. Following are some of the techniques to be used in this initial inspection. They apply to all properties.

- Review and list in advance the anticipated mechanical or physical hazards.
- Let the inspection follow the job process whenever possible. For example, when buses or trucks are to be serviced, note what equipment is being used as vehicles are being refueled, checked, and cleaned. Is any of this equipment unsafe to use?
- Avoid disturbing or distracting those at work by not ceremoniously writing notes or memorandums in their presence. Make notes quickly or make them afterwards. A compact cassette recorder would be useful here.
- Don't pass up an opportunity to instruct in the safe procedure if this is necessary. Usually it is best to bring the matter to the attention of the proper supervisor or superintendent after the inspection has been completed, unless there is an emergency that requires immediate action.
- Be as alert as possible when making an inspection.

Look for signs of poor housekeeping, poor maintenance, inadequate tools, unsuitable equipment.

Listen for sounds of escaping compressed air, steam, water, oxygen, and acetylene. Listen for unusual sounds like thumps, squeaks, and squeals.

Feel for equipment or machinery that is vibrating unnecessarily. Carefully check for sharp points or edges that may cut, puncture, or tear. Check for hot surfaces that may burn or radiate, causing discomfort.

Smell for odors of leaking gas, spilled gasoline or diesel fuel, or other flammable gases or liquids.

Taste drinking water as it comes from drinking fountains or other forms of dispensers. Taste the quality of products dispensed from coffee urns or soft drink dispensers. Is the temperature proper?

On this first inspection, it might also be desirable to call in trained personnel or contract for their services for appraisal and inspection of fire extinguishing equipment and of elevators and pressure vessels, if this hasn't already been done. Such inspections are usually required by a city, county, or state ordinance or code, and by insurance carriers.

Chapters 3 through 7 of the National Safety Council's *Accident Prevention Manual for Industrial Operations, Administration and Programs Volume,* 8th ed., discuss safety organization and inspection methods. Chapter 24 of the same book lists private organizations and government agencies of both U.S. and Canada that offer help. It would be a good idea to consult this book for the nondriving safety aspects of fleet safety management.

Freight and passenger terminals

In freight terminals, specifically, check for condition of the docks, floors, lighting, freight-handling equipment (such as forklift trucks, dollies, pallets, conveyors, hand trucks), weighing scales, storage racks, bins. A checklist accompanies this section.

In passenger terminals, check condition of baggage-checking facilities, ticket counters, waiting room and officer furniture and equipment. Usually, such inspections are made in conjunction with the inspection of public-passenger facilities in waiting rooms, rest rooms, and boarding and alighting areas. It is far better to seek and detect probable injury-causing conditions than to find them the cause of an accident.

A checklist is given on these pages. More details are given in the section "Establish Safe Practices," pages 102 to 118.

Mechanical and Physical Hazards To Look for When Making a Safety Inspection

QUALITY OF SHOP, STATION (TERMINAL), OR GARAGE HOUSEKEEPING

1. Are yards and outdoor premises clean?
2. Are roadway markings, lane numbers, markings for parking areas kept freshly and neatly painted or outlined?
3. Are buildings kept attractively painted?
4. Are windows clean? Are missing, broken, or cracked window panes renewed?

5. Are skylights clean? Are missing, broken, or cracked panes renewed?

6 Are building entrances unobstructed?

7. Are indoor traffic lanes kept freshly painted?

8. Are floors kept clean of oil, grease, water, dirt, or trash?

9. Are aisles kept clear?

10. Are stairs kept clear?

11. Are fire escapes unobstructed?

12. Is loose material left around building columns or walls or under benches?
    Soft drink bottles?
    Discarded lunch boxes?
    Short pieces of pipe?
    Defective automotive parts?
    Timbers or wooden blocks no longer needed?

13. Are approved container or waste or trash cans or bins provided?

14. Are they emptied regularly and often?

15. Are automotive maintenance or overhaul pits satisfactorily clean?

16. Is the area under automotive hoists kept clean?

17. Are lighting fixtures dirty?

18. Are work benches and tool carts kept satisfactorily clean?

19. Are tools kept in a designated place when not in use?

20. Is portable equipment kept in a designated place when not in use?

21. Is material stored or piled neatly and safely?

22. Is firefighting equipment kept in a well-known, well-marked place?

23. Is firefighting equipment kept free of obstructions?

24. Are old brooms, mops, ladders, and other gear disposed of when no longer usable?

25. Are bulletin boards stripped periodically of out-of-date notices, letters, greeting cards, and the like?

26. Are locker rooms, change rooms, rest rooms, washrooms kept neat and clean?

27. Are there any protruding nails, bolts, wire, splinters, glass, or other sharp objects?

28. Are warning or caution signs in good condition?

29. Are hose and portable electric cords allowed to become a tripping hazard when they could be kept overhead?

30. Are sawdust or metal chips allowed to accumulate on the floor?

31. Are office areas kept neat and free of samples, experimental materials, defective parts, catalogs, and discarded clothing?

32. Are desks and shop work benches neatly maintained?

33. Are clock faces kept clean?

34. Is the area around soft drink dispensers and candy bar dispensers kept neat and orderly?

QUALITY OF SHOP, STATION (TERMINAL), OR GARAGE MAINTENANCE

1. Are floors and stairways in good condition?

2. Are handrails provided on stairways, and kept in good condition?

3. Are aisle and work area markings provided, and well maintained?

4. Are machine tools kept well painted?

5. Are moving machinery parts well guarded?

6. Is materials handling equipment kept in good repair:
   Cranes?
   Hoists?
   Conveyors?
   Forklift power trucks? Pallets?
   Hand trucks?
   Wheel barrows?
   Carts?
   Dollies?

7. Are ropes, chains, cables, and slings in good condition?

8. Are elevators and manlifts well guarded and in good repair?

9. Are platforms and scaffolds in good condition?

10. Are ladders in safe condition; equipped with safety shoes?

11. Are pressure vessels regularly inspected?

12. Is compressed air equipment and piping in good condition?

13. Is gasoline and diesel oil dispensing equipment in good condition?

14. Is lubricating and transmission oil dispensing equipment O.K.?

15. Is venting equipment in good condition?

16. Is heating equipment in good condition?

17. Is general overhead lighting system adequate? Well maintained?

18. Is pit, storeroom, and other special lighting adequate? Well maintained?

19. Is firefighting equipment adequate? Well maintained?
    Fire extinguishers? (CO_2 or dry powder?)
    Fire hose?
    Overhead and "beneath vehicle" sprinklers?

20. Is safe storage provided for flammable liquids? Well maintained?

21. Are there adequate and sufficient facilities for storage of used oils, lubricants, and solvents?

22. Are containers of solvent labeled to show hazards of improper use?

23. Are material safety data sheets (MSDS) for all hazardous materials readily available?

24. Have all employees using hazardous materials been informed of the location of the corresponding material safety data sheets?

25. If a vendor is contracted to dispose of used oils, solvents, and other materials, is he properly licensed?

26. Are doors and windows kept in easy operating condition?

27. Are sufficient work benches provided? Well maintained?

28. Are vises, grinders, and welding equipment in good condition?

29. Are portable electric tools safely grounded? Checked periodically?

30. Are tool rooms provided and are they properly supervised?

31. Is first aid equipment kept in an accessible place? Checked periodically?

32. Are washroom and locker room facilities adequate? Well maintained?

33. Are storage tanks provided? Well maintained?

34. Are tire storage facilities provided? Well maintained?

35. Are waste disposal drums or bins provided? Well maintained?

36. Is adequate personal protective equipment provided and well maintained?
    Safety hats or caps? Respirators?
    Goggles, safety glasses, eye shields, face shields? Gloves?

37. Is personal protective equipment being used by employees?

38. Do roofs leak?

Follow-up

Following this inspection, the committee should summarize all unsafe conditions observed and make recommendations for their correction. Management should then issue the orders necessary for the correction of these conditions. The safety director should follow up on each recommendation to make sure it is carried out within a reasonable time.

Establish Safe Practices

There are certain fundamental safe practices that should be followed by everyone. These should be formulated, published, and disseminated to all employees in the form of logical and enforceable safety rules. A rule that is not logical or that cannot be enforced may seriously impair the effectiveness of other rules. Once definite safety rules have been selected and made known to employees, the company safety policy should state explicitly that they must be observed.

General safety rules should cover the following subjects after first stressing the need for safety rules for operating and maintaining a safe fleet.

- *Employee responsibility* for conducting oneself in a safe manner at all times, for reporting to the supervisor all unsafe practices and unsafe conditions observed, for asking the supervisor for specific instructions about unusual hazards not covered in the rule book, and for observing all signs and notices.
- *First aid.* Discussion of available first aid facilities, essential telephone numbers (such as those for a doctor and for an ambulance), and the injury-reporting system. The subjects of infection, artificial respiration, heat sickness, and all other first aid information pertinent to terminal, garage, or highway can be given through courses.
- *Firefighting.* Location and description of emergency firefighting equipment in the plant, how to reach the local fire department, the specific procedure to be followed in case of fire or other emergency, an explanation of the emergency alarm system, and information on fire prevention.
- *Electrical equipment.* Hazards associated with certain types of electrical apparatus and the appropriate precautions to be taken during maintenance and repair of defective equipment. How to deal with electrical fires.
- *Work clothing.* Detailed item-by-item descriptions of what is safe and unsafe work clothing, and that wearing of rings, for example, is prohibited in the work areas.

• *Personal protective equipment.* Eye protection, foot protection, respiratory equipment, hand protection, head protection, and so on. Tell whether specific items are recommended or required and the circumstances under which required equipment must be used.

• *Good housekeeping.* Personal cleanliness. Hygienic use of toilet, shower, washroom, locker room, and lunchroom facilities; safe methods of piling material; and other aspects of good housekeeping.

The company rule book should be given to all employees and its contents discussed at one or more safety meetings. It should also be given to new employees, and its material should be incorporated in the company's training program.

A general safety rule book, unfortunately, cannot cover everything. Instruction in specific job-safety practices is, therefore, the responsibility of the immediate supervisor. Performance is the responsibility of the employee.

To determine the specific job hazards, use the systematic procedure known as a job safety analysis (JSA). Not only should the safety director learn this technique, but all safety supervisors should also. The reader will find details in Chapter 14.

Some of the more important job hazards found in fleets are as follows:

1. Hazards to eyesight

Probably the most tragic injury short of death is total loss of eyesight. This need not occur if eye protection is required by safety rules, and consistently used. This safety habit can be acquired.

Employees who must wear prescription eye glasses should be required to wear prescription safety glasses because these will generally withstand an impact from eight to twelve times greater than ordinary glasses can without cracking or shattering.

Because glasses will not afford sufficient eye protection for every job duty, other types of protection is available. Here is a suggested list of the type of eye protective equipment that should be worn for specific job duties:

Wear safety goggles or eye shields when:

Grinding
Using impact wrenches and air drills
Chipping, scraping, or scaling paint, rust, carbon, or other materials
Using punches or chisels
Cutting rivets
Cutting or breaking glass

Chipping or breaking concrete
Using paint remover
Servicing air conditioning equipment with refrigerants
Soldering
Cleaning dust or dirt from motors, generators, compartments
Removing hard putty from sashes
Using metal-cutting lathe, shaper, drill press, or power hack saw
Steam cleaning
Washing vehicles or parts with soaps or solvents
Working under vehicles

Wear face shield when:
Working around battery acid
Pouring Babbitt or other molten metals
Buffing with wire brush wheels
Repairing brake linings
Grinding body filler

Wear safety goggles with light green lenses when:
Metallizing

Wear hood with clear lenses when:
Sandblasting out in the open
Pouring acid from carboys

Wear hood with dark lenses of proper shade when:
Cutting or welding metal
Doing electric welding or assisting an electric welder

2. Health hazards

The primary health hazards to garage employees are spray-painting equipment, solvent hazards, carbon monoxide poisoning, dermatitis, hearing damage from noisy work, inhalation of metal fumes when metallizing, and inhalation of asbestos dust when working on brake or clutch linings.

Spray-painting hazards can be overcome through the design and adequate maintenance of ventilating systems. Ventilating systems will remove most of the exhaust fumes and gases produced by gasoline or diesel engines operated within buildings. Solvent vapors can be controlled through the use of properly designed equipment. Gloves, aprons, and other protective clothing can shield the skin against solvent absorption. Wearing ear plugs or other noise attenuators will protect the ears from hearing damage caused by excessive sound. Respirators can prevent employees from breathing harmful asbestos and other dusts, fumes, or mists. Again refer to the Council's *Accident Prevention Manual* and *Fundamentals of Industrial Hygiene.*

3. Hazards of lifting autos, trucks, and buses

Three major hazards are associated with hoisting or raising automotive equipment: (*a*) having a vehicle fall off a hoist or a ramp because it had not been properly positioned, (*b*) having a hoist drop suddenly due to a loss of pressure, or binding and dropping suddenly due to a stuck or jammed piston inside of a hydraulic cylinder, (*c*) striking one's head against some part of the hoist or the vehicle on the hoist.

Install only hoists specifically designed to handle all automotive equipment used. Do not use makeshift setups.

Competent periodic inspection of all hoisting equipment and a high quality maintenance program will minimize hoist failure.

To avoid striking one's head, workers should wear a "bump-type" safety cap, which will not limit their ability to work in close quarters. Along with the wearing of suitable head protection is the necessity of using safety goggles, eye shields, or face shields to prevent eye injuries from dislodged dirt or other foreign matter. Vapor-proof lights should be used around these areas.

4. Burn hazards from chemicals, hot water, or steam

Oil-soaked, grease-covered, and dirt-covered parts have to be cleaned from time to time to permit accurate, expeditious maintenance or overhaul of automotive equipment. Special steam-cleaning equipment is used for the purpose. The hazard of using steam arises out of its accidental misdirection or having a steam hose burst or come loose while under pressure. National Safety Council Industrial Data Sheet No. 238, *Cleaning with Hot Water and Steam,* gives details.

Boilers and other pressure vessels must be constructed according to the *Boiler and Pressure Vessel Code* of the American Society of Mechanical Engineers,* be properly installed and fitted with all required safety devices, and be inspected regularly and conscientiously as required by the insurance underwriter and state or local laws. Burns arising out of accidental contact with hot surfaces can be avoided by using suitable insulation, barricades, railings, or enclosures. Check local codes also.

When a heated caustic solution is used for cleaning, it presents a chemical burn hazard. This may be safeguarded against by wearing suitable safety goggles, eyeshields or face shields or hoods, gloves, and aprons. Acid burns from handling, servicing, or charging of storage bat-

---

*American Society of Mechanical Engineers, 345 East 47th St., New York, N.Y. 10017

teries can be prevented by using proper personal protective equipment such as hoods and rubber gloves and aprons. Those people handling cleaning chemicals can be protected from dermatitis by wearing similar protective gear. See the *Supervisors Safety Manual* for detailed information.

5. Hazards of removing or replacing very heavy unit parts

When handling engines, transmissions, clutches, front and rear axles, dual tires and rims and brake drums, air conditioning equipment, and all other heavy automotive parts, use jacks, dollies, hoists, or cranes. When rope or steel slings or forklift trucks are used to handle these heavy loads, all equipment should be handled by properly trained and supervised personnel. There should be a high safety factor in the equipment used to handle the heavy weights involved. Equipment should be properly maintained.

Certain hazards are likely to be overlooked when using powered materials handling equipment. Be careful when raising, lowering, and tilting the hoisting ram and guides of forklift trucks. Also, as the ram ascends or descends, it can pinch off fingers unless pinch points are well guarded.

Monorail hoists and traveling cranes must have their interlocks checked periodically to make sure the stop dogs will readily drop to prevent running off the rail. Hoist load blocks and hooks should have a sheave guard to prevent fingers, hands, or arms being caught between the sheave and the wire rope. When jacks or table hoists are used to raise or lower metal parts, metal-to-metal contacts may slip and permit movement of whatever is being raised or lowered. Use a piece of cloth or properly fitted wood blocks to separate metal from metal.

6. Hazards of mounting heavy-duty tires and rims

The obvious hazard in mounting tires and rims is that of blowing off the rims, flanges, or lock rings as high-pressure, heavy-duty tires are being inflated. Blowoffs can occur with such violence that they can kill a person instantly. To safeguard against this, deflate tires *before* any other operations are performed, and use a correctly constructed metal cage to contain the lock ring should it accidentally blow off during inflation. For complete details on how to combat this hazard, see the Council's Industrial Data Sheet No. 411, *Mounting Heavy-Duty Tires and Rims.*

Another hazard involved in handling heavy truck and bus tires comes from mishandling impact wrenches used to loosen or tighten wheel lug nuts.

Still another hazard that frequently causes skinned knuckles and hands is the close clearance between tires and fenders. Therefore, keep hands low when pulling tires and rims. One ever-present hazard is that of being struck by a falling heavy-duty tire, or by dual-mounted tires. They must be moved carefully and must be left in a very secure position if laid aside.

7. Hazards of machine tools

Two principal hazards when using metal working tools are:

- Power transmission equipment such as pulleys, sheaves, belts, gears, and clutches, and
- Point-of-operation hazards.

Both hazards can be safeguarded against by the use of well designed and well maintained guards or barricades. (The *Accident Prevention Manual for Industrial Operations, Engineers and Technology* volume, contains many ideas about guarding.)

8. Hazards of welding equipment

Welding equipment can produce accidental burns (due to contact with the heat source or with hot metal), and eye injuries (due to exposure to ultraviolet light or popping slag). Fumes or vapors from certain metals like zinc can also produce ill effects. All of these hazards can be effectively guarded against by wearing proper protective equipment (hoods, jackets, leggings, spats, gloves, goggles, and respirators) and by having adequate ventilation.

Be sure all employees are protected from the harmful rays of electric arc welding equipment. Welder's helpers must be required to wear tinted safety goggles. Screens and barricades should be erected around welding operations to trap all harmful light rays. Welding booths must be ventilated adequately to protect those working inside. (More welding hazards are discussed in Section 10, following.)

Also, wear clear lens flash goggles under the helmet to prevent hot slag from popping into eyes when hood is temporarily raised. (see Section 1 in this chapter and the chapter on "Welding and Cutting" of *Accident Prevention Manual for Industrial Operations, Engineering and Technology* volume, for more details.)

9. Hazards of powered hand tools

The use of portable electric drills can result in eye injuries or electrical shock. Not only can hot chips or turnings cause burns, but the drill can puncture hands, arms, or legs. Therefore it must be handled with care.

To avoid accidental electric shock from drills and other electric hand tools that are not double insulated, an auxiliary grounding wire must be connected to the frame of the drill. This is usually done through a three-wire electric cord.

In general, it is preferable to have compressed air supply lines and electric extension cords ceiling-suspended, if possible, on automatic takeup reels in order to eliminate tripping hazards.

10. Hazards due to explosive vapors

Both acetylene gas and petroleum vapors are highly explosive in critical air/gas ratios. But unless acetylene welding equipment has developed a leak, there should be no explosion hazard. Care must be taken with welding hoses to prevent cutting or burning a line.

Petroleum vapors can be extremely hazardous when an attempt is made to weld an "empty" oil drum or gasoline tank that is not thoroughly vapor-free. Prohibit use of gasoline for cleaning automotive parts, because, aside from the defatting effect on skin and the ever-present possibility of spilling it on clothing, there is the possibility that, during the winter months, an explosive mixture will accumulate in confined areas and be detonated. In place of gasoline, use kerosene or a safety solvent for cleaning. Use them as sparingly as possible and with adequate ventilation. There are many safety codes regarding this subject. See the *Accident Prevention Manual for Industrial Operations,* and *Fundamentals of Industrial Hygiene,* for technical data.

11. Hazards of vehicle movement

Personnel must always watch the movement of vehicles inside garages, shops, and terminals as well as outside. Drivers must permit buildup of proper air pressure for the safe operation of power brakes; otherwise there is always the possibility that a vehicle that is being moved may not only crash into the vehicle ahead, but also trap and crush someone between the two vehicles.

One particularly hazardous operation is washing the rear of motor vehicles, because the person doing this job will have his back turned to the next vehicle moving up the line. He must train himself to always be alert for the movement of vehicles behind him. The penalty for failing to do so may be crushed legs or thighs.

Legs can also be crushed when working under a vehicle while on a "creeper." If the mechanic's legs and feet stick out, they can be run over by another vehicle, particularly one that is being backed up without a watcher assisting the driver.

12. Other hazards to shop and garage personnel

Major sources of injury are jumping across open inspection pits, falling off ladders, hurting backs while trying to move supplies and equipment, and using hand tools improperly. Prevention of all work injuries requires proper selection and training of employees, careful supervision of their work habits, review of all injury causes, and the creation of safety-mindedness in all employees, such as discussed in previous chapters.

13. Hazards in terminals

Many of the hazards described in the previous section also apply to freight terminals and docks. In addition there is the ever-present hazard to employees of being crushed between a truck and a loading dock, of being crushed between two vehicles, of being hurt by falling merchandise or equipment, of being run over by forklift trucks, or being hurt on conveyors.

Appropriate use of "highway yellow" marking paint in and around freight terminals can minimize the possibility of drivers and freight terminal employees bumping objects or falling off places. For example, a yellow or white line painted six inches from the edge of a loading dock can deter persons from accidentally walking off the elevated area or driving freight-handling equipment off the edge of the dock.

Check the DOT and state regulations governing the contents and color mixes of marking paints before using a highway yellow-type paint in a public or municipal area.

Trailer movement. To reduce injuries to employees assigned to move freight in or out of truck trailers, the National Safety Council fully endorses and encourages the use of wheel chocks. Chocks provide an extra margin of safety against possible defects or deficiencies in the braking system of a trailer, which could interfere with the safe loading operations. All trailers, including those with spring brakes, should be blocked or chocked at the dock. (See Figure 7-1.)

Trucks or trailers may be edged away from the dock as a result of the movement of heavy freight in and out of the trailer or truck body or even from an accidental bump by a lift truck. Many dock workers have been seriously injured in falls between the vehicle and dock. In some cases, lift truck operators have actually fallen under the forklift. Wheel chocks, placed firmly ahead of the rear wheels, are the best safeguard against trailer movement.

If sliding trailer tandems are left in a forward position, a heavy load, especially on a lift truck, may lift the front end of the trailer and force it away from the loading platform. This will, of course, affect the stability of the freight already in the trailer, the load on the lift truck, and the lift truck itself, which can result in an avalanche of freight, seriously injur-

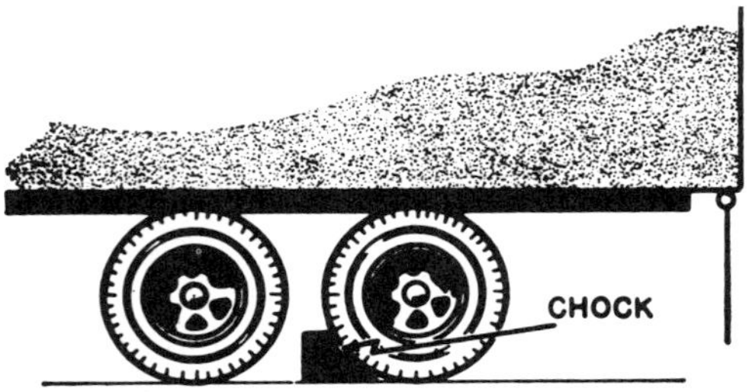

Figure 7-1. *Preferred position for placing chock.*

ing the dock worker. If sliding tandems are forward, the back of the trailer should also be supported by stands or the tractor should be hooked up to prevent seesawing as weight is moved in and out of the trailer.

Whenever heavy nose loading of a trailer is expected, a tractor should be hooked up or the nose supported by stands. Too much weight ahead of the landing gear of unsupported trailers can cause a nose-dive and result in severe injury to workers inside.

Bridge plates. Bridge plates (or dockboards) used in loading operations pose a tripping hazard and affect the stability of freight and equipment moved across them. In addition, the edges of these plates become sharpened on concrete floors and can cause serious injuries if not kept flush with the surface of the dock and trailer. If they are not built in, loose plates may be driven away from the dock by the wheels of a lift truck or be knocked aside by cars, thus exposing workers to danger in the unbridged threshold. Workers should not assume that the plate is secure just because it is properly positioned. They should make certain it is properly anchored.

Bridge plates should be kept clear of water, grease, ice, and other material that could create a slipping surface and result in injury to a dock worker. Also, the bridge plates should be wide enough and able to support any load that crosses them. Power truck operators should be instructed to drive over them slowly.

Handholds, or other effective means, shall be provided on portable bridge plates to permit safe handling. Heavy plates should be moved by forklift.

Additional information on dockboards will be found in *(a)* American National Standard, "Loading Dock Levelers and Dockboards," ANSI/ASME MH 14.1-1984, and *(b)* in the National Safety Council Industrial Data Sheet No. 318, *Dock Plates and Gangplanks.*

Interior trailer. Inadequate lighting in a truck-trailer will hide jagged edges, splintered crates, and various other hazards on the floor or walls. Many dockworkers have tripped over unseen material in a dark trailer or cut their hands on rusty nails left in the floor where blocking timbers had been. If the front bulkhead of an empty trailer cannot be seen, or if a worker has difficulty in reading labels on the freight he is unloading, more light is required.

When rigging additional lighting, it should be set up to minimize the possibility of bulb breakage or other damage to the lighting fixtures. Wires should be placed where they will not be run over. Also, all dockworkers should know where to obtain replacement bulbs and how to rig the portable lighting equipment, when needed.

The interior surfaces of a truck-trailer are not always smooth and uniform. Loose, dangling roof supports, jagged punctures in the sheet metal sides, holes in the floor, damaged posts, and holes in plywood sides have caused many injuries. Such defects may be found even in the newest trailers. Dockworkers must thoroughly survey the trailer body before unloading or loading in order to spot hazards before they cause injury. When defects are discovered, immediate action should be taken by the workers to minimize the danger until a permanent repair can be made.

In addition, dockworkers should be instructed to report all defects in the trailer they have been assigned to work. No damaged trailer should be loaded without first being repaired.

Some freight to be unloaded from a truck-trailer can give off particles of matter, harmful mists, or vapors. After trailers have been sealed for a period of time, a high concentration of contaminants may build up within them. The effects on the human system cannot always be predicted and can be a serious health hazard.

Dockworkers should be instructed to check the working atmosphere before entering any trailer. If a worker believes the air is contaminated, he should notify his supervisor. Company policy should be established on the type and amount of protective equipment to be maintained at each terminal. The company policy should include detailed descriptions of the conditions under which contaminated trailers may or may not be loaded or unloaded.

Dock cleanliness. The immediate surroundings and the path over which materials are to be moved are of considerable importance if injury and lost time are to be avoided. Keep working docks swept clean. A neat, clean, orderly dock usually allows an efficient operation to be performed. Tripping and slipping hazards must be avoided. Steel bands, splintered boards, and other trash can accumulate around the dock area and should be picked up. This should be done on a routine basis, depending on the operation. Grease and other liquids must be cleaned off the floor immediately. There should be a specific place to put all materials handling equipment. When equipment is used, workers should be held responsible for its return.

Illumination is also important to the moving of freight. Be certain that necessary lighting is available. Minimum recommended illumination on loading docks is 20 footcandles (decalux); inside truck bodies, minimum illumination is 10 footcandles (decalux), according to the Illuminating Engineering Society.

Good housekeeping is a habit-forming practice and a very important part of an effective fleet safety program.

Scattered debris. Freight and equipment are sometimes carelessly left lying in and around the working area by the previous shift. Unchecked freight, tools, wrappings, bottles, and loose dunnage are all traps for the wheels of a hand truck and for unwary feet. These traps often become more than just a nuisance to be stepped over or avoided. They have been the cause of almost every imaginable kind of personal injury from simple bruises and abrasions, through cuts and broken bones, to concussions. The first duty of any dock worker, before beginning any actual work, is to make his work area safe. This means that all dunnage and tools not in use should be replaced in their respective storage racks; all trash should be deposited in the receptacles provided; and all unchecked freight left scattered about should be checked and removed. Unloaders (strippers) should know that an "empty trailer" should be *completely* empty. Stripping is not completed until the floor of the trailer is swept clean of all trash, nails left in the floor have been removed, and the bridge plate has been pulled and stored.

Cargo shifting. Safe loading of motor vehicles and protection against shifting or falling cargo can do much to prevent highway and industrial accidents. Because trailers are designed for uniform load distribution, the cargo should be distributed equally between the rear tires and the fifth wheel which transfers the trailer's load to the truck-tractor. In addition, weight of the freight should be distributed equally on each side of the trailer. A heavy load at one side will overload the springs and tires at that side. The cargo should be placed so that weight is equal on the rear tires and thus eliminate possible twisting of frame and overloading of axle housing and wheel bearings. Heavy containers, equipment, or machinery large enough to occupy the width of the trailer floor should be loaded with the center of weight over the center line of

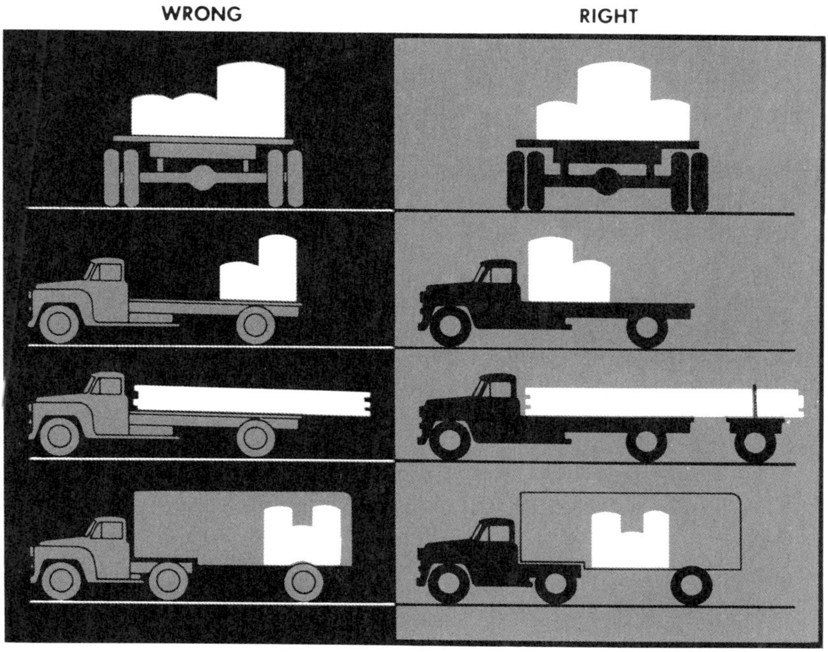

Figure 7-2. *For proper load distribution, analyze. . . equalize. . . distribute. Analyze each truck or tractor-trailer unit according to tire size—the axle carrying capacity of the tires—and distribute the load accordingly. Equalize the loads on each axle according to the carrying capacity of the tires. Distribute loads, on semi-trailer units, so each axle and the fifth wheel carries its share according to carrying capacities of tires.*

the trailer. Freight should be secured in a manner which will prevent its shifting.

Top-heavy articles, such as machinery and other equipment, should be blocked and braced to prevent tipping and damaging other freight or affecting operation safety. Such articles will generally require bracing near the top in addition to floor blocking. Blocks and bracing should be used to eliminate slack space. All cargo should be secured so it will not come in contact with doors; this precludes the load from shifting or rolling while in transit. Properly seasoned and undamaged lumber, free of dry rot and knots, should be used for blocking and bracing freight in the trailers. Bracing and blocking material and construction should be capable of withstanding loadings representative of the forces that may act upon them during emergency application of the brakes. The Federal Highway Administration's Bureau of Motor Carrier Safety regulations for the safe loading of motor vehicles and protection against shifting or falling cargo should be observed. (See Figure 7-2.)

On buses, baggage, freight, or express should be stowed and secured in a manner which will assure protection of occupants against injury resulting from the falling or displacement of the articles being transported. The articles should not interfere with the driver's freedom of movement or proper operation of the bus. In addition, baggage or freight should not obstruct any occupant's access to any of the exits.

Materials handling. More workers in the motor transportation industry are injured by improper handling of shipping materials than from any other single source. Strains, sprains, and other injuries frequently cause long layoffs from work, and can be costly to both the worker and the company. The need for knowledge of material handling, therefore, is obvious.

The handling and stowing of objects and materials is not always as easy as it appears. It is, therefore, wise to stop and reason out every intended operation. The fleet supervisor should instruct his workers to carefully inspect each load for its weight and slivers, nails, sharp edges, and weak bottoms.

If the load is too big to handle alone, the worker should be instructed to get help or, if available, use equipment designed specifically to handle the load. When handling rough or sharp-edged objects, protective gloves should be worn. Also, cartons should be gripped away from seams so that the hands do not come in contact with sharp staples. Bare hands should be kept off steel and wire banding. Since material can fall out of open or weak-bottomed cartons, workers should be encouraged to wear safety shoes. Recommended hand protection and safety shoes are a must on most jobs involving handling materials. Some companies require wearing goggles and/or safety hats.

Lifting is a part of almost everyone's job, but too often it's done in the wrong manner. Injuries caused by improper lifting can be very easily prevented if workers follow a few simple rules covering proper body position and lifting practices. (See the illustration, Proper Way To Lift, on pages 116 and 117.)

When lifting heavy objects, keep the back straight, and arms and elbows tucked into the side with the weight of the body centered over the feet. Lift with the legs. Twisting during a lift is a common cause of back injury. By simply turning the forward foot out and pointing it in the direction you intend to move, the greatest danger of twisting will be avoided.

Move drums with a barrel truck whenever possible. Drums should not be rolled on edge, because of the precarious balance such a maneuver requires. Avoid pinch points near the top of the drum, and keep feet clear of the bottom seam. Because drums often contain hazardous materials, take great care to avoid puncturing the drum or spilling its contents. Clean up any such spills as soon as possible and before they are allowed to spread.

In handling sacks (paper and cloth), avoid cuts from wire stapling at the bound end. Lift by gripping underneath the sack, and using the legs as jacks. If a large number of sacks are to be moved, two people should work together—one at each end of the sack. Do not throw sacks carelessly; keep the dust level down. If sacks are damp or warm there is the possibility that a chemical action is taking place.

In handling bundles, watch out for short, sharp ends of steel strapping used to bind the bundles. Keep fingers out from between the individual lengths in a bundle. Use dock equipment to move them whenever possible; bundles are often coated with protective grease at the factory which makes them hard to grip. When raising lighter bundles to load as top freight (for example, plastic tubing), try to keep both ends level; otherwise, an individual length is likely to slide back at the worker on the lower end, hitting his face, chest, or leg.

Hand trucks. When handling freight with hand trucks, instruct the worker to place the "blade" of the hand truck completely under the load, then pull it back slowly until the weight is entirely balanced over the axle. Always push, never pull, hand trucks. The freight should be loaded on the hand truck only as high as the top crossbar so that visability is kept clear. When pulling freight back to the siderails of the hand truck, never grip the steel strapping, wire binding, or twine of the freight. Reach across the top of the load and grip the far edge.

If using barrel trucks, handle the freight in the same safe manner as the hand trucks. It is, however, especially critical that the weight of the drum be centered exactly over the axle of the barrel truck. Liquid sloshing in the drum might destroy this balance, so move cautiously—especially at turns.

Freight should be loaded on four-wheel carts so that the worker can see over the top. Carts should be pushed so the leading edge of the cart cannot run up against the dock worker's heel, and should be pulled only when moving downgrade, as when coming out of a trailer down an inclined dockplate. The dock worker, then, must face the cart and brace against it for control. Two workers may be required to control heavily loaded carts.

Most "J" (Johnson) bar injuries occur when the handle is driven up with great force into a worker's face or jaw. The body should be kept in a position where it will not be struck if the grip is lost.

Proper Way To Lift

Lifting is so much a part of everyday jobs that most of us don't think about it. But it is often done wrong, with bad results: pulled muscles, disk lesions, or painful hernia.

Here are six steps to safe lifting.

1. Keep feet parted—one alongside, one behind the object.
2. Keep back straight, nearly vertical.
3. Tuck your chin in.
4. Grip the object with the whole hand.
5. Tuck elbows and arms in.
6. Keep body weight directly over feet.

FEET should be parted, with one foot alongside the object being lifted and one behind. Feet comfortably spread give greater stability; the rear foot is in position for the upward thrust of the lift.

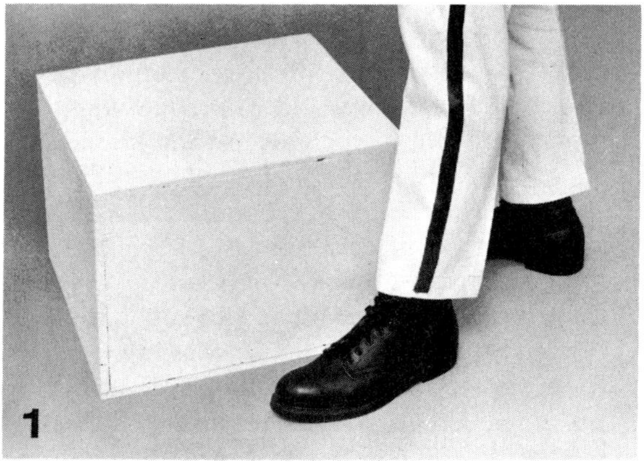

1

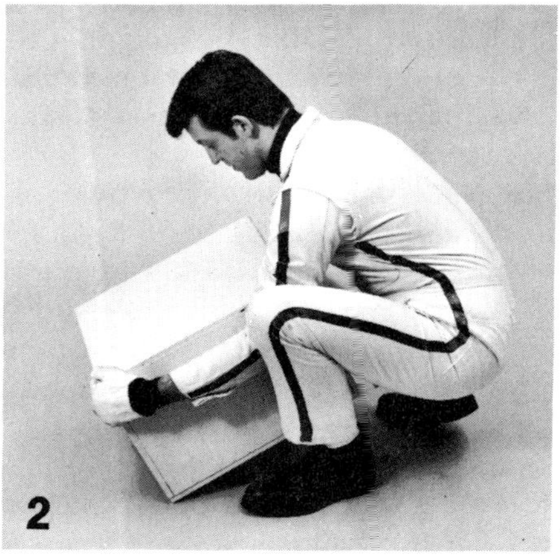

2

BACK. Use the sit-down position and keep the back straight —but remember that "straight" does not mean "vertical." A straight back keeps the spine, back muscles, and organs of the body in correct alignment. It minimizes the compression of the guts that can cause hernia.

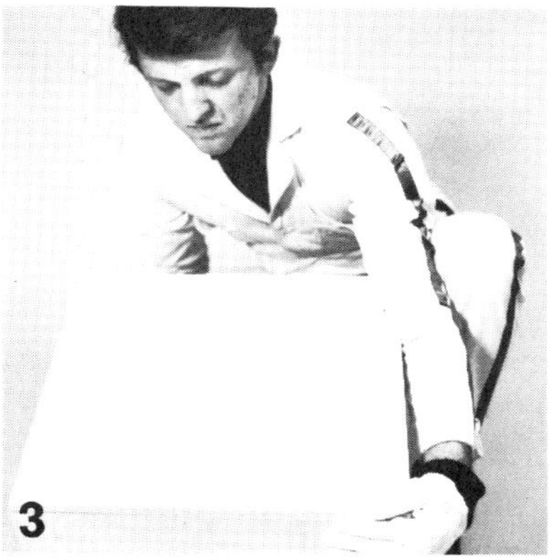

3

Arms and elbows. The load should be drawn close, and the arms and elbows should be tucked into the side of the body. When the arms are held away from the body, they lose much of their strength and power. Keeping the arms tucked in also helps keep body weight centered.

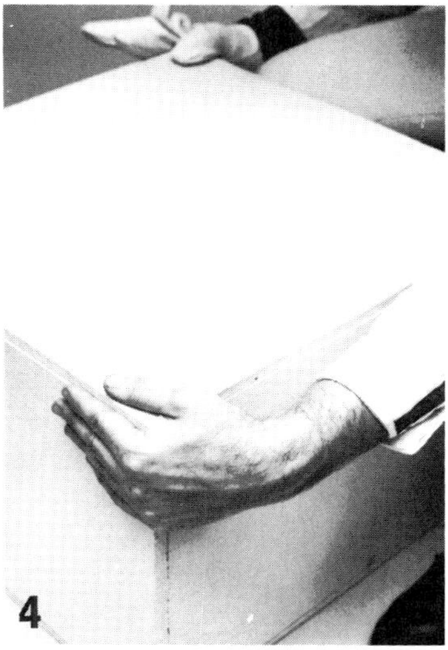

4

Palm. The palmar grip is one of the most important elements of correct lifting. The fingers and the hand are extended around the object you're going to lift. Use the full palm; fingers alone have very little power. Glove has been removed to show finger positions better.

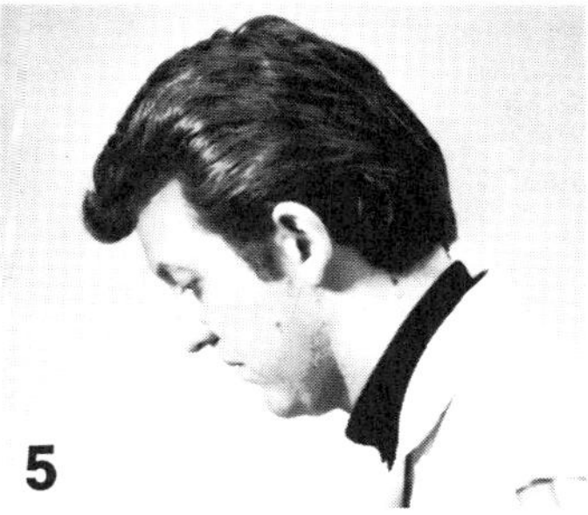

5

Chin. Tuck in the chin so your neck and head continue the straight back line and keep your spine straight and firm.

Body weight. Position body so its weight is centered over the feet. This provides a more powerful line of thrust and ensures better balance. Start the lift with a thrust of the rear foot.

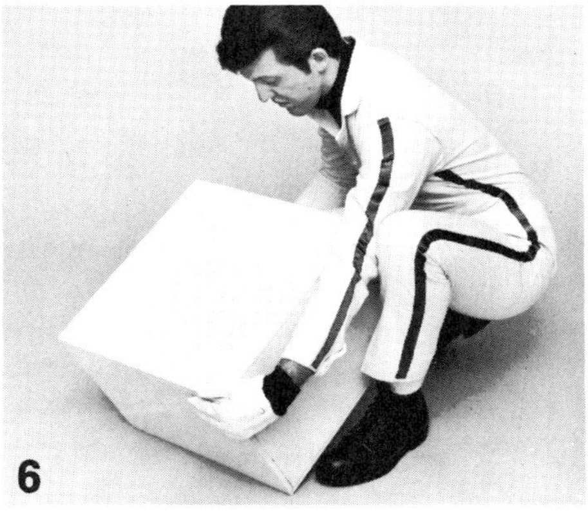

6

Powered industrial trucks. As in the use of any machine, certain safety rules and regulations must be observed and carefully followed to prevent serious injury. The supervisor and lift truck operator should be familiar with the safety rules and regulations of the American National Standard *Safety Standard for Powerered Industrial Trucks—Low Lift and High Lift Trucks,* ANSI/ASME B56.1-1983, and *Powered Industrial Trucks,* ANSI/NFPA 505-1981. OSHA requirements Title 29, *Code of Federal Regulations* §1910.178 still references the ANSI Standard B56.1-1969.

14. Job hazards of truck and bus operators

Bus and truck operators must not only avoid traffic accidents but also public relations problems that can arise out of dealing with the general public. Defensive driving practices (described in Chapter 9) can generally prevent motor vehicle collisions; considerate, friendly handling of the public can usually prevent strained relations (discussed in Chapter 10).

In addition, there is the possibility of a driver being hurt in a non-driving accident. Operators are frequently injured when they fall while boarding or alighting from a vehicle, within their vehicle, or when they fall at terminals and rest stops. Drivers should be taught to always have at least three limbs in positive contact with the steps or hand holds. The possibility of hand, wrist, arm, shoulder, or back injuries arises when a vehicle's front wheel strikes an object or drops suddenly into a depression causing the steering wheel to jerk or spin. Injuries to operators frequently arise from adjusting the operator's seat, opening or closing doors, operating gear shift levers, or handling windows and ventilators and changing route and destination signs (if there are any).

If operators must handle merchandise, they must take care to avoid sprains, or muscular overexertion, and to avoid receiving foot injuries due to falling or shifting objects. If an operator cannot handle himself safely, how can he be counted on to handle passengers, merchandise, or freight safely?

In order to focus attention on driver safety records, accident statistics must be maintained, reviewed, and discussed, and recommendations made as to how these injuries can be avoided. If this can be done in open safety meetings, group discussion will focus attention on injury-causing conditions or practices. If they cannot be handled this way, then the supervisor can discuss them with individual drivers. The only good that can result from an accident is its educational value.

We cannot attain safe operation without working for it. The motivation and desire for a real safety program must originate with management, which was discussed earlier in this chapter and in Chapter 2.

Maintain Interest in Accident Prevention

Even though all facilities have been brought up to high safety standards, all jobs have been subjected to a hazard analysis, safe work procedures have been devised and are enforced, and an accident reporting and analysis system has been set up, one important task remains—to stimulate employee interest in accident prevention. Employees should want to work safely at all times. Here are ways to do this:

1. Management interest and example

Management's sincere interest in accident prevention is one of the strongest incentives for good safety performance. This holds true for all levels of management—each must reflect an interest in company safety objectives and set a good example of compliance with safety rules, because a person will believe in safety only to the same degree he thinks his boss believes in it.

Supervisors should often talk personally to each of their subordinates about safety. Managers should seek every opportunity to be identified with the safety program, such as by attending safety meetings and rallies and signing bulletins and announcements. Serious accidents should be personally investigated by management, and the employee interviewed by them. Above all, management personnel at all levels must set examples of safe action, both at work and off the job.

2. Safety meetings and rallies

Periodic safety meetings and rallies keep interest high. Safety meetings should be small and should be conducted by the immediate supervisor. Meetings should be confined to a definite subject and deal with specific problems. For example, a safety meeting for drivers and mechanics might be devoted to discuss the safe way of getting in and out of various vehicles. Meetings can also be held to explain a new safety procedure, announce a new contest or campaign, review a specific accident, or discuss the overall safety performance of the group.

Large rallies attended by all employees, including members of management, are helpful in celebrating safety achievements such as winning an award or working a specified number of hours without a disabling injury.

3. Awards for work safety

Employees like to be recognized individually for safe work performance. A good method of doing this is to establish a "Safe Driver Award" or "Safe Worker Award" program (see Chapter 10). Although this program is available from the National Safety Council, companies may create their own. Awards are usually presented for working a calendar year without a disabling injury. If the worker has a disabling injury he does not receive an award for the year. Usually awards are cumulative, thus a worker can earn a 1-year, 2-year, 3-year (or higher) award for working that number of years without a preventable accident or a disabling injury. (For publicity value, see Appendix A.)

4. Safety contests

Various contests can be held: working the highest number of hours without a disabling injury, or achieving the lowest frequency rate within a specific period of time. Contests can be between units within the same fleet or between fleets in different areas.

Contests should be well promoted for maximum interest. Workers should understand the method of scoring and be kept informed of the standing of the various contestants—either individuals or units.

There should be no contest penalties for reporting very minor injuries, otherwise these may not be reported and infected wounds may result.

Safety contest and award projects are a means of generating enthusiasm, cooperative effort, and a "safety awareness" within the company. As effective as they are, contests and awards cannot substitute for a well-run safety program, established and backed by management, and administered by all levels of supervision in a firm and impartial manner.

5. Posters

A good poster program can do much to maintain interest in safety—even the best employees need reminding. Aside from the actual message of the poster, the mere fact that there are well maintained poster boards with fresh posters tells employees that management has a continued interest in safety. In addition, this helps give a terminal, dock, or driver room the look of a safety-minded company.

Special bulletin boards can also aid various safety subjects. Actual photographs of broken safety glasses which saved an eye, photographs of unsafe practices and award presentations, safety announcements, and awards can all be exhibited.

A special bulletin board showing number of days worked since the last lost-time injury can also promote interest so long as it is faithfully kept up to date.

Planning and administering a good poster program requires careful consideration of (*a*) kinds of poster boards used, (*b*) number and placement of poster locations, (*c*) selection of posters, and (*d*) regularity and frequency of change.

Poster boards. Mounting may be as simple as thumb-tacking to a wall, or as "complicated" as placing in an illuminated, glass-enclosed bulletin board. The latter is more desirable because it is not only more dignified and attractive but it also protects the posters from being tampered with.

Black-enameled metal poster frames, available through the National Safety Council at a nominal cost, are large enough to permit cardboard backing and a glass (or plastic) shield. They come in 8½ by 11½-inch ("A" size) and 17 by 23-inch ("B" size) sizes, and are especially useful when display boards are not feasible or when a single poster must be spotted at a strategic point.

Number and placement of poster locations. Like ads, posters also must be seen to be effective. This means bringing posters to employees, not employees to posters. Knowing the pedestrian traffic patterns helps in planning poster locations. So will answering these questions:

- Where will most employees see a poster most frequently?
- Will all employees see it during their normal work day?
- How many locations will be required to make sure that all employees are exposed to a poster program?
- Where are the most effective locations for posters discussing specific work hazards? (Safe driving posters should be seen mostly by drivers; posters devoted to proper lifting techniques should be seen especially by dock and maintenance workers.)

At these optimum locations, place posters at eye level—centered about 53 in. (1.35m) from floor. Make sure poster has sufficient light and is free from obstructions so that employees can focus their attention on it. Avoid placing posters at stairways, doorways, or other places where a person may have an accident if his attention were diverted from seeing a potential hazard.

Selecting posters. Posters may be obtained from the National Safety Council by two methods:

- Request a monthly supply of preselected posters be sent you. Council safety engineers will select posters that apply to your special type of operation—intercity bus, truck terminal, intracity truck, or what have you.
- Select posters from the Council's Annual Poster Directory or from the new poster listings that appear in each issue of *National Safety and Health News* and *Traffic Safety* magazines. Choose posters that refer to your most common injury problems.

Automatic mailings assure a constant supply of carefully selected

***Figure** 7-3. Motor fleet safety posters from the National Safety Council can be chosen to point out areas of needed improvement.*

posters that touch the principal sources of accidents, and are balanced in their appeal. They range from humorous cartoons to those pointing to personal consequences of unsafe acts. "Automatic poster service" sets are available in "A" and "B" sizes. Multiple or fractional sets can be ordered depending on the number of drivers and other employees covered.

Water-resistant jumbo posters (11 ft 8 in. × 9 ft 11 in.) and indoor or outdoor safety banners (10 ft × 3½ ft) are also available from the Council. These huge safety reminders can be displayed at entrances, in parking lots, and near docks. They're an effective way to raise the safety awareness of employees.

Personal selection of posters allows choice based on actual accident experience or for special safety campaigns. Both methods can be combined. (Some fleet posters are shown in Figure 7-3.)

Regularity and frequency of change. Posters are most effective when used singularly and changed or alternated frequently. If left in place too long, they become part of the background and their message is not noticed. It would be better to use four posters per month—one each week—than to put all four at one location and leave them there for a month. Changing or alternating posters weekly gives a sense of movement to a poster program.

Administration of a poster program requires the personal attention of a capable employee. The safety director should check to make certain poster sites are kept in good condition and that posters are changed according to a prearranged schedule.

6. First aid training

Many companies give all employees first aid training because they find employees work more safely when they are qualified at first aid. Also, OSHA requires personnel trained in first aid be on each work shift where emergency care is five or more minutes away. The American Red Cross can schedule special first aid classes for a company at a modest fee.

Chapter 8

Driver Selection And Hiring

People differ in their ability to act and to drive safely. Because we know little about *why* this is true or how to rate a job applicant's future on-the-job safety performance with any degree of accuracy, this situation challenges the fleet personnel officer. Few occupations involve a greater need for safety than that of the motor vehicle operator, especially since the work is done almost without supervision. A properly selected, trained, and motivated driver can usually avoid accidents that inflict property damage or injure persons.

General Abilities and Aptitudes

The general abilities and aptitudes required of a driver vary with the individual job. For example, the physical demands made on school bus drivers and delivery vehicle drivers are very different. Figure 8-1 illustrates a method of grading the component abilities and aptitudes required in specialized driving jobs. The importance of correct driver selection is apparent after taking a closer look at items 6, 7, 8, and 12 on the Evaluation of Driving Job worksheet.

RESPONSIBILITY FOR VEHICLE (Item 6). It is possible for the professional driver to damage or demolish his vehicle in an accident. The cost can range from $8,000 for a compact passenger car to $100,000 for a city bus or line-haul trailer-tractor combination.

RESPONSIBILITY FOR SAFETY OF CARGO OR PASSENGERS (Item 7). It is possible to inflict damage to costly cargo, especially human cargo which is priceless. As to the value of cargo, it's not unusual for a semi-trailer truck to haul freight worth over a million dollars.

RESPONSIBILITY FOR SAFETY OF PEDESTRIANS AND OTHER MOTORISTS (Item

WORK SHEET

EVALUATION OF DRIVING JOB

Inter-City Truck, Semi-Trailer	Taxicab
Inter-City Truck, Straight	School Bus
Inter-City Bus	Passenger Car
City Truck, Semi-Trailer	Utility Truck
City Truck, Straight	Route Delivery Vehicle
City Bus	Other ________

	High		*Average*		*Not Important*
JOB FACTOR	1	2	3	4	5
1 Education					
2 Experience					
3 Technical Training					
4 Physical Demand					
5 Mental Visual Demand					
6 Responsibility for Vehicle					
7 Responsibility for Safety of Cargo or Passengers					
8 Responsibility for Safety of Pedestrians and other Motorists					
9 Contacts with Customers					
10 Responsibility for Company Funds					
11 Driving and Working Conditions					
12 Personal Hazards					
13 Supervision Received					

Figure 8-1. *Relative abilities and aptitudes for various driving jobs can be compared on this form.*

8). Every vehicle operator has the potential to injure pedestrians and collide with other motorists.

PERSONAL HAZARDS (Item 12). It is certainly possible for any professional driver to suffer injury in a traffic accident.

Because any driving job is potentially dangerous, one of the essential requirements for drivers is the ability to avoid accidents.

Accident repeaters

Any discussion of individual differences related to the ability to avoid accidents must first deal with the problem of accident repeaters. It appears that some persons have repeated accidents while others can work or drive for years without having any accidents at all. It has also been learned that *everyone* is potentially an accident repeater and can become a temporary accident repeater under certain conditions of stress.

The supervisor must select drivers with the best potential for driving safely, train them in the techniques of safe driving, and provide the kind of supervision that will maintain safe driving performance at a very high level. Thus the relationship between management and drivers must be different than ordinarily found between management and employees, supervisor and supervised. The relationship is more akin to that which exists between the players on a big league baseball team and the coaches and managers: club managers not only must select good players, they must work closely with individual players to keep each in good physical and psychological condition. Thus management must field a group of carefully selected and highly trained safe drivers. The safety program and the supervisory program must keep the drivers conditioned to turn in a high level of safe driving performance.

Selecting safety-conscious drivers. Can the safe driving potential of an applicant be predicted at the employment office? The answer is a qualified "Yes." It is possible to screen out many of the poor risks, and a selection program that succeeds only in doing this has already made a substantial contribution. However, predicting safe driving ability is less exact. The best approach is to hire experienced drivers having established records that can be verified.

Once the obviously bad risks have been screened out, selection should stress hiring the whole person without limiting the screening to potential ability to drive safely. Matching the total person to the total job holds out the best promise for success.

Profile of the good driver

What, then, is a good driver? An analysis reveals that the good driver must be able to:

- Drive well
  a. Avoid accidents
  b. Follow traffic regulations
  c. Care for the vehicle
  d. Avoid schedule delays
  e. Avoid irritating the public
- Perform the nondriving parts of the job
- Find satisfaction in the job
- Get along with others
- Adapt to meet existing conditions.

Driving experience. Previous experience in driving as a professional driver or as a private motorist is the best indicator of potential ability to drive safely. It has been fairly well established that a driver who has had frequent motor vehicle accidents in the past will continue to have frequent accidents in the future. This is one of the oldest and most reliable predictive factors. It means that one of the most important facts to be ascertained about the applicant is how many motor vehicle accidents has he had and how many times has he been cited for traffic violations. Since the applicant will ordinarily try to minimize or conceal a record of past accidents and traffic violations, his word alone is not sufficient evidence. Previous employers and state license records should be consulted.

The fact that an applicant has had past accidents should not be considered as automatic disqualification for employment. Each instance should be discussed with the applicant in an effort to determine his attitude toward the preventability of such accidents and the importance he attaches to observance of traffic rules and regulations.

The amount of previous driving experience to require of the applicant will depend much upon the scope of the company driver training program and the personnel philosophy of the fleet.

Ordinarily, previous experience in driving ought to be viewed as a valuable asset in a new employee, particularly if it is experience driving the same kind of vehicle the applicant will drive on the job. Fleets which lease equipment from owner-drivers often do not have training programs. In such cases, the management should carefully examine the applicant's past driving experience, accident record, and demonstrated ability to drive safely.

Skill. The degree of driving skill possessed by the applicant can sometimes be determined from an examination of his past driving experience. When this cannot be done satisfactorily, the only way to judge skill is through a work-sample test; that is, put the applicant behind the wheel of a vehicle and observe his driving ability over a prescribed course. Drivers hired in interstate commerce since 1970 must be given a road test or state licensing equivalent, as outlined in paragraph 391.31 of the Federal Motor Carrier Safety Regulations.

Fleet safety administrators support two types of driving tests, one involving that kind of test—referred to as "driving range test"—which determines whether or not the driver is aware of the physical limitations of the vehicle; his ability to make starts, stops, turns, and various other maneuvers. The other type requires the applicant to drive through traffic wherein he is subjected to various kinds of traffic patterns. In both cases, an attempt should be made to standardize the testing procedure as much as possible.

It must be borne in mind, however that this test is an attempt to make a determination as to how skillfully the applicant can handle equipment. Based upon available studies, it has no correlation to the accident experience that might be anticipated of the applicant.

The weight that is placed on the applicant's performance on these skill tests should depend on the extent of subsequent driver training. If no driver training is offered, the applicant's performance during the test may prove to be qualifying or disqualifying. If the training program is comprehensive, even a driver who shows below-average skill can gain the necessary skill for his job during the training program.

Ability to avoid accidents is the paramount criterion for judging driving performance. No matter how well qualified a driver may be in his other job requirements, repeated accidents can soon make him a bad investment. Even a "star salesman" can become a liability because of too many accidents. Ability to avoid accidents is largely a result of the driver's natural ability, strengthened with training and conditioned by good supervision. The good driver learns also by observing the errors of *others.*

Ability to follow traffic regulations. Observance of traffic rules and regulations is important to good driving. No company can afford to keep drivers who repeatedly violate traffic rules and regulations. Even though company policy may require the driver to pay any fines himself, his behavior as a law violator makes him a public relations liability. There is also a close correlation between repeated traffic violations and repeated accidents.

Ability to care for the vehicle. Drivers differ in their ability to conserve a vehicle. Fleets that assign the same vehicle to the same driver every day have found that some drivers get more miles between overhauls than do others. The smooth operator also consumes less fuel. When fleet operating costs are figured to the decimal point per mile of operation, ability to drive smoothly shows up as a substantial factor in fleet economics and a relevant measure of driving ability.

Ability to meet schedules. The fleet motor vehicle represents a capital investment whose purpose is to produce transportation service and resulting revenue. There is a time and distance dimension involved in such a service. The fleet dispatcher knows what he can reasonably expect in terms of production output per vehicle per day. The driver who dawdles at stops, is unduly slow in negotiating traffic, and wastes time in other ways, is not meeting his production schedule and is not getting maximum return on the company's investment. In city bus service, for example, failure to stay on schedule creates difficulties and headaches for other bus operators on the line and is a direct factor in producing accidents. It is obvious that schedules must be carefully drawn up with safety and traffic conditions in mind. After this is done, however, it is reasonable to consider ability to meet schedules as a factor in rating driving skill.

Avoiding irritating the public. Most fleet vehicles are painted in distinctive colors and carry the company name. Because of this, they are traveling billboards whose advertising value to the company, if duplicated in conventional advertising media, would require the expenditure of huge sums. But this advertising value can become a negative factor if the vehicle is operated in an unsafe manner. Tailgating, speeding through residential areas, racing the engine at traffic stops to hurry pedestrians out of the way, unnecessary use of the horn, bulldozing through traffic and many other such discourteous actions on the part of the fleet driver can irritate, frighten, disturb, and otherwise alienate the public. Ability to drive a vehicle with courtesy and consideration for pedestrians and for other motorists is important.

Nondriving parts of the job. In many professional driving occupations—involving such things as meter reading, appliance servicing, food delivering, and route selling—the nondriving part of the job takes more time than the driving portion. Employees must be able to do the nondriving job well, because if they are insecure or nervous about it, unsafe driving will result.

Ability to find satisfaction in the job. The employee who doesn't like his job will be a poor performer, and will quit or be discharged. The process of recruiting, selecting, and hiring an employee can be quite costly. If the worker does not prove satisfactory and quits or is discharged after a short time, this investment is lost. Added to this is the inevitable confusion and disruption created when it becomes necessary to end a driver's employment.

Selection is, therefore, a two-way street. Not only must the person be suited to the job, but the job must also be one that he finds suitable for his personal needs.

When considering an applicant for the driving job, the minimum and maximum levels of ability should be considered. An applicant with too high a level of ability for a given job can be just as frustrated by his work as one whose level of ability is too low. Be sure the over-qualified applicant is really seeking a driving job. At the same time, it is not uncommon for overly educated people to seek the high-paying driving jobs; and if they can show a successful prior work history in driving, they should be considered as valued applicants with future potential in company management.

The factor of an applicant's needs for personal status should be considered. Usually, there is an implicit level of status attached to any given job. Thought should be given to whether the driving job offers the applicant the degree of status that will satisfy him. If there are any indications that the applicant might not be satisfied with the job, he may not be a good candidate.

Ability to interact with others. The ability to successfully interact with others adds to a person's value as an employee and enhances his total job performance. Hiring a new employee is an all-or-nothing proposition. One cannot hire merely skills and aptitudes; one hires the whole person, including whatever positive or negative personality traits he may have. Personality is considered here in terms of the candidate's likeableness and ability to get along with others. One negative person can upset an entire employee group.

It is, therefore, relevant to ask, "How well will the applicant fit in with the other employees he will have to work with? Will he feel superior, or will he accept his fellow workers as equals? Will they accept him? How well will he get along with customers and other members of the public he will meet as a representative of the company?"

The ability to clearly and quickly determine an applicant's potential usefulness to the company is a skill that develops through experience. The hiring officer can improve his decision-making capabilities by observing the company's competent employees to find the common traits that seem to imply personal responsibility and dependability. Fair-hiring laws have made it necessary for the hiring officer to rely more heavily on his own assessments.

Fair-hiring guidelines

Because of antidiscrimination laws and possible lawsuits, the hiring officer should not request personal information, during the interview and on the written application, unless it can be proven that the answers were necessary to establish occupational qualification.

State and federal agencies publish pre-employment inquiry guidelines. These guidelines show how to phrase the questions to be within existing laws. For example, the State of Illinois, Department of Human Rights, publication, *Pre-Employment Inquiries,* suggests that the hiring officer not ask questions regarding citizenship, or ask for proof of legal entry status, before hiring. After hiring, however, the hiring officer can directly ask if the employee is prevented from lawfully being employed in this country because of visa or immigration status. He can then request proof of the employee's citizenship or legal entry status.

For the safety director, or other hiring personnel, it is essential to have a working knowledge of fair-hiring laws before beginning the selection process.

The Selection Procedure

The hiring of a new driver is an important decision. Because it must be done carefully and thoroughly, the fleet manager should be willing to allocate as much time and personnel to this activity as is required. Normally it should take from three days to several weeks between the time the applicant applies for a job and the time he is actually hired.

The selection procedure is designed to uncover facts about the applicant on which a decision can be made as to his suitability for employment. This data will come from a number of sources: what the applicant says about himself, from his past employers and employment records, from business and personal associates, and what objective tests and medical examinations reveal about him. Since the gathering of such information involves an expenditure of time and money, the procedure should be organized into a successive hurdle sequence designed to discover as quickly as possible those applicants who do not meet the job requirements and who, therefore, can be eliminated from consideration without further processing.

While each fleet must find its own best sequence based on the number of techniques used in the selection procedure and the volume of hiring, the following steps are suggested:

Step 1—Recruiting

It should be remembered that applicants can only be selected from the group that applies for jobs. If only poorly qualified applicants apply for work, the most elaborate selection procedure will still yield a poor employee. The selection procedure must therefore begin by attracting an adequate number of well-qualified persons to apply for employment.

a. Referrals from present employees. An excellent source of applicants is the friends and acquaintances of present employees. Many companies have established a policy which prohibits the employment of relatives of present employees. Objections raised on this issue, however, do not prevail in the employment of friends and acquaintances of present employees. If it is known to employees that their friends will receive due consideration, they will tend to refer them to the company for employment. They will try to send better-qualified ones because this is a reflection on themselves.

b. Industry contacts. Establish contacts with other fleet supervisors. This can be another dependable source of applicants. Trade association meetings are good places to meet your peers.

c. Other sources. Driving schools, vocational schools, and other similar places are additional sources of recruitment.

Step 2—Application form

The employment application form is usually the hiring officer's most complete source of information about the applicant. It can be used to quickly select candidates who appear to be qualified and eliminate unsuitable candidates.

The hiring officer should choose or construct an application form best suited to his company's needs, taking into consideration the type and size of the operation, the specialized requirements of the job, the fair-hiring laws of his state and the federal government, and regulatory agency requirements, if any apply. The final application might be a preprinted general form, a special company form, a regulatory agency form, or any combination of the preceeding.

Regulatory agency forms. Driver employment forms used by motor fleets falling under the jurisdiction of the Federal Bureau of Motor Carrier Safety should be Department of Transportation (DOT) approved. The physical, medical, and other minimum qualification standards of the DOT differ from those required by most other motor fleets.

General forms. Preprinted employment application forms can be purchased at local office supply stores or through business form pub-

APPLICATION FOR EMPLOYMENT

Company ____________________

Address ____________________

City ____________ State ________ Zip ________

(answer all questions - please print)

In compliance with Federal and State equal employment opportunity laws, qualified applicants are considered for all positions without regard to race, color, religion, sex, national origin, age, marital status, or the presence of a non-job related medical condition or handicap.

Date of application ____________

Position(s) Applied for ____________________

Name ____________________ Social Security No. ____________

Last First Middle

Address ____________________

Street City

____________________ Phone ____________

State Zip

ADDRESS FOR PAST THREE YEARS

____________________ How Long? ________

Street City State & Zip Code

____________________ How Long? ________

Street City State & Zip Code

Date of Birth ____________ If hired can you provide proof of age? ____________

In case of emergency notify ____________________

Name Address Phone

Have you worked for this company before? ______ Where? ____________

Dates: From ________ To ________ Rate of Pay ________ Position ________

Reason for leaving ____________________

Are you now employed? ______ If not, how long since leaving last employment? ________

Who referred you? ____________________ Rate of pay expected ________

PHYSICAL HISTORY

List any handicap that prevents you from doing certain kinds of work ____________________

____

____

____

Are you physically capable of heavy manual work? ____________________

Ever injured on the job? ______ Give nature and degree of such injuries ____________

____

How much time lost from work in past three years for illness? ____________

Would you be willing to take a physical examination? ____________

Figure 8-2. *Shown here, and on the following three pages, is a good example of a preprinted employment application form.*

J. J. Keller & Associates, Inc., Neenah, Wis.

lishers. A good example of a preprinted application designed for the trucking industry is shown in Figure 8-2.

Company forms. The individualized company form should be carefully drawn up, and frequently revised to reflect only those facts

EMPLOYMENT FOR THE PAST 3 YEARS

(ATTACH SHEET IF MORE SPACE IS NEEDED)

LAST EMPLOYER NAME ______________________________
ADDRESS ______________________________
POSITION HELD ______________ FROM ______________ TO ______________ SALARY ______________
REASONS FOR LEAVING ______________________________
SECOND LAST EMPLOYER NAME ______________________________
ADDRESS ______________________________
POSITION HELD ______________ FROM ______________ TO ______________ SALARY ______________
REASONS FOR LEAVING ______________________________
THIRD LAST EMPLOYER NAME ______________________________
ADDRESS ______________________________
POSITION HELD ______________ FROM ______________ TO ______________ SALARY ______________
REASONS FOR LEAVING ______________________________

MILITARY STATUS

HAVE YOU SERVED IN THE U.S. ARMED FORCES? ________ BRANCH ______________ DATES FROM ______________ TO ______________

RANK AT DISCHARGE ______________________________ DATE OF DISCHARGE ______________________________

EDUCATION

CIRCLE HIGHEST GRADE COMPLETED 1 2 3 4 5 6 7 8 HIGH SCHOOL 1 2 3 4 COLLEGE 1 2 3 4

LAST SCHOOL ATTENDED ______________________________
(NAME) (CITY)

EXPERIENCE AND QUALIFICATIONS — DRIVER

	STATE	LICENSE NO.	TYPE	EXPIRATION DATE
DRIVER				
LICENSES				

A. Have you ever been denied a license, permit or privilege to operate a motor vehicle? YES ________ NO ________
B. Has any license, permit or privilege ever been suspended or revoked? YES ________ NO ________
IF THE ANSWER TO EITHER A OR B IS YES, ATTACH STATEMENT GIVING DETAILS

DRIVING EXPERIENCE

CLASS OF EQUIPMENT	TYPE OF EQUIPMENT (VAN, TANK, FLAT, ETC.)	DATES FROM	TO	APPROX. NO. OF MILES (TOTAL)
STRAIGHT TRUCK ________				
TRACTOR AND SEMI-TRAILER ________				
TRACTOR - TWO TRAILERS ________				
OTHER ________				

LIST STATES OPERATED IN FOR LAST FIVE YEARS ______________________________

____

SHOW SPECIAL COURSES OR TRAINING THAT WILL HELP YOU AS A DRIVER ______________________________

WHICH SAFE DRIVING AWARDS DO YOU HOLD AND FROM WHOM? ______________________________

ACCIDENT RECORD FOR PAST 3 YEARS OR MORE (ATTACH SHEET IF MORE SPACE IS NEEDED)

DATES	NATURE OF ACCIDENT (HEAD-ON, REAR-END, UPSET, ETC.)	FATALITIES	INJURIES
LAST ACCIDENT ________			
NEXT PREVIOUS ________			
NEXT PREVIOUS ________			

that the hiring officer deems pertinent to the driving jobs in the particular company.

Since it is a form that just one company will use for hiring its drivers, it should reflect the needs of the company. The hiring officer

TRAFFIC CONVICTIONS AND FORFEITURES FOR THE PAST 3 YEARS (OTHER THAN PARKING VIOLATIONS)

LOCATION	DATE	CHARGE	PENALTY

(ATTACH SHEET IF MORE SPACE IS NEEDED)

EXPERIENCE AND QUALIFICATIONS — PLATFORM

LIST TYPES OF PLATFORM EXPERIENCE AND YEARS OF EACH ____________________

LIST PLATFORM EQUIPMENT YOU CAN OPERATE (LIFT TRUCK, ETC.) ____________________

SHOW COURSES OR TRAINING IN PLATFORM WORK ____________________

EXPERIENCE AND QUALIFICATIONS — MAINTENANCE

LIST TYPES OF MAINTENANCE EXPERIENCE AND YEARS OF EACH ____________________

SHOW EQUIPMENT YOU CAN OPERATE	CHECK	YEARS OF EXPERIENCE	EQUIPMENT	CHECK	YEARS OF EXPERIENCE
Woodworking Equipment			Electric Welder		
Sheet Metal Equipment			Oxyacetylene Welder		
Clutch Rebuilding			Paint Spray Gun		
Differential Rebuilding			Wheel & Tire Balancing Machine		
Transmission Rebuilding			Tire Recapping Mold		
Body Work			Engine Dynamometer		
Frame & Axle Straightening Equipment			Chassis Dynamometer		
Electrical & Ignition Repair			Magnetic Crack Tester		
Engine Rebuilding Equipment			Vacuum & Air Brakes		
Diesel Injection Equipment			Other:		

LIST COURSES AND TRAINING IN MAINTENANCE WORK ____________________

EXPERIENCE AND QUALIFICATIONS — CLERICAL

INDICATE TRAINING AND SHOW EXPERIENCE IN THE FOLLOWING:

INDICATE WORDS PER MINUTE	TRAINING (CHECK)	YEARS OF EXPERIENCE		TRAINING (CHECK)	YEARS OF EXPERIENCE
Typing			Rates		
Shorthand			OS & D		
Billing			Interline		
TWX			Claims		
PBX			Cashier		
Key Punch Operator			Accounting		
Calculator			Dispatcher		
Dictating Machine Transcriber			Tabulator		
Bookkeeping Machine			Mimeograph		
Adding Machine			"Indicate tariffs with which you		
Other:			have worked		

LIST COURSES AND TRAINING FOR OFFICE WORK ____________________

should know the kinds of information he can expect from the job applicant that will be relevant to the particular job.

No questions or blanks should be permitted on the form unless they are justified. The hiring officer can apply this test to each item:

EXPERIENCE AND QUALIFICATIONS — OTHER

SHOW ANY TRUCKING, TRANSPORTATION OR OTHER EXPERIENCE THAT MAY HELP IN YOUR WORK FOR THIS COMPANY ______

LIST COURSES AND TRAINING OTHER THAN SHOWN ELSEWHERE IN THIS APPLICATION

LIST SPECIAL EQUIPMENT OR TECHNICAL MATERIALS YOU CAN WORK WITH (OTHER THAN THOSE ALREADY SHOWN)

TO BE READ AND SIGNED BY APPLICANT

This certifies that this application was completed by me, and that all entries on it and information in it are true and complete to the best of my knowledge.

I authorize you to make such investigations and inquiries of my personal, employment, financial or medical history and other related matters as may be necessary in arriving at an employment decision. I hereby release employers, schools or persons from all liability in responding to inquiries in connection with my application.

In the event of employment, I understand that false or misleading information given in my application or interview(s) may result in discharge. I understand, also, that I am required to abide by all rules and regulations of the Company, as permitted by Law.

______ Date ______ Applicant's Signature

PROCESS RECORD

APPLICANT HIRED ______ REJECTED ______

DATE EMPLOYED ______ POINT EMPLOYED ______

DEPARTMENT ______ CLASSIFICATION ______

(IF REJECTED, SUMMARY REPORT OF REASONS SHOULD BE PLACED IN FILE)

THIS SECTION TO BE FILLED IN BY RESPONSIBLE OFFICER OR COMPANY REPRESENTATIVE

	SUPERIOR	GOOD	FAIR	BELOW AVERAGE	POOR	WRITTEN RECORD ON FILE
1. APPLICATION						
2. INTERVIEW						
3. PAST EMPLOYMENT						
4. WRITTEN EXAM						
5. ROAD TEST						
6. POLICE AND TRAFFIC RECORD						

SIGNATURE OF INTERVIEWING OFFICER ______

TRANSFERS

FROM ______ TO ______
DATE ______
REASON FOR TRANSFER ______

FROM ______ TO ______
DATE ______
REASON FOR TRANSFER ______

FROM ______ TO ______
DATE ______
REASON FOR TRANSFER ______

FROM ______ TO ______
DATE ______
REASON FOR TRANSFER ______

TERMINATION OF EMPLOYMENT

DATE TERMINATED ______ DEPARTMENT RELEASED FROM ______

DISMISSED ______ VOLUNTARILY QUIT ______ OTHER ______

TERMINATION REPORT PLACED IN FILE ______ SUPERVISOR ______

- Why do I need this information?
- Am I likely to get a correct and honest answer from the applicant?
- From the information likely to be given, what will I be able to

discern as to the applicant's ability to satisfactorily perform the job for which he is being considered?

There may be certain background information about the applicant that will be useful to the personnel department only if the applicant survives the selection process and ends up on the payroll. These details can be left off the application form. Later, this information can be provided to the personnel office on a special form designed for this purpose.

No matter who makes the form, it is important to realize there are strong fair-hiring laws (discussed in the previous section) that require careful construction of the application form. The criteria for rejection of an applicant must also be carefully drawn. This is an area where the safety person must get qualified help. It is an area where innocent, well-intentioned actions can lead to expensive fines, and occasionally force a company into hiring a poor driver.

Completed application forms should be carefully studied by the hiring officer to determine applicants who appear most promising. Those people should be called in for the next step in the selection procedure. Those who are rejected deserve to be notified promptly. Any applicable provisions of the Fair Employment Practices Act must be complied with.

Step 3—Driver-written test

The employment application is itself a kind of written test. Many companies will not use any other. However, for some applications it is valuable to give a general test (either oral or written) of familiarity with trucking terms and perhaps a test of facility with DOT log books. Drivers who work with numbers might be given a standard clerical aptitude test. Companies operating in interstate commerce must give the DOT test prescribed in paragraph 391.35 of the Federal Motor Carrier Safety Regulations.

Step 4—The employment interview

The employment interview between applicant and hiring officer is normally the most decisive step in the selection procedure. While not the final step, it is the one at which a provisional decision is made as to whether the applicant, barring any disqualifying information developed subsequently, should be hired or not.

Prior to the interview, the hiring officer will have looked over the information on the employment application form and will have noted and considered any test scores achieved by the applicant in the testing program. He will try to form a mental image of the applicant's total qualifications in terms of the job demands. He will conjecture what the applicant's strong and weak points might be and what lines of questioning to pursue in the interview to verify or probe into the applicant's background.

The setting for the interview should provide privacy. No other person should be in the room but the interviewer and the applicant. The room should be quiet. It should be arranged beforehand that the interview proceed to conclusion without distraction. The interviewer's manner should be friendly and informal.

It should be remembered that an interview is a conversation with a purpose. The interview should develop the following information about the applicant:

• Verify or expand on information shown on the application blank. It is especially important to close all gaps in the employment time record, and reduce entries to factual data.

• Enable the interviewer to form an opinion about the applicant's personality, appearance, attitude toward employment, and attitude toward safe driving.

• Give the applicant an idea of what the job involves and what working for the company would be like.

The interviewer should keep in mind that the employment interview has many weaknesses as an objective device for measuring the potential capabilities of an applicant. Studies have shown that interviewers are frequently influenced by their prejudices and biases for or against an applicant. Equally competent interviewers frequently disagree in the appraisal of the same applicant. The interview often results in inaccurate information about the applicant.

In spite of its weaknesses, the interview remains a primary employee selection tool. All other selection procedures are designed to develop information on which the interviewer can make a final decision as to the suitability of the applicant for the job.

The interviewer should, therefore, approach the task with objectivity. He should attempt to be unbiased in his appraisal of the applicant's abilities, and should keep his mind focused on the requirements of the job. He is not a politician handing out patronage jobs to his friends. He is more like a purchasing agent bent on finding quality raw material for the enterprise.

The interview is a complex social encounter. The technique itself has produced extensive literature. The conscientious personnel officer will avail himself of all the literature he can find on the subject, study it, and strive to put it into practice. Successful interviewing is a difficult art, and proficiency can be attained only through conscious study and practice.

After interviews have been completed, the hiring officer makes a further appraisal of candidates. Those who have not been selected as a result of the interview should be notified. For the others the next step in the selection procedure, that of checking references, should be undertaken.

The interviewer must be very careful not to mislead an applicant at this point. If the applicant feels he has the job and that other steps are mere formalities, he may leave another position or, at the very least, get his hopes up. He should be told only that there are other applicants, but that he is certainly in the running.

Step 5—Checking references

Thus far in the selection procedure, the hiring officer has pretty much relied on what the applicant has said about himself and what objective tests have revealed. Most of what the applicant has said about himself can be taken at face value; but it is only human to exaggerate good points and minimize or conceal anything in his background that would hurt his chances of getting the job.

It is, therefore, very important to consult other persons who have known the applicant in the past and who can provide details about his professional abilities and general character.

The most important source of this information is previous employers. These can provide information as to length of employment, type of work performed, number of accidents, and general character. The applicant should be asked to provide names and addresses of his past three employers or of only his previous employer if he was employed for a period of ten years or more. (Some fleet supervisors say five years.)

There are three methods of checking with past employers; the telephone check, the form letter, and the personal visit.

The telephone check should be conducted by the interviewer, using a printed form which serves as a checklist to make sure all pertinent information is requested and also as a form on which to record the information. The call should be made, if possible, to the immediate supervisor of the driver, since this person will sometimes provide more information than will a personnel office. The advantage of this method of checking references is that it is fast. The disadvantage is that previous employers may be reluctant to provide information over the telephone. To double-check a caller, some companies will ask for a phone number and only call back after checking it. (An example of an "Employment Inquiry" checklist is shown in Figure 8-3.)

Checking references by correspondence is perhaps the most frequently used method—usually a printed form and a stamped return envelope are used. The advantage of this method is that it is a routine

EMPLOYMENT INQUIRY

Name of Applicant: ______________________________

Previous Employer: ______________________________

Former Supervisor: ______________ Telephone: ______________

______________ has applied for employment with our firm. May we please confidentially verify some of the information he has given us?

1. When did he work for your company?
   From __________ to __________.

2. What type of work did he do? ______________________.

3. Did he have any lost-time injuries while on the job? ☐ Yes ☐ No.
   How many? __________.

4. Was he involved in any traffic accidents? ☐ Yes ☐ No.
   How many? __________ Were any considered preventable? _____.

5. Was he able to get along well with supervisors? __________.

6. Was he considered to be trustworthy? ________.Honest? ________.
   Punctual? __________. Steady? __________.

7. Why did he leave your company? ______________________.

8. Is he eligible for rehire? ☐ Yes ☐ No. If not, why not? ________
   ____.

9. COMMENT: ______________________________________
   ____.

Date of Inquiry ____________________. By ____________________.

Figure 8-3. *This Employment Inquiry Form is an easy-to-use and easy-to-file checklist.*

clerical operation that results in a written report from the previous employer. The disadvantage is that the previous employer may be reluctant to make any signed report about a former employee, especially if it contains derogatory information. Another disadvantage is that letters are slow, the personnel department may not be able or willing to quickly answer written reference checks. (An example of the form letter reference check is shown in Figure 8-4.)

A personal visit with the previous employer to discuss the past work history of the applicant is perhaps the most reliable method. Previous employers will discuss an applicant much more frankly in a personal interview than they would by other methods. The disadvantages are that it can be costly and time-consuming, and is almost impossible when hiring a large number of drivers, or when long distances are involved.

Professional agencies exist that will conduct personal investigations for a fee. Such investigations usually include checking with the police department, credit agencies, and neighbors and acquaintances of the person investigated.

Always check the applicant's State Department of Motor Vehicles record. This is a vital check on accidents and injuries. Check each state where the applicant has lived or worked in the last three years. Checks by mail are usual, but a personal call to the department is possible in some states. The American Trucking Associations' publication, *How and Where to Check Driving Records,* contains additional information on the subject.

To guard against any legal liability resulting from personnel investigation activities, all applicants should first sign a release which contains the statement:

> I hereby release the __________ company or any agency it may designate or any persons the __________ company or agency may contact in the course of its investigation, from any liability which may result from the conduct of such investigation or from the result of the investigation.

The results of these reference checks are so important that it is very risky to start an applicant on the job before they are received. To be practical, the interviewer will usually make telephone checks, and rely on a letter of personal reference only as a last resort. Applicants cannot be kept "on the hook" until a written check comes back; but putting the driver to work unchecked is foolhardy and can lead to expensive accidents.

Step 6—Physical examination

Motor carrier safety regulations for bus and truck operators (*a*) require a physical examination for all new drivers and (*b*) provide that motor carriers must have on file a certificate showing each new driver to be physically qualified. These regulations also require that the driver carry on his person evidence of such physical fitness.

All applicants for driver positions should be examined by a qualified physician as a part of the employment procedure.

The Bureau of Motor Carrier Safety has set minimum requirements for operation in interstate commerce. Most fleet operators, who are serious about safety, establish physical requirements which are much more selective than the ones set out above.

A physician selected to conduct the physical examination should be familiar with the requirements of the job for which the applicant is being considered. In larger cities, some physicians specialize in industrial practice and, therefore, are conversant with the D.O.T. regulations and requirements, as well as the attitude of state agencies who administer workers' compensation laws. Such physicians can render valuable assistance to motor carriers in establishing standards, conducting examinations, handling workers' compensation cases, and maintaining the physical well-being of all drivers.

After the results of the physical examination are in, and if the applicant has been found to be fit to handle the job, a road and skill test should be given.

Step 7—Road and skill test

Road and skill tests are used to qualify an applicant as a safe, professional driver. The safety director, or other hiring officer, is present as an observer while the applicant demonstrates his vehicle operating and handling skills.

The test may be conducted on a private driving course under simulated conditions, or on a public road in actual traffic.

Michigan State University has developed the Driver Performance Measurement Test.* This test can help assess safe driving ability during selection by pointing out the precise unsafe habits likely to lead to later accidents.

The system requires the preparation of a thoroughly calibrated test course on public roads. As many as 50 traffic situations may be charted

---

*Information can be obtained from Michigan State University, Lifelong Education Highway Traffic Safety Programs; telephone (517) 355-3270.

REQUEST FOR INFORMATION FROM PREVIOUS EMPLOYER

From: *(Sender Company Name and Address)* **Date:** ____________________

TO: *(Company Name and Address)*

Gentlemen:

Mr. ______________________ has made application to this company for a position as ______________________ and states that he has been employed by you as ______________________ from ______________________ to ______________________.

Will you kindly reply to the inquiry below respecting this applicant. Your reply will be held in strict confidence and will in no way involve you in any responsibility.

For your convenience in replying by return mail, we have enclosed a self-addressed stamped envelope.

Very truly yours,

1. Correct dates of employment. From ____________ to ____________
2. What kind of work did he perform? ____________
3. Had he custody of money or valuables while in your employ? ____________
4. If so, were his accounts in order? ____________
5. If a driver, what types of equipment operated? Semi-trailer ______ Full trailer ______ Truck ______
6. Did he receive Workmen's Compensation for any injury? ____________
7. If so, what type injury? ____________
8. Were his habits sober, honest and proper? Above average ______ Average ______ Below average ______
9. Driving accident experience? Above average ______ Average ______ Below average ______
10. Job performance? Above average ______ Average ______ Below average ______
11. Work attendance history? Above average ______ Average ______ Below average ______
12. Reason for leaving your employ? Lack of work ______ Voluntary resignation ______ Involuntary resignation ______ Discharged ______ Other ______
13. Rehire status? Against company policy ______ Eligible ______ Not eligible ______

Other remarks: ____________

Date: ____________ For: ____________
(Name of Company)

By: ____________
(Signature of person supplying information)

(Detach here for your files)

____________ Date ____________
(Former Employer)

You are hereby authorized to give to the ____________
(Name of prospective Employer)
all information regarding my services, character and conduct while in your employ, and you are released from any and all liability which may result from furnishing such information.

Witness: ____________ Signed: ____________

Figure 8-4. Request for Information from Previous Employer form is used for checking applicants' references by mail.

National Committee for Motor Fleet Supervisor Training, East Lansing, Mich.

and correct/incorrect driving procedures determined for each. After the course is validated, it can be used by all nearby companies to test drivers, once they have trained and certified their own observers.

While the test course obviously requires a lot of organization and test time, it does give a standardized measure of driving performance. Any company hiring large numbers of drivers in one area should investigate this test.

Some companies maintain a truck roadeo* type of driving course, where pure maneuvering skill can be measured. This may be important to measure in a city driver who, for instance, may be backing into tight alleys and loading docks from his first day on the job.

Skill course diagrams and tests, and obstacle specifications can be found in the *Driver Trainer Manual,* available from the Private Truck Council of America, Inc., 2022 P Street, NW., Washington, D.C. 20036.

In some trucking operations, job applicants may be tested for skill in nondriving tasks. Experienced tank truck driver applicants may be asked to hook up hoses to pumps. A driver claiming experience with "doubles" trucks may be required to hook up a set of trailers, thus showing his knowledge of procedures as well as his driving skill.

Step 8—Acceptance interview

If the applicant passes the various requirements, he should be called in and either told that he is hired or being placed on a waiting list. This acceptance interview should reinforce the applicant's enthusiasm for the job. It is important that he be made to feel that, although company employment standards are rigorous, he has attributes the company sincerely wants. He should be welcomed to the company as a valued new employee. He should be given further orientation about the company and told what training he will receive, and when and where to report. His wages and working conditions should be finalized at this time.

Legal and Social Restrictions

The motor transportation fleet is a constructive social and economic force in the community in which it operates not only because of the transportation service it renders, but also because of the jobs it provides. Placing a person on the payroll, therefore, has social and economic significance not only to the one who is hired, but also to the fleet and to the community.

In this context, the employer today is no longer as free as he once

*Information on truck roadeo courses can be obtained from the Safety Department, American Trucking Associations, 2200 Mill Road, Alexandria, Va. 22314.

was to hire whomever he pleases. Laws throughout our nation forbid discriminating against job applicants. Society often takes the view that if the employer wishes to avail himself of the local labor market, he must do so with due regard for every applicant's right to fair consideration for the job.

These are not unreasonable restrictions. They should certainly not—in any way—force the employer to hire the unqualified. It is no favor to an applicant to hire him for a position for which he is not qualified and in which he will be a source of accidents, possible injuries, and unproductive work. The hiring officer has a moral obligation to the applicant, to the company, and to the community, to perform his job well. He alone knows the demands of the job and the qualifications required of the applicant. His decision should always represent a choice that is beneficial to the applicant and to the fleet. Such a decision will automatically benefit the company and community.

Chapter 9

Driver Training

One of the most important ingredients of efficient and profitable transportation service is safe-driving skill. A $60,000 diesel tractor is a frozen asset until a driver gets behind the wheel, starts the engine, and puts the vehicle to work.

The degree of skill with which this vehicle is maintained, operated, and managed will affect the amount of and quality of service it will provide, the vehicle's service life span, and the number of traffic accidents in which it will be involved. Management must, then, elevate its standards and take great pains to see that drivers possess a high degree of safe-driving skill.

Following the selection program described in the previous chapter should provide drivers who are capable of meeting management's standard. A good training program will bring the skills to this level, so that good supervision of the drivers (discussed in subsequent chapters) can further improve it.

How much training is necessary?

To what extent is training related to safe driving? Is not the operation of a motor vehicle a fairly common skill? No, it isn't. Safety experts have long known that safe driving ability is far from being a simple skill. It requires the ability to make traffic decisions quickly. This is why driving skill should be acquired through planned training instead of being picked up haphazardly.

The professional driver's skill has an added economic dimension. Regardless of former training, a driver must meet the company's standard of safe driving. Previous training quality cannot be taken for granted. The only sure way to assure a high degree of driving skill is to train each new employee. Training will provide the driver with the knowledge needed to do the job, the skill necessary to do it properly, an appreciation for the importance of the job, and an understanding of the necessity of doing it safely.

Benefits of training

Although training costs money, time, and effort, management can expect to obtain the following benefits from it:

Reduced number or complete elimination of accidents and accident-related costs. The trained driver will be a safer driver who knows both how to be safe and what situations to avoid.

Reduced maintenance costs. The driver who knows the mechanical limitations of the vehicle and develops an attitude of vehicle conservation will develop smooth operating habits, will take better care of the vehicle, and will cooperate more fully with the maintenance department.

Reduced absenteesim and labor turnover. Training develops an understanding of both job and fleet problems, which helps the driver gain job satisfaction.

Reduced supervisory burden. Training establishes a standard of performance and a basis for effective corrective action by supervision when needed. The well-trained driver usually requires less supervision because he understands these standards clearly and knows how to meet them without continued reminders from the supervisor.

Improved public relations. The driver represents the company in daily contacts with customers and other users of the highway. Good training is obvious and reflects credit not only on the driver but also on the company.

Development of a Training Program

Because there are many different approaches to training, the detailed development of the fleet training program is highly individualized. Factors to be considered include the philosophy of fleet management, personalities involved in driver training, the function of the fleet, the time allotted to training, and labor union relations.

Developing a training program is much like writing a speech. Each person must write his own, but can use material from many sources. The program must cover the subject thoroughly and interestingly. Since it will be presented over and over as new drivers are hired, it must be constantly revised in terms of audience reaction, trainee success on the job, and the changing needs of the fleet.

The following ideas should help build a good driver-training program.

When to teach

Training should be thought of as a process of personal development that begins when the driver is hired and continues until he retires. The most effective time for extensive, systematic training is right after the driver has been hired and before he is assigned to a vehicle.

How long to teach

The amount of time devoted to initial training will depend on the selection program, the type of person that is hired, his background, and the amount of usable training and experience he brings to the job.

The only practical gage for determining initial training time is that it should be adequate to bring the knowledge and skill of the new driver up to that necessary to perform his job properly.

Refresher training is often needed. This usually consists of one or two days of classroom instruction in which initial training material is reviewed or updated material (designed to familiarize drivers with new equipment, operating problems, or regulations) is presented. Refresher training is given annually or as needed.

A special type of refresher training is presented by a large city bus company 90 days after a new operator has finished his initial training. The theory is that during the initial training, trainees accept material pretty much without question because many of them have had no actual experience driving a bus. After 90 days on the job they have faced situations not fully covered before and now have many questions. This refresher course lasts one day and is devoted mainly to discussion periods.

Remedial training is another type of instruction that is provided for drivers who have had a certain number of accidents. Best results occur when course content is related to the type of accidents the repeaters have been having and the discussion technique is used. One technique is to describe an accident that one member of the class has had and have the other members discuss how it could have been prevented; in this way, all learn a lesson from it. Remedial training has been

Figure 9-1. *The most effective training is done in a specially designed training room. This room is equipped to accommodate lecture and demonstration classes and audio-visual presentations.*

successful in improving the performance of accident repeaters and is well worth the effort.

Education should be continuous and should go on day after day to provide the driver with a continuous exposure to safety information and ideas. This type of education utilizes safety posters, dash cards, bulletin boards, safety booklets, and driver letters, in addition to classwork.

Where to teach

The most effective training is done in a *specially designed training room*—something every fleet should have (see Figure 9-1). If a separate room is not feasible, then a place should be found that can be adapted. The training room should be soundproof, well-lighted, and ventilated. It should be equipped with tables and comfortable chairs, because if trainees are not comfortable, the environment will not be conducive to learning and a good deal of training effort will be wasted.

The training room should be equipped with a chalkboard, a magnetic board for showing traffic situations, and model vehicles (these can be 2- by 6-inch slightly pointed 1/4-in. boards, with two concealed magnets in them), and other aids to training.

Care taken in the layout, design, decoration, and equipment of the training room will pay off in better-trained drivers. Also, the room can be used for training other employees, for committee meetings, and for management conferences. In fact, the training room can be a very important communications center for the entire organization. The costs for setting up and maintaining a training room can be jointly budgeted from the safety, sales, mechanical maintenance, and other departments.

Behind-the-wheel training is also important. Only by riding with the driver can the supervisor observe his driving habits and his responses to different traffic situations. The usual pattern is for the trainee to drive the vehicle over a prescribed course while the supervisor rides as observer (Appendix C shows a test course layout). The supervisor refrains from pointing out errors until the completion of the test drive, at which time he discusses any driving errors observed and points out the correct method.

A special type of behind-the-wheel training is known as "commentary driving." Here the supervisor also rides with the driver, but the driver talks about what he sees in the traffic situation ahead and how he plans to adjust to it.

Such commentary could go like this: "The speed limit sign says 35 miles per hour. I'm well under that speed. There is an unregulated intersection ahead. A blue station wagon is pulling into the intersection. I think it is going to stop. Now I see it isn't, so I'm reducing my speed. He is now clear of the intersection and I can resume speed. My turn is up ahead. I can see no vehicles following in my rear view mirror, but I am putting on my right turn signal anyway. I am edging over to the curb lane, slowing down to make the turn. . . ."

Commentary driving allows the supervisor to gage how much a driver notices in any traffic situation; it also teaches the driver how to use his eyes more effectively and take note of all the elements that enter into any driving situation.

Another place for driver training is on a closed test course in a vacant parking lot or driving range. Driving problems requiring close clearances and careful maneuvering are practiced. Because trainees are shown how to maneuver their vehicles between barrels, flags, wooden horses, and pavement marks, these sessions are sometimes referred to as skill drills. (See Appendix C.) Drivers should be permitted to practice on the test course until they become proficient.

Skill drills are also used as a basis for driving contests or "roadeos" in which drivers match their skills.

The safety supervisor's office is another setting for training. It is especially effective when the safety director and a driver discuss an accident in an attempt to determine whether it was preventable or not. This is an excellent training situation and should be regarded as such rather than as a disciplinary action.

Appendix B gives details of training meetings.

Training is continuous

While there are special times and places for training, it can be effectively carried on at any time and in almost any place. The good trainer or supervisor will know when and where to take advantage of training opportunities as they arise.

What To Teach

The most important part of a training program is its subject matter. Because training is useful only when it fills a need, the subject matter should cover what the driver needs to know to do his job well. Before assembling any training material, the instructor should first outline the things he wants the trainee to learn and decide on their relative importance:

1. *Vital subject matter*—absolutely essential to success on the job;
2. *Important subject matter*—provides basic understanding of the job;
3. *Helpful material*—related to the job and gives a broader base of understanding on which to build performance; and
4. *Incidental material*—"nice to know" but not necessary to job performance.

It is not always easy to decide into which of these categories any piece of training material may fall. In making his final selection, each driver should use his own judgment. The training material outline along with the teaching method (see page 160) and the training aids choices (see page 161) make up a training session plan (see Appendix B).

The amount of time devoted to each area will also be a matter of individual determination. The trainer will have to assemble the individual facts and details of subject matter from the available literature on the subject.

Here is a guide to subject areas that should be covered. Much of this is covered in the Council's "Driver Improvement Program."

The motor vehicle accident problem

Describe the national traffic accident problem: number of fatal accidents, and the number of property damage accidents and their cost. Show both direct and indirect cost of traffic accidents to the company. Show how rates are determined, and how company rates compare with those of other fleets and those throughout industry. Show how the direct and indirect costs of accidents alter the company's profits and, therefore, its ability to stay in business and provide top wage, benefit, and bonus programs to its employees.

Describe cost of accidents to the driver himself: possible disablement or death, and loss of earnings should he be hospitalized or disabled for an extended period.

Describe how safe driving performances contribute to community safety: by reducing number of accidents, and setting a good example to other drivers. Show how it contributes to the health of the company: reducing costs, improving efficiency of service to customers, creating a favorable impression on the general public. Describe safe driving ability in terms of employee welfare: how it ensures job security and continuity of earning power.

Stress that the company has high standards of performance in everything it does, including safe driving. State that the company expects not just average safe driving performance but award-winning safety performance because it knows that this is possible. Read and discuss the company's written safety policy (see Chapter 2).

Be sure that the material provides the driver with a strong basic motivation to develop and maintain safe driving skills.

Traffic regulations

Cover state and municipal traffic laws and ordinances. If the fleet operates in interstate commerce, Bureau of Motor Carrier Safety regulations that affect drivers should be taught, and copies of these regulations distributed.

Review traffic signs and correct use of hand and automatic signals.

Stress that the company—as well as the law—expects all drivers to observe all traffic rules. Explain the company's attitude should a driver be arrested or cited for a traffic violation.

This training should not only give knowledge of traffic rules and regulations, but also develop understanding and respect for them.

Causes of traffic accidents

Develop the principle idea that motor vehicle accidents are not the result of chance, but are caused by factors, most of which can either be controlled or compensated for by the driver. These factors are the physical, mental, and emotional condition of the driver, the mechanical condition of the vehicle, and the acts of pedestrians and drivers of other motor vehicles. Discuss such other accident factors as road surface conditions, weather conditions, and light conditions.

Stress that the trainee is expected to be alert to all these accident-producing factors, to recognize how they can contribute to accidents, and to take the proper precautions in regard to each so as to avoid an accident. This lesson should build in the trainee a strong conviction that motor vehicle accidents are preventable and that, as a driver, he can do the most to prevent them.

Personal traits affecting driving

To build a renewed respect for the relationship of good health habits to safe driving, describe how the physical, mental, and emotional wellbeing of a driver affects safe driving. Tell what the driver should do.

A number of psycho-physical testing devices are available to demonstrate how a trainee measures up in each trait so that, if need be, he can acquire compensating habits. For example, if the trainee has a very narrow peripheral vision, he can compensate for it by forming the habit of moving his head from side to side to observe traffic conditions. Psycho-physical devices may be purchased from the American Automobile Association through any affiliate office.

The trainee should be impressed with the importance of keeping himself in good physical condition, avoiding extreme fatigue, avoiding the use of drugs or medications that might adversely affect his driving ability, and keeping his mind free of worries and unnecessary distractions.

Defensive driving

An entire unit of instruction should be devoted to one of the most important safe-driving concepts—that of defensive driving.

Defensive driving, essentially, requires both the desire and the ability of a driver to control the accident-producing situations he meets in order to avoid an accident. To practice defensive driving, a driver must acquire a proper attitude and refine certain components of his driving.

The defensive driving attitude is one that accepts responsibility for being on top of accident-producing situations and avoiding accidents, rather than passively surrendering to an adverse situation. It is a positive attitude; namely, that the driver can prevent accidents by taking the initiative.

But attitude alone is not enough. The defensive driver must implement it by his alertness, foresight, knowledge, judgment, and skill. All of these qualities lend themselves to development in the training program and can be further improved by experience.

The National Safety Council's "Defensive Driving Course" teaches the techniques to drive to save lives, money, and time in spite of the conditions around you and the actions of others. This program could be used in conjunction with an off-the-job safety program (see Chapter 15).

Preventable concept. Closely allied to defensive driving are the terms "preventable" and "nonpreventable" used in describing an accident. These two terms measure the defensive driving skill exercised by the driver in a given accident. If he did everything he *reasonably* could have done to prevent the accident and it still happened, then the accident is graded "nonpreventable." If he failed to do so, then the accident is graded "preventable." The trainee must know the ground rules under which he will be judged, and how he can appeal an adverse decision.

These two ideas (defensive driving and accident preventability) dovetail and thus make possible a third idea of equal importance to the safety program; a workable and enforceable standard of safe-driving performance: *the standard of safe driving performance is driving without a preventable accident.* This standard must be thoroughly understood by top management, by supervisors, and by drivers, if there is to be effective safety supervision.

These three ideas are sometimes difficult for drivers to comprehend at first. But they are so essential to the development of professional safe driving attitudes and skills, that time should be allotted to explain them clearly. Once the rules are understood, drivers will acquire a new respect for safe-driving ability, will be more receptive to safety information, and will develop a personal concern for their own safety records.

Two-vehicle collision prevention

Another unit of training should be devoted to demonstrating how two vehicles can collide from each of six positions, and what defensive measures apply in each situation.

Traffic offers problems of such variety and complexity that unless these situations are grouped, the training program could easily become an exhaustive list of impossible-to-remember "do's" and "don'ts."

Fortunately there are several ways to unify these problems to make the subject more manageable. One of these is the six-positions of the most frequent type of traffic accident—collision between two motor vehicles.

From the standpoint of *our* vehicle, there are only six positions that the *other* vehicle can take relative to ours from which both vehicles can collide: (1) it can be ahead of us, (2) behind us, (3) approaching us from an angle, (4) approaching from the opposite direction, (5) passing us, or (6) being the vehicle that we pass.

Backing accident prevention

Because backing accidents occur frequently, this subject belongs in the driver training program. Even though the severity of this type of accident is usually minor, the cumulative cost mounts up. Sometimes, however, a backing accident can have serious results.

Drivers should also be taught that backing should be avoided whenever possible, that backing around corners or out of driveways or alleys is especially dangerous, and that—if there is a choice—backing out of traffic is safer than backing into traffic.

Stopping distance demonstration

The brake detonator is a device that will vividly show drivers the distance it takes to stop their vehicle. Because most drivers firmly believe it is a mark of driving skill to be able to stop their vehicle on a dime, this misconception is hard to dispose of without convincing proof. The brake detonator dramatically demonstrates stopping distances.

The device, equipped with two firing chambers for firing chalk marks onto the pavement, is attached to the vehicle's front bumper. The first charge is fired by the instructor at his discretion when the vehicle has attained a predetermined speed. This makes a mark on the pavement and also signals the driver to apply his brakes and stop his vehicle in the shortest possible distance. When the brakes take hold, the second charge is fired and makes a second mark on the pavement. When finally the vehicle is stopped, the driver and his instructor get out and mark the point on the pavement that is even with the front bumper.

There are now three marks on the pavement: the first, the point where the instructor fired the first charge and signaled the driver to stop; the second, the point at which the vehicle's brakes began to take hold. The distance between these two marks—*the reaction distance*—is how far the vehicle traveled while the driver was responding to the signal and getting his foot on the brakes. The third mark is that made where the vehicle stopped.

The distance between the second and third marks—known as *the braking distance*—tells how far it took the brakes to stop the vehicle. The two measurements represent total stopping distance required in every stop a driver makes from that speed. Tests can be run at different speeds.

Sometimes all drivers can be tested. When time will not permit this, volunteers are selected while the rest of the training class observes. Even to observers, this demonstration of stopping distances convinces them that they cannot "stop on a dime."

This demonstration teaches drivers that they must follow a vehicle at a safe distance, be alert for sudden stops, and start braking as soon as they anticipate that they might have to stop. Brake detonators can be purchased from the American Automobile Association, through any affiliate office.

The driver and his vehicle

The driver should know the mechanical principles of the gasoline or diesel engine, the power transmission train, the braking system, the electrical system, and other components of his vehicle. Even drivers with many years of experience can profit from a review of these subjects. When new vehicles are added to the fleet, differences of the new equipment should be reviewed with drivers. They should be familiar with the new vehicle's characteristics before they take it on a run. The drivers should be encouraged to give their opinions on the handling qualities and running economics of new (and existing) fleet vehicles.

Of course the driver is not expected to be a trained mechanic, but he should know enough about his vehicle to recognize and describe mechanical defects when they arise and to know how to avoid abusing his vehicle. He should be able to know when trouble is serious enough to warrant assistance.

This training unit should include practice drills in the step-by-step procedure to be followed in making a pretrip inspection and how inspections should be made en route. (see Chapter 12.)

Basic driving maneuvers

The basic driving maneuvers are starting the engine, shifting gears, starting, steering, and stopping the vehicle, backing, turning, and parking. The correct method must be mastered if driving is to be smooth, safe, and efficient. If the vehicle has several speeds forward, training should also cover double clutching, if necessary, when gearing up or down.

The instructor should demonstrate to each trainee the correct method of performing each of these tasks and then have the trainee do it himself. The instructor should correct any errors, make suggestions, and then allow the trainee to practice until he can perform it correctly and with ease.

The trainee must understand that he becomes skillful only when he can perform these maneuvers the right way *every* time.

Driving in traffic

Allot time for the trainee to test drive the type of vehicle to which he will be assigned. The best time is near the end of the training program, after the trainee has had the benefit of classroom instruction and has been checked out on the basic driving maneuvers.

The test drive should be conducted under the supervision of a driver trainer and the route selected should include a variety of traffic situations: controlled and uncontrolled intersections, residential and congested areas, narrow streets and freeways, railroad crossings, and dock areas.

The same route should be used for each test drive so that the instructor can become familiar with the situations that cause the trainee the most trouble and best test his skill. This will also enable the instructor to better help the trainee and be more consistent in grading him.

The test drive builds the trainee's confidence in his ability to handle the vehicle properly and safely, and it lets the instructor observe the trainee under actual road conditions so that he can decide whether the trainee is sufficiently trained.

If the trainee passes the test, he may be assigned to a regular run, with or without an instructor. In bus operations, the new driver is often placed on a regular run with an experienced operator riding with him for several days as a final check on his competence, and to make certain he knows the routes.

Should the trainee fail the test, a decision must be made: provide additional training or practice, assign him to a nondriving job, or terminate his employment.

Procedure in case of accident

Although training is designed to keep drivers out of accidents, they should also be carefully taught the correct procedure to follow if they are involved in an accident with a company vehicle. Review the accident procedures discussed in Chapter 4.

Include practice in completing the company accident report form by giving case histories of actual accidents with the information presented just as it might be in such a situation. The trainee uses this to compete an accident report form.

Trainees should be taught to make out a report for every accident, no matter how minor it may seem. Because one purpose of the accident report is to learn more about accident prevention, much can be learned from even a minor accident.

The cause of a good accident reporting discipline, so essential to the success of any safety program is aided greatly if this subject is taught thoroughly and well.

Handling passengers. Drivers of passenger-carrying vehicles should be taught how to prevent passenger accidents. This will include how to position the vehicle for safe boarding and alighting of passengers, how to drive smoothly and slow down gradually in order to avoid on-board falls, and how to look for and remove tripping and slipping hazards aboard the vehicle.

If passengers are hurt, medical assistance should be sought, if possible, and the police should be informed of the injuries.

Handling freight. Any applicable regulations to loading or transporting cargo should be taught. Loads should be braced so that a sudden stop will not send freight flying toward the driver.

Drivers should be taught what to do if an accident scatters cargo about. It is important to:

- Minimize damage to other vehicles (because of broken glass, spilled liquids, scattered boxes in the road).
- Notify police of a specially dangerous cargo. People in the area and other motorists must be warned if necessary. Any vehicle carrying hazardous materials must, under DOT regulations, carry a shipping document describing the load and its hazard. If the quantity or hazard is great enough, the vehicle will carry a hazard placard on all four sides. Firefighting instructions must also be posted when the cargo is especially hazardous.
- Take steps to prevent (or minimize) theft of, or additional damage to cargo, such as covering the cargo with tarpaulins to prevent damage from exposure, and posting a guard at the accident site if feasible and necessary.

The company safety program

Because each driver will be in daily contact with the safety program, he should develop an understanding and cooperative attitude toward it. Time devoted to explaining it will pay dividends.

Trainees should know why the safety program is necessary, its main elements, what safe driver awards or bonuses are offered under it and the rules for earning these, and what fleet contests the company has entered and the rules governing these.

How To Teach

Teaching is more than telling or exposing the trainee to information: the trainee must exert mental effort. The process is like playing ball. The instructor makes the pitch, but the learner must make the catch. The responsibility for the success of the exchange, however, is always the instructor's. It is up to the teacher to motivate the trainee to learn. This he can do by making his presentation clear, interesting, memorable, and of personal value to the trainee.

The new trainee has a natural motivation to learn because he is embarking on an important venture—a new job. If he has been selected wisely, he will be the kind of person who will be anxious to learn to do his job well. In spite of this, the trainee may have certain barriers to learning, which the instructor must anticipate: the trainee may feel that he already knows the subject, he may feel that the instructor is exaggerating the importance of the subject matter, or he may find that the material is too difficult to understand.

The good instructor is sensitive to these attitudes and develops ways to overcome them. He understands that his job is to present the material and encourage the trainee to learn. The instructor must be a salesman, have an attractive personality, and be full of energy and enthusiasm for his subject. He has something to sell, but until the trainee buys, there is no sale.

Just as every good leader is also a teacher, every instructor is a leader. As a leader, he should exemplify the qualities he seeks to transfer to the trainee. By his manner, he must demonstrate that he has pride in himself, pride in his job, and pride in his company. He should be neat in appearance. He should be fair in his relationship, but still friendly.

Teaching methods

Having decided what material to present, the instructor must then organize it into lessons.

Lessons have dimensions in time and space. A good *time* dimension is 50 minutes, with a 10-minute break between sessions to allow the class to relax. The *space* dimension refers to the amount of material to be covered in a given session, and should always be based on the amount of material the trainees can comprehend. Four or five main points are about all an average trainee can learn in one lesson. To attempt to crowd more material into it will usually result in less learning rather than more.

The lecture method (in which the instructor stands before the class and tells about and explains the material) is the most commonly used teaching method because it can cover a great deal of material in a short time. The danger is that the lecture can become monotonous and boring.

To guard against this, the instructor must strive to make his lecture interesting by keeping to a few basic points, selecting good examples or anecdotes, utilizing audiovisuals, asking rhetorical questions, changing the pitch and speed of his delivery, making clear transitions from one main point to the next, and summarizing the material at the end of the lecture.

Demonstration is another teaching method, usually used in conjunction with other methods. Here a physical object is displayed to the class to show how it works, why it works, or how to work it.

Discussion is a third effective teaching method. This allows the class to participate by answering questions, relating their own experiences, or thinking through a problem under the guidance of the instructor. Although this is a slower method of covering a subject, it arouses good interest in the trainees, provides a more vivid learning experience, and fosters a spirit of unity in the group. A short discussion period can be used to end a training lecture or demonstration.

Allow trainees to practice what they learn. The instructor first *explains* how the job is done—for example hooking up a tractor to a trailer—he then *demonstrates how* it is done. He then allows the trainee to try it himself, correcting the trainee's performance when necessary. Then he has him repeat the correct procedure. The trainee is then given additional time to practice the procedure until the right way becomes a habit.

Examination is actually another teaching method. It may be oral, written, or of the performance type, but whichever type, it permits the trainee to show what he has learned and gives him a sense of accomplishment. It is a form of repetition or review that intensifies the learning process, and should be used throughout the training program. Even a question put to a trainee during a lecture is a form of examination. Through use of the examination technique, the instructor is able to evaluate what the trainee has learned. The trainee is permitted to demonstrate what he has learned, and often finds out what he still needs to learn. Examination results can be kept confidential or posted. Choose whichever seems more effective.

Reading should not be overlooked because it plays an important part in both shortening and enriching the training program. Reading is usually done after course hours and on the trainee's own time. To make sure the trainee has read and understood the material, reading assignments should be followed up by classroom discussion or written examination, or both.

Training aids

Because it is not always possible to express ideas vividly or quickly enough by the spoken word alone, audiovisuals should be used to supplement the lecture. In a discussion of accident costs, for example, writing the figures on the chalkboard will aid the trainee in appreciating the dollar amounts involved. Graphs or bar charts can be used to show quantitative relationships. Although key words or points in a lesson written on the chalkboard help in remembering the ideas presented, diagrams can save precious minutes of explanation.

The instructor has available to him a wide range of visual aids. He should learn how to use each effectively. He must always remember that training aids are aids only. They should never be used just because they are available, but rather because they contribute to the instructor's objective in training. Whatever aids are chosen, it is important to list them in advance in a training session plan (see page 257) to ensure that they are available and set up before the class begins. A missing chalkboard or projector will sabotage the best presentation.

Chalkboard. One of the first and still most widely used visuals is the chalkboard. This can be used to show key words, phrases, or points in the lecture. It can be used for making diagrams, graphs, and sketches that will help the trainee understand what is being discussed. Whether writing is placed on the chalkboard before class, or written there as the instructor comes to the point in his lecture, make sure it is large enough for all to see clearly. The instructor should stand at the side of the chalkboard and face the class as much as possible. The instructor can use colored chalk to add further interest to the presentation.

Flip chart. The flip chart has somewhat the same uses as the chalkboard. However it contains a number of successive pages and will accommodate a great deal more prepared material than a single chalkboard. If the chart will be used over and over again, the instructor can afford to make each page as attractive and informative as possible. Words can be carefully lettered (see Figure 9-2), diagrams drawn to scale, sketches painstakingly drawn, and colored inks used to add interest and readability to the chart. Each successive page should help to develop the lesson.

Sometimes blank flip charts are used, the instructor writing on the pages with a colored crayon or marking pen. This can be dramatic but since the pages cannot be erased, they must be discarded after each lesson. This is an asset, however, in a discussion. Old pages serve as a record.

Flannel board. The flannel board combines some of the features of the chalkboard and the flip chart. It is usually about the size of a medium-size chalkboard. The material to be placed on the flannel board can be used over and over again so the instructor can afford to construct the material with care. Objects to be placed on the flannel board include strips of cardboard on which key words, points, or phrases are printed or carefully lettered. A variety of other objects can be used: photographs, clips from a magazine, shapes, sample forms.

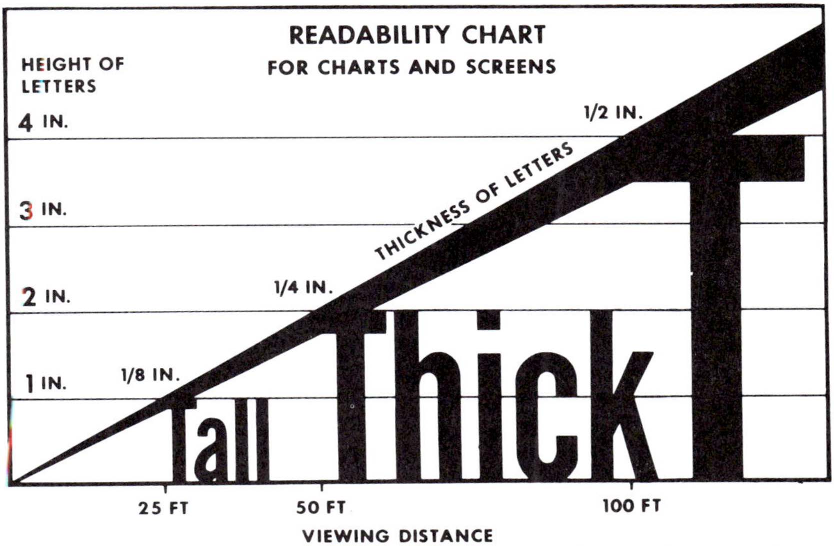

Figure 9-2. *This chart shows the heights and thicknesses letters and symbols should be for easy viewing of non-projected and projected visuals.*

The flannel board allows the instructor to put complicated material on the board and take it off as needed. He can add material to the board as his lecture progresses, in order to develop his lesson as he would build a pyramid, by adding building blocks as he goes along.

Magnetic board. Every driver training program should have a magnetic board showing a standard traffic layout with magnetized model vehicles that will stick to the board wherever they are placed.

The magnetic board can be used to explain the correct driving maneuvers, to reconstruct accidents for class discussion, or for reenacting an accident when counseling with the driver involved to determine its preventability. A magnetic board can be combined with a chalkboard or flannel board.

Accident demonstration board. Miniature automobiles and demonstration boards can also be used for portraying accidents. An excellent vertical demonstration board that can be constructed at little cost is made by thumbtacking different colored pieces of felt on drywall or pressed board. The felt pieces can be sized to indicate curb lines, view obstructions, signal lights, and buildings. Miniature vehicles (obtained at toy stores) are fitted with pins for moving about on the board. Several types of vertical demonstration boards are currently on the market that use a simple adhesive process to hold materials to the board. They allow diagrams to be shifted and illustrations to be moved about easily.

Demonstration mockups. Talks given in conjunction with demonstrations using actual equipment (or a model) are effective in holding the interest of employees. An actual setup or model of the vehicle's braking system, showing master cylinder, brake lines, brake cylinders, shoes, and drums, can help the student to learn how the brakes operate. Other subjects particularly adaptable to demonstrations are ignition, cooling system, headlights, tires, electrical equipment, and carburetion. Persons giving these demonstrations should be experts in their fields.

Abused equipment. Actual tires can be displayed as an example of what results from climbing curbs when making turns or the amount of rubber that can be worn off a tire in an unnecessarily fast stop. Worn mechanical parts can also be displayed to show the results of careless operation. Actual replacement cost figures are also effective communicators.

Driver testing equipment. Although no definite relationship has been established between psychological and physiological test results in accident proneness, drivers do like to compete for honors in demonstrating their ability to operate such equipment and tests may be conducted as part of the safety meeting program. Some insurance companies and automobile clubs have testing equipment available and are glad to cooperate in giving tests. The educational value of these tests lies in explaining the compensation and correction necessary for offsetting the deficiencies indicated by the tests. Therefore, they should be given with extreme care by trained examiners.

Slides. The slide projector opens another rich source of visual material that can aid in teaching. The instructor can take color slides of vehicles, traffic situations, accidents, damaged equipment, unsafe practices, and many other scenes, and then show them to the class.

Some trainers take pictures (slides or movies) of bad driving practices when the offending driver is unaware he is being photographed. Later, the proper practices are staged and photographed for presentation with the former. Films of this character have an excellent effect on the drivers. The cost of photographic equipment is not great and reasonably good pictures can be produced with a little practice. When homemade slides (or movies) are used, the safety department should prepare a short talk discussing the practices shown and emphasizing the correct methods. Slide projectors which are integrated with cassette tape decks

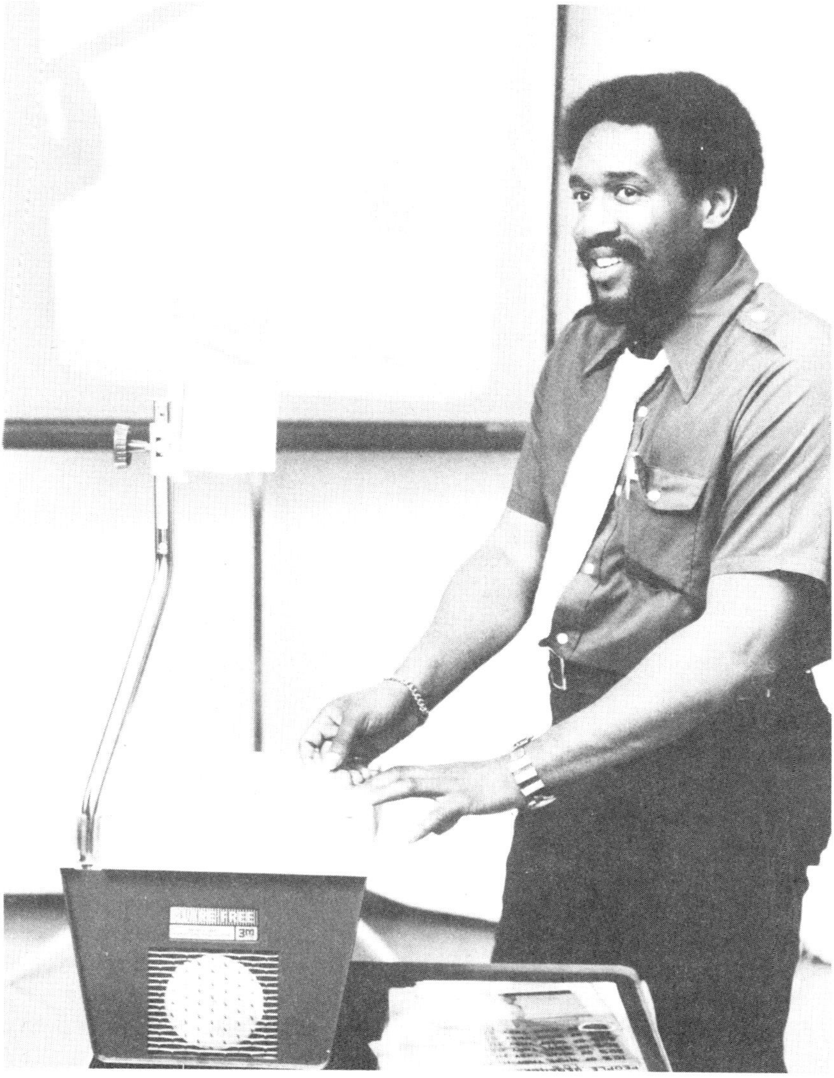

Figure 9-3. *The overhead projector can be set up and used as needed during a training session. It permits the instructor to maintain good eye contact with his audience—he can see his visual without having to turn his back on them. A pencil or other marker in the instructor's hand shows as a "shadow pointer" on the screen behind. He could also write on the transparency.*

are available, and are not too expensive. With such a system, a sound and slide presentation can be made and shown at different company locations. The message will always be the same because the narration is taped.

The slide projector can also be used like a giant flip chart. Pages of a flip chart, company report forms, graphs, and many other subjects can be photographed for projection before the class.

Many slide shows are also available for training. They are useful in clarifying technical discussions and, because they combine a visual and spoken message, make a lasting impression on the employee.

Overhead projectors. Overhead projectors are similar to slide projectors, a main difference being that the transparencies used for projection can be prepared using materials available in most offices. Printed or typewritten materials can be transferred to the clear acetate sheets by running them through a dry process photocopy machine. Pictures, charts, and graphs can be drawn on the 8½- by 11-inch transparencies using black or colored marking pens, crayons and inks.

Because the overhead projector is designed to be used in a fully illuminated room, the safety instructor can use it to emphasize critical points during his lecture or demonstration training sessions (see Figures 9-3 and 9-4).

Films. The driver training movie can make an important contribution to the training program. Even though the film may make only a limited number of points, it focuses attention on the problem and promotes discussion or further instruction.

Since the driver training film usually runs from 10 to 20 minutes, it cannot carry a very heavy training load by itself. To make a film-based training session effective, the instructor should first describe the film, tell why it is being shown, and then direct the attention of the trainees to certain points in the film before it is shown. Following the screening, the main points are reviewed and discussed and the material applied to particular problems. Following this, a quiz can be given to further reinforce the lesson. The quiz can be discussed at the end of class, or at the beginning of the next class.

A film or other audiovisual should be selected and reviewed before showing it in a training session. If possible, the vehicles and scenes depicted should be very similar to the vehicles used and the conditions encountered by your drivers. Drivers of vans, for instance, tend to ignore training materials aimed at tractor-trailer drivers, and vice versa. Both groups often reject materials directed to passenger car drivers.

However, that does not always mean that the trainer must pass up a good film because it does not deal with the specific operations of the

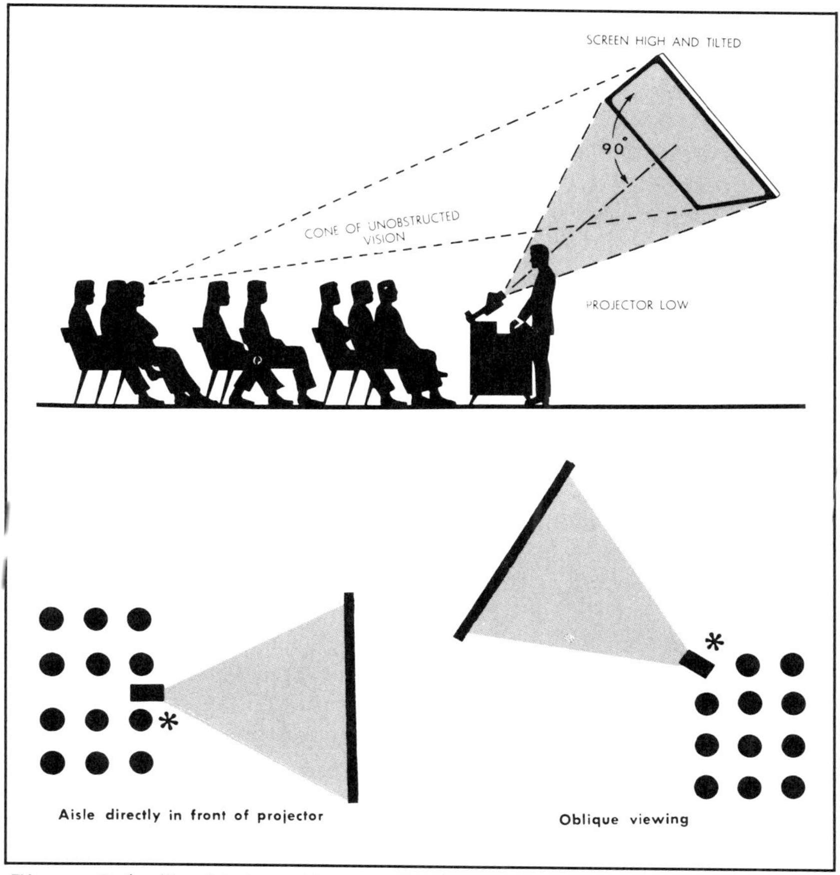

Figure 9-4. *To obtain optimum viewing area, especially when instructing large groups, tilt the overhead screen (shown at top) or place it toward the corner of the room* (lower right). *Both placements reduce the possibility of the instructor and equipment blocking the vision of some viewers, as might be the case when the projector is located in front of the group* (lower left).

fleet. But the instructor can point out that while the film features passenger cars, there are many valid ideas in it for truck drivers. The good instructor often can take an appropriate passenger car film and make it the basis for an effective lesson for truck drivers or take a truck driving film and use it to good advantage in teaching passenger car drivers.

Tape recorders. Tape recorders can add variety, interest, and emphasis to a training program: trainees can listen to the actual commentary of a driver during a trip, trainees can play back counseling interviews in which the preventability of an accident was determined. The resourceful instructor will think of many other ways in which the tape recorder can be used as an effective training aid.

Video. A novel approach to safety training programs was mentioned in the Council's recent book release, *Introduction to Occupational Health and Safety* (see Appendix E, "Bibliography and Additional References"). The author suggested that computerized video equipment be placed in an employee lunch or rest area and used to play a continuous safety message. In addition, a software package would be provided that would allow an employee to play a "space invaders" or similar arcade game, but only after that employee had correctly answered a short series of safety questions. Such questions would be changed as necessary to reflect the company's current safety and health emphasis.

Additional help

Remember that any training program must be designed to fit the training need—not fit the training aids available. Ask "What is the trainee expected to do as a result of this training?" and "What behavioral change is expected?" Then decide (*a*) the method of instruction, (*b*) the training aids to use, and (*c*) how all-inclusive to make the program.

The choice must be made to best fit the subject to the audience. Be sure to check the advantages of all types of audiovisuals before deciding. National Safety Council publishes a series of Industrial Data Sheets to help do just that. Refer to *Motion Pictures for Safety* (No. 556), *Nonprojected Visual Aids* (No. 564), *Photography for Safety* (No. 619), *Posters, Bulletin Boards, and Safety Displays* (No. 616), and *Projected Still Pictures* (No. 574).

A number of films and other training aids are available from the Council. Write for information on how you can obtain a catalog.

Chapter 10

Driver Supervision

Supervision is not only the art of getting things done through people, it is the art of getting them done well.

Most driving jobs require two duties: those that relate to driving, of course, and those that don't. Both pose different supervisory problems.

What Is Driver Supervision?

In some instances, nondriving duties can be supervised by ordinary techniques used throughout industry. The special techniques for supervising the driving part of the job, however, are most complex.

Drivers are capable of committing any number of errors that can be costly to the company. The driver supervisor must know (*a*) what these errors are, or could be, (*b*) how they can be spotted, and (*c*) how to prevent them. The supervisor must enforce a high standard of performance—one that does not condone accidents that could reasonably be prevented. This chapter is designed to tell him how.

Who is the driver supervisor?

The driver supervisor is responsible for the quality of driver performance. In the small fleet, this person may be the fleet manager or owner, in a large common carrier fleet, several persons may share supervisory responsibility, each having some authority (sometimes overlapping).

For example, the terminal manager is usually thought of as the driver's direct supervisor. But the dispatcher shares some of the supervisory load because the dispatcher both (*a*) assigns runs and vehicles to the driver, and (*b*) makes sure these runs are completed on time and correctly.

The safety director (who is responsible for overall safety performance) should work through the supervisor at the driver's home terminal. Additional supervision may be provided by a safety road patrol—supervisors who can make on-the-spot observations of driving performance and report these back to company headquarters for follow-up. In some instances, this road supervisor may be authorized to stop a vehicle and correct the driver.

But what about that ancient rule of supervision that a person cannot serve two masters? How, then, can a driver please so many different people who all seem to have something to say about how he is doing his job? Because these supervisory practices are created by the operating conditions of a motor transportation fleet, unity is achieved only *if all supervisors agree on how the driving job should be performed.*

Most safety programs ultimately depend on the immediate supervisor to get results. If this person undercuts safety through his words or actions, little can be achieved. However, the strong safety director may get results from even a reluctant supervisor through the judicious use of pressure. It is better to have a motivated manager actively pushing the program; but sometimes the safety director must settle for less.

How To Prevent Accidents

Because motor vehicle accidents represent a great potential for loss in terms of human life, bodily injury, and property damage, the primary responsibility of supervision is to prevent accidents before they happen.

There are certain techniques that the supervisor should learn and use for spotting substandard performance that often results in accidents. For example:

• Personally observe the driver's performance and check driver trainer reports, road patrol reports, arrest records, and comments from other drivers and employees.

• Review complaints from other drivers or pedestrians as a possible barometer of driving performance. If more than one incident takes place, the supervisor who knows his job can usually spot the behavioral actions—such as belligerence or indifference—that can lead to an accident. The supervisor should try to find the reason for this change in behavior and seek to help solve the problems that may have brought about such change in the driver's characteristics. Sometimes a driver can do nondriving work if he is emotionally disturbed.

• Be alert to personality and performance changes before they reach the incident stage by making frequent personal contacts with the drivers.

A safety supervisor should watch for these typical symptoms of accidents in the making:

1. Errors in performance of work
2. Changes in everyday behavior and manners
3. Changes in simple habits of a routine nature
4. Near-accidents.

These reflect mental and emotional feelings and can fluctuate with various factors: resentments stemming from childhood, weariness, fatigue, a series of disappointments. Sometimes these feelings lead to an accident.

This does not mean that the driver supervisor must be a psychiatrist. He should be aware, however, that much substandard performance has a psychological base so that he can be more understanding and effective in dealing with it.

Dr. A. R. Lauer, a leading authority on driving behavior, offers this advice to the driver supervisor:

> Drivers seem to improve when approached about their difficulties and these are discussed with them in a semiclinical way. Because it appears that they realize they can compensate for their weaknesses, this may be the important factor in improving their record. An objective check of a driver, followed by a careful and confidential discussion of the deficiencies noted, will result in improved driving behavior and a corresponding reduction in accidents.

Errors fall into a number of main categories, we shall discuss the importance of each category along with the specific errors that a supervisor should watch for. These errors may not be of equal importance to all fleets. The driver supervisor should adapt the list to fit his operation.

Errors that lead to accidents

Driving errors that frequently lead to accidents were compiled by means of a survey of more than 150 of the nation's top fleet safety directors. The driver supervisor can adapt this list to aid his own fleet operation—especially in training drivers.

1. Upon starting

- **a.** Failure to first check clearances, front, rear, overhead
- **b.** Failure to signal when pulling out from curb

c. Failure to check for a break in traffic before moving

2. **Speed control**
   - **a.** Too fast for volume of traffic
   - **b.** Too fast for condition of road surface
   - **c.** Too fast for condition of visibility (due to weather or road)
   - **d.** Too fast for condition of light (dusk/darkness)
   - **e.** Too fast for neighborhood or roadside environment
   - **f.** Too fast for street/highway layout and traffic signals
   - **g.** Too slow for speed of traffic stream

3. **Lane Usage**
   - **a.** Failure to select proper lane
   - **b.** Failure to drive in middle of lane
   - **c.** Abrupt lane change
   - **d.** Failure to signal intent to change lanes
   - **e.** Weaving

4. **Passing**
   - **a.** Misjudging speed and nearness of oncoming vehicle
   - **b.** Failure to check to the rear before pulling out to pass
   - **c.** Overtaking and passing too slowly
   - **d.** Cutting in too quickly after passing
   - **e.** Failure to signal intention of passing
   - **f.** Unnecessary passing
   - **g.** Racing other vehicle trying to pass you
   - **h.** Passing in an intersection

5. **Turning**
   - **a.** Turning from wrong lane
   - **b.** Failure to let oncoming traffic clear before turning left
   - **c.** Failure to block area to right of vehicle on right turns
   - **d.** Running over curb on right turns
   - **e.** Abrupt turn on slippery road surface causing vehicle to skid
   - **f.** Failure to signal intention to turn

6. **Stopping**
   - **a.** Failure to make smooth gradual stop
   - **b.** Failure to signal stop
   - **c.** Failure to stop in time
   - **d.** Abrupt braking on slippery road surface causing a skid

7. **Parking**
   - **a.** Parking in unsafe or illegal place
   - **b.** Parking with front or rear of vehicle protruding into traffic
   - **c.** Failure to secure unattended vehicle on hill
   - **d.** Failure to properly mark disabled vehicle

8. **Specific signaling errors**
   a. Failure to signal
   b. Signal too late
   c. Wrong signal
   d. Failure to use horn
   e. Excessive or improper use of horn

9. **Errors in clearance judgment**
   a. Following vehicle ahead too closely
   b. Failure to check clearance to rear when backing
   c. Failure to check right side clearance
   d. Failure to check left side clearance
   e. Failure to check top clearance
   f. Failure to yield space in any traffic encroachment

10. **Errors in observation**
   a. Failure to observe object or pedestrian in path of vehicle
   b. Failure to observe traffic at rear of vehicle while moving
   c. Failure to observe to left and right of vehicle at locations from which vehicles or pedestrians could enter path of vehicle
   d. Inadequate observation, failure to see vehicle or pedestrian approaching
   e. Observation too late
   f. Failure to anticipate parked vehicles pulling out

11. **Lack of personal control**
   a. Inattention—any cause
   b. Distraction—any cause
   c. Driving while drowsy
   d. Reacting emotionally to driving situations
   e. Driving under the influence of alcohol or drugs
   f. Driving while ill

12. **Lack of knowledge and awareness of equipment, load, route**
   a. Failure to inspect equipment (before, during, after trip)
   b. Being unfamiliar with equipment
   c. Being unfamiliar with load
   d. Being unfamiliar with route
   e. Failure to secure doors or cargo

Check Traffic Rule Compliance

Because fleets must use public streets and highways, they have a special obligation to always operate within the law. Violation of traffic laws cannot be condoned. Even a single violation may reflect badly on the company; a long record of noncompliance can damage the public relations image of the entire industry and may lead to more restrictive legislation. For individual companies, repeated violations may result in revocation of their operating rights.

Fleets usually do not pay traffic fines incurred by drivers, nor do they put up bonds for them. A record of traffic violations is kept in the driver's personnel folder and repeated violations are the basis for disciplinary action or discharge.

Following are some of the most frequent driving errors that are also legal violations:

1. **Running errors**
   - **a.** Speed in excess of the legal limit
   - **b.** Speed too fast for conditions
   - **c.** Speed too slow for conditions
   - **d.** Following too closely

2. **Passing errors**
   - **a.** Passing at illegal place
   - **b.** Passing at unsafe place
   - **c.** Unnecessary passing
   - **d.** Returning to lane too soon after passing

3. **Intersection violations**
   - **a.** Failure to yield right-of-way at unmarked intersections
   - **b.** Running red light
   - **c.** Coasting through stop sign
   - **d.** Failure to reduce speed for intersection
   - **e.** Failure to yield to oncoming traffic when making left turn
   - **f.** Failure to yield right-of-way to pedestrians

4. **Improper lane Usage**
   - **a.** Failure to select proper lane
   - **b.** Turning from wrong lane
   - **c.** Sudden change of lane
   - **d.** Failure to signal a lane change
   - **e.** Failure to make sure next lane is clear before entering.

5. **Parking and stopping errors**
   - **a.** Illegal stopping on street or roadway
   - **b.** Obstructing traffic
   - **c.** Double parking
   - **d.** Failure to secure parked vehicle.

Check Vehicle Abuse

About 10 to 25 percent of the annual fleet maintenance cost is due to faulty operation or abuse of the vehicle by the driver, which in turn stems from carelessness, lack of training, or inadequate supervisory control.

Not only can excessive repair bills be an index to substandard driving performance, but they are directly related to the number of accidents. A "rough" driver has a high accident potential; a "smooth" driver is usually more alert and able to avoid accident hazards and to be ready for any emergencies.

Rough operation—including fast starts, delayed braking, and sudden stops—can indicate a bad attitude toward authority and be symptomatic of an attitude that may produce an eventual accident. It may also indicate driver inexperience. *Lack of aptitude* and *poor attitude* should be spotted in the selection process because they are usually irremediable faults; even if the driver is retained, he will probably cause the company excessive accident expense. *Lack of training* as a cause of rough operation can be corrected.

Freedom to abuse an expensive vehicle is not a fringe benefit. The company has the right to expect its drivers to act as guardians of company property by showing respect for equipment put in their charge.

Following is a list of driving abuses that lead to undue wear of the vehicle.

1. **Engine (motor) abuse**
   - **a.** Excessive acceleration of cold engine
   - **b.** Stopping engine suddenly after a long run
   - **c.** Operating overheated engine
   - **d.** Operating engine with low oil pressure
   - **e.** Racing engine
   - **f.** Failure to keep checking the instrument panel gages
2. **Clutching errors**
   - **a.** Riding the clutch
   - **b.** Snapping the clutch
3. **Errors in shifting gears**
   - **a.** Starting out in wrong gear
   - **b.** Rapid acceleration from stops
   - **c.** Scraping and jerking the gears
   - **d.** Shifting gears into neutral and coasting down hill
   - **e.** Failure to double clutch, if necessary, when changing gears
   - **f.** Lugging—operating in improper gear
4. **Errors in use of brakes**
   - **a.** Failure to fully release hand brake when moving
   - **b.** Abrupt stops
   - **c.** Delayed braking
   - **d.** Excessive brake applications
   - **e.** Running downhill in too high gear

   f. Failure to understand and use spring parking brakes and other elements of brake systems

5. **Errors in tire care**
   a. Operating with flat or under-inflated tires
   b. Driving over curbs or objects, and into potholes
   c. Rubbing tires against curbs in parking
   d. Letting air out of tires for a smoother ride
   e. Unnecessary spinning of tires on ice or snow
   f. Running with flat tires until a repair facility can be reached

6. **Tampering with equipment**
   a. Overriding governors
   b. Stopping up the fuel return line to try to get more power
   c. Tampering with trip recorder
   d. Abuse of cab interior
   e. Tampering with electrical system

7. **Lack of maintenance responsibility**
   a. Driving unit even though it needs repairs
   b. Failure to write up defects and repairs
   c. Failure to inspect equipment properly before each trip
   d. Inability to recognize signs of an en route problem

Set Good Schedules

The motor transportation fleet cannot conduct its business without schedules. However, a schedule is only a piece of paper until a driver and his vehicle translates that schedule into on-time transportation. Observance of schedules is therefore a prime ingredient of driving skill. Failure of a driver to observe schedules can be regarded not only as poor production, but probably as a symptom of a bad underlying attitude toward the job, or a personal problem which is interfering with efficiency. If the average driver can maintain the given schedule, then the supervisors should find out why this driver cannot.

Following are driving errors which result in schedule delays:

1. **Errors in departure procedure**
   a. Reporting late for scheduled run
   b. Excessive time spent in preparation for departure
   c. Pulling wrong trailer
   d. Taking wrong freight bills
   e. Stopping at home for personal business following departure
   f. Not getting proper rest before run, resulting in having to stop for sleep along road

2. **Errors leading to delays en route**
   a. Accidents
   b. Arrests
   c. Excessive and prolonged coffee stops
   d. Excessive time at meal stops
   e. Excessive time at scheduled stops
   f. Excessive time at weighing stations
   g. Failure to follow designated route
   h. Failure to call in for instructions
   i. Stops at unauthorized places
   j. Exaggerated caution in bad weather, in hopes of getting overtime

Remember Your Public Relations

When a truck is painted attractively and shows the company name, it becomes a traveling advertisement. A like amount of advertising purchased through regular advertising media would cost a great deal of money. But there is one difference—the advertising on the truck can be good or bad, favorable, or unfavorable, depending on how the driver behaves toward other motorists and pedestrians. Driving with courtesy and consideration for the public is therefore an important part of the driving job. Courtesy can build public goodwill for the company and, as a consequence, influence its ability to compete for and increase its business.

Here are some of the discourtesies drivers commit that tear down their company's good public image.

1. **Errors in speed control**
   a. Exceeding speed limit and passing motorists who are abiding by the law
   b. Speeding through towns and residential areas
   c. Backing up traffic by driving too slow

2. **Errors in following**
   a. Following passenger cars too closely
   b. Tailgating by two or more trucks
   c. Following too close at night without dimming lights

3. **Errors in passing**
   a. Passing when unnecessary
   b. Cutting in too sharply after passing
   c. Creating excessive splash and spray while passing

4. **Errors in lane use**
   a. Crowding center line
   b. Straddling two lanes

c. Drifting across lane dividers
d. Weaving from one lane to another
e. Running two or three abreast on limited-access highways
f. Use of wrong lane for speed or traffic flow

5. **Errors that block traffic**
   a. Blocking crosswalk
   b. Double parking in heavy traffic
   c. Not pulling off road to allow builtup traffic to pass
   d. Failure to use designated truck lanes especially on steep hills

6. **Errors in noise and smoke abatement**
   a. Excessive diesel smoke
   b. Excessive engine noise, or unnecessary use of noisy engine retarders
   c. Unnecessary use of air horns
   d. Racing engine to hurry pedestrians across intersection
   e. Splashing pedestrians in sloppy weather

Encourage High Performance

It should not seem that the negative aspects of supervision have been overemphasized because the observation of performance involves finding and correcting faults. Although this is an essential part of any supervisor's job, it is by far the lesser part.

For high performance, management (through supervision) must offer the driver more than good wages and fear of being discharged or disciplined. the true test of the supervisor's skill is the ability to provide the conditions under which a driver will maintain high standards because he wants to. Here are some methods and techniques that a supervisor can use to motivate drivers.

Set performance standards deliberately high

Setting job standards high is one way of securing compliance. High standards are challenging: a driver feels a keen sense of pride—an espirit de corps—when meeting them. On the other hand, when mediocre standards do not inspire respect, they are just as difficult to enforce as are high standards.

Set a good example

The driver supervisor must set a good example, he or she should radiate pride in the company and be dedicated to it; should never say or do anything that would indicate a lack of pride in the company or disloyalty to its officers and objectives.

Build a sense of participation

Give drivers a sense of participation in their company. Keep them informed of company plans. Let them know how they are meeting their objectives. They feel that they are their part of the company when they share in information about the company.

This sense of participation is fostered when supervisors welcome suggestions for improving company services or overcoming specific problems. Drivers often have suggestions that can lead to important cost savings.

Many companies have formal systems that require suggestions to be submitted on a specially prepared form. These are numbered and carefully considered by a committee. Later, the driver is told what has happened to the suggestion. In some cases, cash awards are made.

Whether or not a suggestion program exists, a driver should get personal recognition for any idea used. If practical (and the driver OK's it), recognition should be made publicly.

Good communications

Communication is vital to good human relations and scientific management because it is a two-way street: management keeps drivers informed and drivers, in turn, feel free to offer suggestions. No matter which way communications travel, the receiver must understand the intent of the sender, otherwise it is not real communication.

But right now we are more concerned with *what* to communicate than *how*. The most important message that management can communicate to drivers is that they hold a unique job in the company—that their job is vital. This builds pride and satisfaction in the job and improves performance.

Promote a competitive spirit

Additional job interest can be created by appealing to the competitive spirit. Safety contests between fleet divisions, or with outside fleets (such as in the National Fleet Safety Contest), generate this interest when drivers understand the rules and are kept informed of contest ratings. Company publications, special posters, contest score boards, bulletin board displays, and safety meetings all promote this. Contests are not limited to large fleets. Small fleets can also use this tool.

Motivate through recognition

Individual safe driving awards are a powerful incentive to better driving performance. Because drivers generally do the same type of work, and because they are usually covered by a uniform union contract (that spells out wages, work conditions, special assignments, and seniority),

NATIONAL SAFETY COUNCIL SAFE DRIVER AWARD RULES

1. Award Plan

1.1 RECOGNITION

The National Safety Council Safe Driver Award is the recognized trademark of professional drivers who have proved their skill in avoiding traffic accidents. The more than six million drivers who have earned the award since 1930 have made it the highest award for professional safe driving performance.

1.2 PERFORMANCE

The award plan is more than a means of rewarding drivers with good safety records. The rules spell out what is expected of professional drivers in the way of safety performance—driving a motor vehicle without having a preventable accident. The award rules constitute a yardstick by which drivers can measure their own performance and by which supervisors can measure the performance of individual drivers. When this standard of performance is clearly understood by both drivers and supervisors, it becomes a logical, fair, and workable basis for effective safety supervision.

1.3 DESCRIPTION OF AWARD

The Safe Driver Award consists of a wallet-size certificate showing name of driver, name of employer, name of safe driving years represented by the award and the date earned. An award lapel pin is also available for special purchase. The School Transportation Safety Service includes both certificate and pin.

Award Lapel Pin, and Wallet Certificate

2. Eligibility Requirements

2.1 ELIGIBLE ORGANIZATIONS

Only organizations receiving the National Safety Council's Motor Fleet Safety Service or School Transportation Service either through membership or under a service contract through a member organization such as a local safety council, trade association, etc., may certify eligible employees for National Safety Council Safe Driver Awards.

2.2 ELIGIBLE DRIVERS

Only employees of eligible organizations who drive a company owned or leased vehicle as part of their regular daily assignment are eligible to earn the Safe Driver Award.

Figure 10-1. *More than six million National Safety Council safe driver awards have been earned since the program began in 1930.*

an individual driver finds it unusually difficult to distinguish himself. Safe driver awards provide an opportunity for a driver to distinguish himself.

The National Safety Council conducts safe driver award programs. The well-respected Council program originated in 1930 and since then has presented more than six million awards. (See Figure 10-1.)

Many associations also offer driver award programs. The American Trucking Association has one, and frequently, the insurance carrier for a fleet will offer awards to show its interest in safe driving. A very popular award program among trucking companies is the Million Miler Program that recognizes the outstanding drivers with 10 years or more free of preventable accidents. One company using this criterion recognized over 800 million milers, 105 two million milers, and 12 three million milers.

Awards work best when the rules are carefully explained to drivers and when decisions on accidents are consistently fair. Fleet management should take special pains to present the awards in a dignified manner that makes it plain that these are emblems representing important, worthwhile achievement.

There is publicity value in awards. See Appendix A for details.

The Challenge of Driver Supervision

The continuation of our society's high standard of living and ensuing high technological change depend primarily on the mass production of goods and availability of services—which is not so much a matter of working harder as it is of *working smarter.* To organize their resources, business and industry depend upon management—the skill of the millions of supervisors who are in direct charge of workers and whose skill in human relations increases production. Transportation is one of these vital resources.

Motor fleets play a big part in meeting our nation's transportation needs. Efficient and cost-effective fleet operation demands faultless driving: driving that is as free as possible from errors that incur unnecessary waste.

To achieve this excellence, the industry must depend upon its driver supervisors, whatever their title and wherever they serve. Driver supervision is therefore a most worthwhile occupation. It should be approached by the driver supervisor with a positive attitude and determination to succeed.

Chapter 11

Establishing the Accident Review Committee

The two key factors in any safety incentive program are: (*a*) a high standard of safety performance, and (*b*) a method of recognizing all individuals who meet this performance standard.

Standards Must Be High

If management is satisfied with mediocre standards of performance, it will get nothing better. Setting high quality standards involves no more difficulty than setting low standards. The same amount of supervisory time and effort is involved in either case. However, when standards are set high an additional incentive is created—a challenge to each individual worker. The skilled workers have a chance to show their ability. Their example spurs the rest of the group to *improved performance*—the objective—which shows up on the profit side of the profit and loss statement.

Recognition Must Be Given

Nothing discourages or annoys a skilled driver more than lack of recognition after he has met the standards of safety performance prescribed by management. Positive recognition is one of the chief job satisfactions of the skilled driver. It does not matter greatly what form this positive recognition takes—only that it be given promptly and impartially whenever it is earned. Negative recognition such as penalizing a driver for an accident he could not prevent is worse than overlooking a preventable accident.

A Standard of Safe Driving Performance

How can we define a standard of safe driving performance? *Perfect safety performance* is operation of a bus, truck, or other commercial vehicle without having any accidents at all. Obviously such a standard may be too high, yet some drivers do it. Drivers may become involved in accidents over which they have no control, and for which it would be unfair to penalize them. In most cases, however, it takes two drivers to make an accident. Usually one of the drivers has violated some traffic ordinance, whereas the other driver has violated some defensive driving principle relating to alertness or safe speed. Either driver could have prevented the accident; therefore, both are at fault.

Here then is a workable definition of standard safe driving performance: While we cannot reasonably penalize drivers for all accidents they might become involved in, we can with reason penalize them for accidents that could have been prevented. Our standard of safe driving performance is therefore *the ability to drive without having preventable accidents.*

A preventable accident

A *preventable* accident is defined in the rules of the National Safety Council's Safe Driver Award Plan as: "any accident involving a company vehicle which results in property damage and/or personal injury, regardless of who was injured, what property was damaged, to what extent, or where it occurred, in which the driver in question failed to exercise every reasonable precaution to prevent the accident."

The key word in this definition is *"reasonable."* How this word is interpreted when applied to actual accident cases will determine how high the standard of safety performance is going to be in any particular fleet. If it is interpreted too strictly, drivers will conclude that the company expects too much of them. They will be prone to give up trying to meet the desired standard of safety performance. On the other hand, if the word "reasonable" is interpreted loosely, driving errors are likely to be overlooked and go uncorrected, and become the cause of similar accidents. As a result of this loose interpretation, the company safety record will fall far short of its possibilities.

The problem of classifying accidents as preventable or nonpreventable for safe driving record purposes is one of the most important problems the safety director is called upon to solve.

Clear-cut preventability

Most accidents are preventable. As a result of having attended company driver training programs and safety meetings, drivers know what standard of "defensive driving" is required of them. When involved in a preventable accident they will usually be able to point out where they failed and how the accident could have been prevented. The safety director will have little difficulty in explaining to drivers why such accidents are being classified "preventable" and why the driver is being penalized in accordance with existing rules of the company incentive or safe driver award program.

Borderline cases

Some of the accidents in the average fleet, however, are not so clear-cut. Their classification presents a special problem. Whether the driver did everything "reasonable" to prevent the accident depends a great deal on personal opinion. These borderline cases represent the "hot potatoes" in any accident report file. How these cases are handled can spell the difference between a superior safety record and a mediocre one.

Some safety directors feel that the deciding of borderline cases poses no particular problem at all and that the decision should be made by the safety director or the person in charge of the safety program at the particular location. They point out that since he is best informed on the subject of accident prevention and responsible for the safety program, he is the only logical person to decide whether or not an accident could have been prevented.

Borderline accident cases are the most sensitive points in the whole safety program. Whether or not the driver could have prevented the accident is a matter of conjecture, and involved drivers will resent any arbitrary decision by management that it was their fault.

Such an attitude is entirely justified and indicates that these drivers take pride in their safety records. It is a valuable asset and must not be destroyed. When drivers no longer care how their accidents are classified, the safety program will have reached a state of bankruptcy.

The Accident Review Committee

If we expect drivers to continue to take their safety records seriously, we must provide for the classification of accidents in such a manner that drivers will feel that their rights have been scrupulously protected. Deciding such cases on the sole basis of the safety director's opinion risks undermining the safety director's proper relationship with the drivers. The decision on borderline cases should reflect the weight of informed opinion of the entire organization. For these reasons, decision by an accident review committee is preferred.

The special advantages of deciding borderline cases by the committee method can be stated as follows:

- The importance of the individual's safety record is emphasized.
- The help of all departments is enlisted in making the safety program successful.
- The safety director is protected from the possibility of creating ill will among drivers who have had accidents.
- The driver is assured that his rights are being protected.
- For the driver involved, it takes a great deal of the "sting" out of an adverse decision.
- The responsibility for the decision is removed from line supervision.

Who should serve on the committee

Deciding whether an accident could or could not have been prevented is not a matter to be solved by popular vote.

The committee's purpose is to decide borderline cases by the weight of informed opinion. The committee should represent all departments of the organization directly involved in the safety program—safety, transportation, and maintenance—as well as driving personnel. A decision from such a group will satisfy involved drivers, and, if the individual members are carefully selected and trained, it will represent the best and most reasonable thinking of the entire organization.

For these reasons, the following persons should serve on the committee:

One representative from the safety department to serve as chairman, who is trained in the principles of accident prevention and safety supervision. He should be familiar with company safety rules, the content of the driver training program, and the rules of the safe driver award plan or incentive plan.

One supervisory representative from the transportation department, familiar with operating rules pertaining to schedules, routes, speed limits, hours of work, and related subjects. He can advise when a driver claims conflict between operating rules and safe practices.

One representative from the maintenance department, familiar with the mechanical abilities of company equipment and with company maintenance policy. He can advise when a driver claims faulty equipment as the cause of the accident.

Two drivers—since drivers are thoroughly familiar with traffic conditions and the everyday hazards of the job. If given the opportunity, they often can explain authoritatively how accidents can be prevented.

It has been suggested that drivers should outnumber so-called "management" representatives on the committee. This suggestion seems to inject the view that the accident review committee is an arena for labor-management controversy. Nothing could be further from the truth. The accident review committee is not a joint labor-management function. It is a supervisory tool and as such should be controlled by management to advance the accident prevention program. Management should never relinquish control to the point where the committee is no longer capable of producing decisions that management finds essential in sustaining a high standard of safe driving performance.

The first committee

Members of the first accident review committee should be selected with special care, since the way they perform their functions will set a pattern for future committees. The supervisory representative and the maintenance representative should be selected for their proven interest in furthering the accident prevention program. Drivers selected should have superior safety records and command the respect and confidence of their fellow drivers.

The chairman should instruct the members of this first committee with great care. The chairman should define a preventable accident and the meaning of defensive driving. Usually a "dry-run" is advisable; that is, the chairman selects an accident report from the file, has the committee discuss it and come to a decision, then tells them how the accident was originally classified and why. When members are thoroughly familiar with the "defensive driving" point of view toward accident prevention, they are ready to decide actual cases.

Rotating committee membership

Insofar as possible, the chairman should try to share the educational benefits of serving on an accident review committee by rotating its membership. Members who have served on the committee will take this experience back to their various departments. This process alone will in time build a high degree of safety-mindedness throughout the entire organization. However, only one new member should be taken on the committee at a time. This allows the new member to absorb some of the experience of the senior members before another member is rotated.

Committee Procedure

Three recommended committee procedures should be adhered to:

- The name of the driver involved in the accident should not be revealed to committee members.
- The driver involved should not be called before the committee to

discuss the accident. His accident report should represent him.

- The committee's decision should be arrived at by secret ballot.

Presenting the facts

As chairman of the accident review committee, the safety representative presents the facts about each accident under review, and guides the discussion.

The chairman should refer to the accident by file number only. Introducing the driver's name would tend to bring personalities into the discussion. Members might be swayed by their prior knowledge of the man's driving habits and general conduct. The fact that the accident is being considered without reference to names enables the committee to be more objective.

The committee should not call the driver before it for questioning. The driver should have already written all he knows about the accident on his report. The facts are there. If called before the committee, he has an opportunity to argue, cloud the issue, and sway the judgment of the committee by his "salesmanship" (or lack of it). It is unfair to the driver and all other drivers.

The facts of each accident presented to members of the committee should come from the following sources:

- Driver's report of the accident
- Police investigation reports
- Insurance company investigation reports
- Facts based on an investigation by company representatives
- Statements of witnesses
- Diagrams, photographs, and any other available evidence

Guiding the discussion

After presenting the facts, the chairman should guide the discussion. The only question before the committee is "Could the driver have prevented this accident?"

The answer to this question depends on the kind of defensive driving philosophy that has come to be accepted in the company. This in turn depends on how good a job the safety director has done in indoctrinating the entire organization in the principles of accident prevention.

But how far can any safe driver be expected to go in attempting to foresee and compensate for the driving errors of others? The standard must be high, but it must also be reasonable. It must be the product of the safety training program initiated and maintained by the safety director. It must reflect a meeting of minds of the line organization as to what is reasonable and possible in the realm of accident prevention.

It should be remembered, however, that when a particular accident is declared nonpreventable, a precedent has been set and the committee is obliged henceforth to render the same decision on similar accidents occurring under the same circumstances. A decision of nonpreventable absolves the driver of all blame for the accident. There will undoubtedly be other accidents of this type and the committee should not hesitate to judge them "nonpreventable." However, such a decision must be sound. If too many accidents are admitted to this classification, the safety program will gradually lose its effectiveness. The chairman should point this out, and should also remind the committee that judging the accident nonpreventable will in effect be saying that if one of them were the driver, he too would be unable to prevent the accident. This tends to remove the element of sympathy and render the decision more objective.

Voting by secret ballot

When the chairman is satisfied that the members of the committee are completely familiar with all the facts of the accident and have discussed it at sufficient length, he should pass out slips of paper and ask for a vote. Members should write "preventable" or "nonpreventable" on the slips of paper and pass them back to the chairman.

The chairman counts the ballots and only casts a vote in case of a tie. Then he announces the majority decision as either "preventable" or "nonpreventable." Experience has shown that when the committee is well indoctrinated, the chairman's vote will be necessary in less than three percent of the cases.

Telling the driver

Following the meeting, the chairman should inform each driver in writing what the committee's decision was and, if the accident was judged "preventable," what the reasons were for classifying it so. Having followed the discussion of the accident, the chairman is familiar with the majority point of view and will be able to summarize it for the driver.

A copy of the written decision should be given to the driver and another copy should be placed in his personnel file. Copies to other interested parties, such as the driver's immediate supervisor, union officials, and others may be provided, if desirable, depending upon company policy.

Usually, it is advisable for the safety director, or the driver's immediate supervisor, to announce the decision to the driver in a personal interview. This should be done immediately. This makes it possible to discuss corrective measures with the driver and to relate the decision to the driver's entire accident record.

Appeal Procedures

Decisions about the preventability of accidents should be made as close as possible to the bottom of the ladder of authority. As was stated before, the vast majority of a fleet's accidents are clear-cut cases and can be decided one way or another by the safety director, the driver's immediate supervisor, or the person directly in charge of safety at the particular location. Only when there is a reasonable doubt or when the person having primary jurisdiction is unable to convince the driver that his accident was "preventable" should an accident be referred to the accident review committee.

But suppose the driver is not satisfied even with the decision of the accident review committee? In some companies, he has no recourse. Other companies, recognizing that the factor of morale is involved, provide an additional assurance of fair play. They take advantage of the National Safety Council's Accident Review Committee. Recommended practice is to allow the driver to make written appeal on any decision from the company accident review committee within 10 days after he has been informed of the decision. In his appeal, the driver is asked to state why he thinks the accident should have been judged "nonpreventable."

In referring to an accident to this committee, six copies of the accident report with all supporting documentation should be forwarded to the National Safety Council with the request that it be referred to the Accident Review Committee for an opinion. *Refer to National Safety Council Safe Driver Award Rules.*

It should be noted that the accident review board represents a unique tool for management: it is a decision method outside the framework of the union contract. Most contracts leave accident judgment to the company. Having a preventable accident means at least a year will be taken off the driver's award record. It cannot be worked off like a warning letter. Years later, the driver will have to say, "I've worked twenty years with this company and have a 19-year safe driving record"; it will be evident that the driver had a preventable accident. A decision of "preventable" is strong discipline to a proud employee, and it is not subject to the political pressures of a grievance hearing.

Chapter 12

The Vehicle and the Safety Program

This chapter discusses some of the influences the vehicle can have on the safety program. When we talk about the vehicle, we enter the domain of the maintenance department and of those people responsible for the purchase and disposition of equipment.

Purchasing Equipment with Safety in Mind

When fleet vehicles are purchased, there are usually a number of conflicting values affecting the decision. The purchaser worries about:

• Cost—How much can be purchased with the available dollars, and are they being spent on the right equipment and accessories?

• Availability—How soon can the new equipment get on the job?

• Standardization—Usually a fleet is better (and safer) if all vehicles are alike. Maintenance is more efficient, drivers know every vehicle, and substitution is easy when a unit goes down. Stocked parts can be purchased in quantity for additional savings.

• Order size—Generally, a bigger order of the same vehicle reduces the cost per unit. However, some purchasers will bargain the price down between competitors, and make minor concessions on the vehicle and equipment if they see a better price. Orders may be split up to favor customers or to spread the purchase cost.

• Maintenance convenience—Some vehicles require less work to repair. Specifying maintenance-free batteries, for instance, may save a lot of inspection and servicing time for the shop.

• Operational convenience—The vehicle is bought to do a specific job. The engine size, gear ratios, etc., should match the job for greatest efficiency.

• Fuel savings—Vehicles are ordered with special fuel-saving components such as high torque/low RPM engines, temperature controlled fans, air shields, and radial tires.

• Optional equipment—Devices that automatically shut down, bring engines to idle, check tire pressure, or warn of overheated cooling systems can help prevent accidents and lower fuel consumption. On-board computers record road speed, engine idling, vehicle stopped time, and fuel consumption. The data is then transferred to the fleet office computer and analyzed to determine driver and vehicle safety and performance.

• Safety—No fleet purchaser will deliberately buy an unsafe piece of equipment. However, the safety department must inform the purchasing department as to what is considered "safe."

The way in which the safety director can be sure to be represented in equipment purchases is to reach agreement, beforehand, that he will be consulted early in the process. Otherwise, in the hectic purchase procedure, he could be overlooked. In addition, the safety director can prepare general safety specs and ask that they be held in the purchasing department files, and referred to before any vehicle purchase. These written specifications should be updated regularly. This is an important matter because, once bought, a vehicle will run at least three years, and often five or ten or more. Mistakes made in the sales office can live on to become accident-producing nightmares.

Getting cooperation

To get cooperation for those who purchase equipment, the safety director should do the following:

• Keep current statistics on accidents or near misses caused by equipment problems, and see that the information gets to the fleet purchaser. Maintain good driver communications so that equipment problems are reported to you.

• Work hard at building good communications and cooperation with the purchaser.

• Keep alert to news about future fleet purchases, and recommend safety items *before* the specifications are frozen in bids.

• Request the chance to go along on sales demonstrations, pilot model inspections, and to trade shows.

• Learn as much as possible about the maintenance, operational, and financial decisions that dictate the order. Often safety considerations can be argued in a way that supports these, instead of undercutting them.

• Keep current on government safety regulations affecting the design, manufacture, and maintenance of parts and equipment. Two examples are the splash and spray control requirements and air brake system changes.

• Take charge of training drivers when new engines or vehicles are ordered. Your help will be appreciated, and it will pay off in driver acceptance and proper use of the equipment.

Safety-related items

Here are some of the safety-related items to consider when ordering new equipment:

• Additional or upgraded right-side mirrors (see earlier discussion).

• Heated mirrors for use in cold climates.

• Safe design of vehicle and accessory controls. Watch for needless protrusions that could cause an injury if a driver is thrown around in the cab.

• Better steps and grab rails on cabs and trailers.

• Shortened or breakaway bumper ends, which will not jam against a front tire and turn a minor collision into a bad one.

• Upgraded comfort features such as bigger heaters, air conditioners, air-ride seats, etc.

• Extra interior lights, fog or road lights, and work lights for hookup or cargo handling.

• Special cab wiring for CB or broadcast radios, to reduce the risk of damage from inexpert splicing to main circuits.

• Truck semitrailer air and electrical hookup on the road side of the nose, reachable from the ground.

• Lifting handles on trailer and converter tongues. Jacks to hold trailer tongues at hookup height.

• Liberal use of reflective tape and/or light paint on equipment, providing better night visibility and a good daytime image.

• Avoid built-in hazards such as cab rear protrusions that are likely to pull trailer air hoses loose on a truck, awkward controls, and weak or unsafe step surfaces such as battery boxes or fuel tanks.

Working with the Maintenance Department

The safety and maintenance departments have so many similarities, they ought to work together well. Neither are specifically profit-oriented. Both are constantly striving for zero defects. Both are at the mercy of operating people who can make their work easy or difficult.

Conflicts arise when a too budget-conscious maintenance worker releases a vehicle that a driver feels is unsafe. Often the driver supervisor ends up in the middle, blamed by both sides.

The solution is simple, but getting there is hard. If the vehicle is unsafe, don't use it. The shop supervisor is the mechanical expert and should know whether or not a vehicle is safe. However, the driver is the one that risks the most and certainly should have the final say. Unfortunately, there are mechanics who cut corners, and drivers who use breakdowns as a means to make money.

The safety director must create a cooperative atmosphere. That means seeing that driver complaints are investigated, and repairs are made if necessary. It also means confronting the driver who has frequent and unfounded complaints, and straightening him out too. It means cooperating to help get "sick but safe" vehicles in to a shop to be fixed, and making sure they are fixed before they go out again.

A good middle ground can be found by believing the complaints and stories of both drivers and mechanics the first few times, but being ready to show doubt when the record shows a lot more than the bad luck a normal employee can have.

A shop and safety department are often on the same side, fighting for more money or an operational change that will allow sufficient shop work to make vehicles safe.

Vehicle Condition Reports

It is essential that good records be kept on each vehicle, including a daily statement by the driver on how it performed. This is required for vehicles in interstate commerce, and recommended for all others. The mechanic can use the "cry sheet" to find out what is going wrong, and the driver can check it later to see what work was done. Nothing improves the trust and cooperation between these workers better than a good, working write-up system.

Pretrip inspection

If the driver is to trust his vehicle, he must be satisfied that it is fit to go on the street, and that means a brief pretrip inspection. Forms for truck and bus inspections are shown in Figures 12-1 and 12-2. Five minutes time is enough to check the major components likely to cause safety problems. Why should the driver have to do this, if the shop is on the ball? Here are some reasons:

- With combination vehicles, the shop doesn't generally have both hooked together when it does its work. Air and electrical problems often stem from the hookup.
- Mechanics often don't have time for a good road check and may

(*Text continues on page 198.*)

DRIVER'S VEHICLE INSPECTION REPORT

AS REQUIRED BY THE D.O.T. FEDERAL MOTOR CARRIER SAFETY REGULATIONS

CARRIER: ____________________

DATE ________ TIME: ________ A.M. ________ P.M.

Check any defective item and give details under "Remarks"

TRACTOR NO. ____________________

☐ Air Compressor
☐ Battery
☐ Body
☐ Brake Accessories
☐ Brakes
☐ Clutch
☐ Defroster
☐ Door Handles
☐ Drive Line
☐ Engine
☐ Fifth Wheel
☐ Front Axle
☐ Fuel Tanks
☐ Heater
☐ Horn
☐ Lights
☐ Loses Water
☐ Mirrors
☐ Oil Pressure
☐ Radiator
☐ Rear End
☐ Safety Equipment
☐ Springs
☐ Steering
☐ Tachograph
☐ Tires
☐ Transmission
☐ Wheels
☐ Windows
☐ Windshield Wiper

☐ OTHER

TRAILER(s) NO.(s) ____________________

☐ Brake Connections
☐ Brakes
☐ Coupling Chains
☐ Coupling (King) Pin
☐ Doors
☐ Hitch
☐ Landing Gear
☐ Lights
☐ Roof
☐ Springs
☐ Tarpaulin
☐ Tires
☐ Wheels

☐ OTHER

☐ CONDITION OF THE ABOVE VEHICLES IS SATISFACTORY

REMARKS: ____________________

____

____

____

____

Driver's Signature ____________________

☐ Above defects corrected ☐ Above defects need not be corrected for safe operation of vehicle

Mechanic's Signature ____________________

Driver reviewing repairs ____________________ (Signature)

Figure 12-1. *This pretrip inspection report form meets DOT regulations.*
J. J. Keller & Associates, Inc., Neenah, Wis.

VEHICLE CONDITION REPORT

USE YOUR SEATBELT

DATE

PRINT EXCEPT SIGNATURE, USED PROPERLY THIS CHECKLIST IS PROTECTION

LOCATION (City) STATE ORGANIZATION TRUCK or TRACTOR-TRAILER NUMBERS

DRIVER DRIVER

INSTRUCTIONS: Drivers will perform necessary inspection. A check (√) indicates satisfactory condition. An "X" indicates unsafe or improper conditions. Items corrected will be circled by management certifier.

INSIDE

☐ Parking Brake (Apply)

START ENGINE

☐ Oil Pressure (Light or Gauge)
☐ Air Pressure or Vacuum (Gauge)
☐ Low Air or Vacuum Warning Device (Air pressure below 40 psi check on pressure build-up. Air pressure above 60 psi deplete air until warning device works). Vacuum below 8 inches Hg. check on build-up. Above 8 inches Hg. deplete vacuum until device works.
☐ Instrument Panel (Telltale lights or buzzers)
☐ Horn
☐ Windshield Wiper and Washer
☐ Heater-Defroster
☐ Mirrors
☐ Steering Wheel (Excess Play)
☐ Apply Trailer Brakes in EMERGENCY
☐ Turn on all lights including 4-way Flasher
☐ Starts Properly

ON COMBINATIONS

☐ Hoses, Connections
☐ Couplings (Fifth Wheel, Tow Bar, Safety Chains, Locking Devices)

SIDE

LEFT	RIGHT	
☐	☐	Fuel Tank and Cap
☐	☐	Sidemarker Lights
☐	☐	Reflectors
☐	☐	Tires and Wheels-Lugs and Serviceability
☐	☐	Cargo Tie-downs/or Doors

REAR

☐ Tail Lights
☐ Stop Light
☐ Turn Signals and 4-way Flasher
☐ Clearance Lights
☐ Identification Lights
☐ Reflectors
☐ Tires and Wheels, Lugs and Serviceability
☐ Rear End Protection (Bumper)
☐ Cargo Tie-downs/Doors

MECHANICAL OPERATION

☐ Engine knocks, misses, overheats, etc.
☐ Clutch skips, grabs, other
☐ Transmission noisy, hard shifting, jumps out of gear, other
☐ Axles — noisy, other

EMERGENCY EQUIPMENT

- ☐ Fire Extinguishers
- ☐ Flags, Standards, Warning Lights
- ☐ Fuses
- ☐ Reflectors
- ☐ Spare Bulbs
- ☐ Chains in Season
- ☐ First Aid Kits

FRONT

- ☐ Headlights
- ☐ Clearance Lights
- ☐ Identification Lights
- ☐ Turn Signals and 4-way Flasher
- ☐ Tires and Wheels-Lugs and Serviceability

INSIDE

- ☐ Release Trailer Emergency Brakes
- ☐ Apply Service Brake-air loss should not exceed 3 psi per minute on single vehicles, 4 psi per minute on combinations.
- ☐ Steering loose, shimmy, hard, other
- ☐ Air, oil, water, leaks
- ☐ Springs broken, other
- ☐ Brakes noisy, pulls, soft, other
- ☐ Speedometer, Tachometer
- ☐ Tachograph, Speed Control Devices
- ☐ Other ______

OTHER

YES	NO	
☐	☐	Equipment Inspection Enroute
☐	☐	Cargo Securing Devices
☐	☐	______
☐	☐	______
☐	☐	______
☐	☐	______

START TIME	SPEEDOMETER	END TIME	SPEEDOMETER

REMARKS/OTHER DEFECTS

DRIVER'S SIGNATURE

DEFECTS CORRECTED (Initial)	DEFECT CORRECTION UNNECESSARY (Initial)	CERTIFIED BY	DATE
DEFECTS CORRECTED ☐ Yes ☐ No		DRIVER'S SIGNATURE (If Defects)	DATE

Figure 12-2. *Pretrip inspection report for buses, trucks, and tractor-trailers.*

Private Truck Council of America, Inc., Washington, D.C.

be relying on a poor write-up done by the last driver.

- The mechanic may have simply done a poor job.

Emergency Equipment

State and federal laws specify the emergency equipment to be carried on trucks and buses. This includes driver safety belts, a fire extinguisher, emergency reflectors, spare bulbs and fuses, and a first aid kit (on buses). Vehicles carrying specified hazardous materials must have additional or larger extinguishers.

It is necessary in some operations to carry a great deal of emergency equipment. Chemical tank trucks normally carry protective clothing, gas masks, cleanup materials, and a breathing apparatus. Drivers have hard hats, face masks, rubber gloves, and rubber boots. Some fleets running in remote areas or in winter may carry blankets, survival suits, and emergency rations on their vehicles.

Unsafe Operational Decisions and the Safety Program

The safety department must be alert to operational decisions that affect the driver and vehicle. Some of the possible pitfalls are discussed here.

Unsafe scheduling and routing. Transportation in the United States is a highly competitive business, more so since deregulation. Competition will force a sales department to make impossible delivery promises and the problem is then turned over to the operations department. If speeding or running long hours is the only way to get the business, strong pressure will be put on the safety department to go along.

This is the point where the safety program must come of age. The only way this can happen is with the strong support of top management, who must insist that unsafe vehicles, drivers, or schedules will not be tolerated. As one wise trucker put it many years ago, "There's no load so hot it won't cool off in the ditch!"

Overloading. Another operational answer to business pressure is to pile more cargo on each vehicle, thus realizing more revenue. Overloaded vehicles wear out more quickly and are difficult to stop. Knowing a lax company attitude toward weight laws, drivers are encouraged to cheat on other regulations.

Safety Considerations in Other Company Vehicles

Often a company will have many nonrevenue vehicles on the highway, along with its trucks or buses. These cars and service vehicles have accidents too, and can create serious image and liability problems.

Company cars

Salespeople and executives may be furnished with company cars for their business and personal use. These cars should be well-maintained and driven in a prudent manner. They should be inspected by the safety department at least four times a year. Accident report kits and maintenance schedules should be in each vehicle. Monthly mailings of safety material will keep the drivers aware; the National Safety Council and many insurance companies can provide these.

Autos should be purchased with safety in mind. In most parts of the U.S., electric rear window defrosters are important. Outside mirrors are vital on the left side and important on the right.

Since the company liability policy is on the line with a car just as it is with a truck or bus, it is just as important to keep these drivers out of accidents. One method is to charge back some of the accident cost in the form of a fine for preventable accidents. The fine itself makes believers out of many drivers, and the act of having their accidents judged by top executives will bring the rest around. (To keep the safety department out of political problems, the judgment should be made by supervisors of the person having the accident.)

Finally, there are some people who should not drive at all. Periodic checks with the State Department of Motor Vehicles will show which company employees are getting citations and having unreported accidents. Discipline may require a great deal of tact and the assistance of the company president. In one case, a sales person with a miserable accident record presented a serious problem, as he was invaluable to the company. The solution was to give him his own chauffer, something even the president didn't have.

Service vehicles

Transportation companies often forget they have small (and sometimes large) trucks on the street to assist the company shops. The drivers may not be checked out for citations, and the vehicles may operate with no controls at all. Sometimes heavy-duty tow trucks, snowplows, and even regular road vehicles are driven by mechanics who don't really know how to safely drive them. The basic company rule should be: "Any company vehicle of any size will only be driven by employees licensed to do so, and checked out by a driver supervisor."

Driver supervisor vehicles

All the comments regarding company cars also apply here. In addition, an attempt should be made to provide extra comfort and driving features, so the driver will not mind long hours on the road.

Generally these vehicles are station wagons or heavier sedans. They may have features like cruise control, adjustable seats, nice radios, a spotlight, and heavy-duty suspension. CB or radio-telephones are often installed. Some fleets install a police speedometer or radar.

These cars need more emergency equipment than do most cars because they respond to accidents and come upon many emergencies during patrol. Include one or two fire extinguishers, a large first aid kit, blankets, a case of assorted fuses, winter and rain gear, a tool kit, flashlights, and perhaps, some small spare parts. The accident kit should contain report forms, measuring tape, a camera, marking crayon, hazard pylons, and a small tape recorder. If hazardous materials are hauled by the company, a cleanup kit with plastic sheets, absorbent material, and a broom might be valuable.

Care must be taken that the vehicle doesn't end up making road calls and hauling tires. It must be controlled and used by the safety department so it will be available for its primary use: accident prevention and investigation.

Vehicle color

Company cars are generally ordered in the color the main user desires. Driver supervisor cars should be light colored, for improved visibility. A company sign in a contrasting color gives winter visibility. If there are several cars, a uniform color is impressive and helps in identification.

It is usually better for the supervisor to be visible to and easily recognized by his drivers. Company signs on cars facilitate this. If the signs are magnetic and removeable, the car can be used incognito when desired. The sign should combine the company name with a reference to the vehicle purpose, which is highway safety. If the supervisor is encouraged to stop and help stranded motorists if his time permits, a powerful public relations tool is created.

Chapter 13

Supervising The Scattered Fleet

Working with widely separated units of a fleet poses special problems. In some respects it is similar to administering a safety program for a collection of small fleets, each with separate local management and problems of its own. If a fleet safety program is to be directed effectively from a central location, each fleet unit must be required to operate on a common basis—observing standardized procedures, and using standard forms, awards, and other program elements established by headquarters.

In all probability, it will take much work to keep safety programming uniform throughout the company. Difficulties often arise because of a breakdown in communications between headquarters and local fleet management. These problems probably will be worse in organizations in which transportation is incidental as its basic function. A bakery, utility, insurance company, department store, newspaper, or other enterprise that uses motor vehicles may find it difficult to create an interest in safe driving.

Yet, the fact remains that companies have gone out of business because they spent more money on accidents then they made in profit on sales.

Profitable operation is safe operation. All segments of an organization must be operated safely too. A good safety record is usually a by-product of good operations throughout the company.

Standardize Policy and Fix Responsibility

Standardization of the safety program at all locations of the scattered units of a fleet is the most effective approach to a good safety program.

Such a uniform program will actually cost less in terms of management and safety staff time and expenses.

Responsibility for safety

One of the first steps to standardization is fixing the responsibility for safety: line management—from top to bottom—is fully responsible for safety results. The safety director is an advisor to management: he serves in a staff capacity.

Functions of a home office safety staff

The function of the home office safety staff should be to help both home and field management by (*a*) counseling them, (*b*) by participating in the establishment of safety objectives, and (*c*) by analyzing, planning, and organizing the safety program to reach these objectives.

Time spent on the various home office safety activities will vary with conditions, but the percentages are often shown in the accompanying table "Safety Director's Time Distribution."

In carrying on these activities, items that most likely will present in-company difficulty in securing understanding and uniformity are:

- Securing the support of the management in uniform, company-wide accident prevention program.
- Securing uniform reporting of accidents.
- Determining whether accidents (or accidental damage) are motor vehicle fleet accidents per the ANSI Standard D15.1—*Method of Recording and Measuring Motor Vehicle Fleet Accident Experience and Passenger Accident Experience,* and then securing acceptance of the decisions about "preventability."*

Establishing a policy for supervisory counseling of employees who violate safe practices or disciplining those who are repeatedly involved in accidental occurrences.

Management committees

A good way to achieve the goals of the safety program is through the use of a management safety committee, discussed in Chapter 2. The committee should include officers (president and vice presidents) of the company. The committee should review the performance of the company, and determine policies, procedures, and features of the safety program. The safety director should counsel and advise this committee.

---

*As explained in Chapter 9 under "Defensive Driving."

SAFETY DIRECTOR'S TIME DISTRIBUTION

Home Office Activities (40 to 95 percent of time)	Percent of Time Spent
1. General duties of developing, establishing, and promoting the program carrying on the necessary correspondence, supervising the reporting, record keeping, and statistics.	30 to 50
2. Preparing for and participating in conferences, and consulting with officers and management people and committees—developing and guiding the acceptance of the safety program	5 to 20
3. Selecting, training, coaching, and appraising the safety staff	5 to 15
4. Reviewing safety orders, regulations, rules, etc., of regulatory agencies	0 to 5
5. Committee work for trade associations or professional societies—such as Private Truck Council, National Safety Council, American Society of Safety Engineers, National Fire Protection Association, American Trucking Associations, and National Committee for Motor Fleet Supervisor Training	0 to 5
Field Activities (5 to 60 percent of time)	
1. Working with company field management on explanation, promotion, and stimulation of safety program, and on inspecting equipment and operating habits	5 to 40
2. Working with official agencies regarding safety orders, rules, regulations, etc.	0 to 10
3. Working with trade associations or professional societies.	0 to 10

Such a committee can establish, with authority, the methods of operation and the elements of the operating and safety program. The committee will assure that the program is practical, and that it will be fully supported as it is carried out down the line as official company policy.

Always remember that it is management's responsibility to support the safety program and to make policy decisions whether they operate through a management safety committee or not. Firms that operate without such a safety committee forego many benefits.

Make the Policy Known

One of the first things management should do is to make known and support the company policy on accident prevention.

Safety policy statement

Although small (one-location) organizations may be able to function without a formal safety policy statement, larger organizations (especially those operating from scattered locations) are at a disadvantage unless they publish their safety policies.

Basic to such a policy declaration are these statements: (*a*) that the company intends to comply with all safety laws and ordinances, (*b*) that the safety of its employees, the public, and its operations are paramount, (*c*) that safety will take precedence over expediency, or short cuts in the operations of the company, and (*d*) every attempt will be made to reduce the possibility of accident occurrence.

The policy declaration should be signed by the president.

The policy should be given wide publicity throughout the company and should set the pace of operations for both field management and employees. Such a policy makes it easier to enforce safe practices and conditions. It makes it easier for supervisors to comply with company policy. It also makes it easier for employees to follow safety instruction. Finally, it makes it easier to obtain good preventative maintenance of equipment or selection of proper equipment when purchased.

Company publications

As a company starts operating in more and more locations, the need for printed procedures, rules, and manuals grows. Field management will be helped by having up-to-date publications that outline company policies and practices covering employee selection, training, and supervision. Methods of investigating and reporting accidental occurrences and detailed outlines (covering such important subjects as counseling, retraining, and discipline) are a must.

A local manager must operate his unit profitably. All the codes, standards, and instructions issued by the main office should be designed to help him make a profit. Manuals must clearly show overall policy and standard methods of procedure, but should not be so needlessly detailed as to reduce the unit manager to a chief clerk.

Make the Policy Understood

The benefits will be reflected in improved performance as new employees are more carefully selected, effectively trained, adequately appraised as to their job performance, and given more effective supervision. Accidents that do occur will be more thoroughly investigated to get the facts, so all can learn how to prevent future accidents.

The safety director should check to see that procedures are complied with, but it's up to management to enforce them.

The safety audit

One of the things a safety director should do both at headquarters and at any other company location is to sample or audit local programs, practices, and procedures, in order to (*a*) check understanding of and compliance with the established and published company policies and practices, and (*b*) to make sure safety inspections are adequate. By checking actual field practice, the safety director will be in a position to help field management to do a better job. Often, while looking for weak points, the safety director can help supervisors improve their understanding of company policies and practices.

The safety director should develop a check sheet for evaluating the safety program and checking conditions or practice during field visits.

Document Program Effectiveness

If a firm is to have an effective program, it must be documented through good recordkeeping, reported accurately and uniformly, and often followed up by visits to scattered fleet units.

Home office records

The home office should keep the official company accident statistical records. However the various locations of the company should keep local counterpart records of accidental occurrences. In many cases, this will be required by law or regulations such as the Bureau of Motor Carrier Safety, OSHA, and Workers' Compensation laws. Central records are desirable, whether required or not, for these reasons:

- To check company accident trends
- To determine those departments or areas that need attention
- To discover what types and basic accident causes are most prevalent
- To determine those employees who have earned safe driver awards
- To learn what safety program features are needed, and
- To calculate how much accidents cost the company.

Even though local statistics will indicate the local accident story, the whole picture will only be available through central reports.

Home office records are necessary because employees transfer from one location to another or from one department to another. Without central records it would be extremely difficult to keep track of changes and records.

Statistical reports

Home office central accident records can be used to compile and issue monthly, quarterly, and annual reports. Such reports are necessary to keep the various branch managers informed of their relative safety performance. Such comparison helps local accident control by encouraging interest in accident prevention and building a spirit of competition between the various units of the company. Special reports, summaries, and analyses of accident experience by type of accidents, basic causes, and other factors should be prepared for management. These were discussed in detail in Chapters 4 and 6.

In general, the areas that should be covered in periodic reports are:

- Injuries to employees at work
- Injuries to employees "off-the-job"
- Injuries to the public (the people who come on company property in their contact with the company and are involved in accidents in which a company vehicle is involved)
- Product liability situation
- Motor vehicle accidents
- Fires
- Loss and damage to cargo or persons
- Theft
- Vandalism
- Other details.

The cost of these during the reporting interval should be included in the report.

As mentioned in these earlier chapters, statistics on motor vehicle accidents should be based on the *Method of Recording and Measuring Motor Vehicle Fleet Accident Experience and Passenger Accident Experience,* ANSI Standard D15.1.

The reports covering motor vehicle accidents should be broken down by operation units and should include at least the following:

- Number of fleet accidents
- Mileage operated by all vehicles (breakdown by types if more than one)
- Frequency rates for each category, and
- Number and percent of fleet accidents judged "preventable."

Statistics on employee injuries may be compiled in accordance with the *Method of Recording and Measuring Work Injury Experience,* ANSI Standard Z16.1, discussed in detail in Chapter 7, "Employee Injury-Prevention Program," or the OSHA reporting criteria.

Special studies of motor vehicle accidents should be made to guide the direction of the accident prevention program. Items that should be carefully analyzed are:

- Types of accidents
- Basic causes
- Geographical location (spot maps are useful)

- Types of vehicles involved (owned by or operated for company)
- Drivers involved
- Hour of day and day of week of occurrences, and
- Other factors deemed significant by repeated occurrence.

"Drivers involved" should determine repeaters. Other significant factors about those who are having the most frequent accidents should be cataloged.

Uniformity of reporting

Uniform accident reporting is essential to conducting a safety program for a scattered fleet. Establishing uniformity may be a time-consuming and difficult undertaking, but it must be done. Any difficulty will probably be due to the program's not being fully understood or accepted by various company units.

There may be a tendency on the part of field management to "cover-up" in order to look good or avoid embarrassment. Sometimes a branch manager will try to protect an employee, rather than to report all facts and conditions.

Whatever the reason, lack of uniformity in reporting accidents hampers the accident prevention program and leads to a vital breakdown in morale and effective supervision.

There are, fortunately, national standards. These should be followed. American National Standards Institute D-15 (already referenced) defines and classifies motor vehicle fleet accidents; the National Safety Council, through its "Safe Driver Award" rules, has established a workable method to determine the preventability of accidents. When all units in a company understand and practice the provisions of these two standards, uniformity of accident statistics will result.

The Council provides interpretation committee service to decide questionable or borderline cases. Individual cases can be submitted to the Council for a decision.

Most companies have established written procedures governing how and by whom accidents will be classified as to reportability and preventability. These procedures vary from company to company but most require that the first decision be made at the local office. When necessary a local committee, usually composed of the employee's supervisor, the supervisor of the garage or maintenance unit, and two fellow employees can review borderline cases or protected decisions. The local decision is then submitted to the home office for a final review. Any decision based on inadequate or biased information should be returned to the local manager for correction if the decision is contrary to company policy. (See Chapter 11 for details.)

Headquarters follow-up

Periodically, headquarters safety staff should personally check the terminals of scattered fleet units. What is the tipoff that a visit is needed? When there is evidence of poor accident reporting and investigation.

Often, poor safety performance goes hand in hand with poor local management. When operational headquarters people find this out, they will usually try to find what caused the local breakdown. The safety director can get in on this audit.

Accidents are frequently one of the "early warning signs" that indicate a local management is going down. Other evidences are: unusual coverages or shortages, unusually high damage claims, and expensive road failures, increased theft, and declining morale.

Characteristics of the Scattered Fleet

Although the units of a scattered fleet resemble, in many respects, the operation of a small fleet, they differ in that each local unit benefits from (*a*) the specialized headquarters staff, and (*b*) well-established company guidelines. Thus, the accident record of local units should be better than the average of a number of small, separate fleets.

The headquarters safety staff can best aid the units of their scattered fleets by (*a*) preplanning schedules for training consultation, driver meetings, and introduction of new systems and equipment; (*b*) systematizing procedures; (*c*) preparing standard forms; and (*d*) establishing inter-fleet contests using comparative records.

When headquarters staff visits the units, they should use their time wisely. Visits should be planned well in advance. Forms and instructions should be sent ahead in sufficient time to allow local supervision to prepare themselves and to review any instructions and new information. This is the time to conduct supervisory safety-training sessions.

There must be a smooth-functioning line of contact between headquarters and the local units. A definite program of visits and followups should be worked out; deviations from this can undermine an otherwise well-planned accident control program.

When headquarters staff (especially safety personnel) visit local units, they must use the highest degree of diplomacy and tact. The safety manager or director must remember that he *advises* management. His is a staff function—he must not assume any line of authority. He should report defects and unsafe practices to line management who, in turn, has the responsibility to correct these situations. At the same time, the safety manager must make it clear that the company standards will be upheld, and he will not allow anything less.

Chapter 14

Job Safety Analysis

To uncover hazards that may have been overlooked in the layout of the terminal, in the design of machinery, equipment, and processes, or may have developed after operations were begun, a continuing program of activities must be carried on. One of the most important of these activities is job safety analysis.

Definition

A job safety analysis is a procedure to make a job safe by:

1. *Identifying hazards* or potential accidents associated with each step of the job.

2. *Developing a solution* for each hazard that will either eliminate or control the exposure.

Once the hazards are known, the proper solutions can be developed. Some solutions may be physical changes that control the hazard, such as placing a guard over exposed moving machine parts. Others may be job procedures that eliminate or minimize the hazard, for example, safe methods of loading cargo.

Some job steps may have no hazards associated with them, but others may each be accompanied by one or more hazards. Some hazards are conditions; some are actions. All are potential causes of accidents.

How To Make a JSA

A job safety analysis can be written up in the manner shown in Figure 14-1. In the left-hand column, the basic steps of the job are listed in the order in which they occur. The middle column describes the hazards or

JOB SAFETY ANALYSIS INSTRUCTIONS ON REVERSE SIDE	JOB TITLE (and number if applicable): Jumping a Battery	PAGE 1 OF 2 JSA NO.	DATE:	☒ NEW ☐ REVISED
	TITLE OF PERSON WHO DOES JOB:	SUPERVISOR:	ANALYSIS BY:	
COMPANY/ORGANIZATION:	PLANT/LOCATION:	DEPARTMENT:	REVIEWED BY:	
REQUIRED AND/OR RECOMMENDED PERSONAL PROTECTIVE EQUIPMENT:			APPROVED BY:	

SEQUENCE OF BASIC JOB STEPS	POTENTIAL HAZARDS	RECOMMENDED ACTION OR PROCEDURE
1. Place the two vehicles in position so that the cables reach from battery to battery.	1. a) Grounding, if two vehicles make contact. b) Vehicles may roll.	1. a) Park vehicles so that they will not make contact. b) Turn off ignition; shift both vehicles into neutral or park; set parking brake.
2. Make certain both batteries are of the same voltage, and both vehicles are similarly grounded.	2. Battery may be permanently damaged or may explode.	2. Check battery for indication of voltage. Conventional batteries (non-maintenance free) have one filler vent cap for each two-volt cell. Check whether the negative or positive terminals are grounded to the vehicle body. If both vehicles are positive ground, follow the standard procedure except using reverse polarity.
3. Check to see that the dead battery has adequate electrolyte (water and acid mixture), and is not frozen.	3. Battery may be permanently damaged or may explode.	3. If battery has vent caps, remove them to check for frozen electrolyte - add water if low. Maintenance free batteries can be tilted or carefully shaken to see if the electrolyte is frozen; making certain not to ground out the nongrounded terminal.
4. Put a cloth over each battery. Uncap a vented battery.	4. Escaping gases from a charging battery are explosive.	4. Cover each battery with a cloth. Keep open flames, cigarettes, and sparks away from the batteries.
5. Identify the positive battery terminals.	5. Connecting the batteries in a crossed polarity can permanently damage or explode the batteries.	5. The positive terminal on a battery can be identified by the color code red, or +, P, or POS on the battery case, post, or clamp.
6. Attach one battery jumper cable between the two positive terminals.	6. One vehicle may be positively grounded instead of negatively grounded.	6. A positive ground system can be identified by the cable leading from the positive terminal of the battery to the vehicle body. In positive-grounded, connect the negative terminals of the batteries instead of the positive terminals.

Figure 14-1. *This Job Safety Analysis shows the safe way to jump a battery.*

JOB SAFETY ANALYSIS

INSTRUCTIONS ON REVERSE SIDE

JOB TITLE (and number if applicable): Jumping a Battery

PAGE 2 OF 2 JSA NO.____

DATE:

☐ NEW
☐ REVISED

TITLE OF PERSON WHO DOES JOB:

SUPERVISOR:

ANALYSIS BY:

COMPANY/ORGANIZATION:

PLANT/LOCATION:

DEPARTMENT:

REVIEWED BY:

REQUIRED AND/OR RECOMMENDED PERSONAL PROTECTIVE EQUIPMENT:

APPROVED BY:

SEQUENCE OF BASIC JOB STEPS	POTENTIAL HAZARDS	RECOMMENDED ACTION OR PROCEDURE
7. Attach one end of the other battery jumper cable to the negative terminal of the booster battery and the other end of the cable to the engine block of the vehicle to be started.	7. a) Final connection may cause potentially dangerous sparks. b) One vehicle may be positively grounded.	7. a) The final connection to the engine block should be at least a foot from the battery and to a clean, unpainted metallic surface. If final connection draws large sparks, you may have polarity wrong. Go back to Step 5.
8. Try to start the vehicle needing the jump.	8. a) Batteries may explode. b) Booster battery may begin to run down.	8. a) Stand clear of batteries while attempting to start vehicle. b) Start the booster battery vehicle to maintain a battery charge.
9. After the vehicle with the discharge battery has started, remove battery jumper cables.	9. a) Sparks may be produced in breaking the jumper circuit. b) Injuries from the vehicle's fan belt may occur.	9. a) Disconnect the last cable connection made to the engine block first, then, the other end of this cable; next, remove the other cable connection to the battery that was jumped. b) Keep cables and tools from making contact with or falling into moving parts.

potential accidents associated with each job step. The right-hand column gives the safe procedures that should be followed to safeguard against the hazards and to prevent potential accidents.

For convenience, both the job safety analysis and the written description are referred to as a JSA.

An outline for making a job safety analysis follows:

1. Priority of job selection. Select the job to be analyzed by its relative risk.
   a. Frequency of accidents.
   b. Severity of injuries.
   c. Potential for accident and injury.
   d. Newly established jobs.
   e. Jobs with procedure modifications.

2. Selection and preparation of the person who will demonstrate the procedure.
   a. Select a cooperative, competent person.
   b. Explain the purpose of the demonstration.

4. Break the procedure into steps.
   a. Be general.
   b. Begin with active verb.

5. Check the breakdown for accuracy.
   a. Get an agreement from the person who performs the job.

6. List the steps on the JSA form.
   a. Record the steps in the first column.

7. Identify the hazards.
   a. Observe the job demonstration for potential accident causes (strain, sprain, slip, fall, etc.).
   b. Observe the demonstration for environmental hazards (vapors, gases, heat, noise, etc.).

8. List the hazards.
   a. Discuss findings and possible changes with operators.
   b. List the hazards in the second column of the JSA form.

9. Develop solutions by presenting controls.
   a. Job change.
   b. Step change.
   c. Environmental change.
   d. Repair or service change.
   e. Check modifications.

Select the job

A job is a sequence of separate steps or activities that together accomplish a work goal. Some jobs can be broadly defined in general terms of what is accomplished. Transporting material, building a plant, mining iron ore are examples. Such broadly defined jobs are not suitable for a JSA. Similarly, a job can be narrowly defined in terms of a single action. Pulling a switch, tightening a screw, pushing a button are examples. Such narrowly defined jobs also are not suitable for a JSA.

Jobs suitable for a JSA are those job assignments that a line supervisor may make. Operating a vehicle, washing a vehicle, piling boxes at a terminal are good subjects for job safety analyses because they are neither too broad nor are they too narrow.

Jobs, even though they fit the description just given, should not be selected at random for analysis. The most hazardous and those with the worst accident experience should be tackled first. This approach will yield the quickest possible return from a JSA program.

In selecting jobs to be analyzed and in establishing the order of analysis, top supervision of a department should be guided by the following factors:

- *Frequency of accidents.* A job that has repeatedly produced accidents is a candidate for a JSA. The greater the number of accidents associated with the job, the greater its priority claim for a JSA.
- *Production of disabling injuries.* Every job that has produced disabling injuries should be given a JSA. The injuries prove that preventive action taken prior to their occurrence was not successful.
- *Severity potential.* Some jobs may have no history of accidents but may have the potential for severe injury.
- *New jobs* created by changes in equipment or in processes obviously have no history of accidents, but their accident potential may not be fully appreciated. A JSA of every new job should be made as soon as the job has been created. Analysis should not be delayed until accidents or near misses occur.
- *Existing jobs* with recent procedure modifications can present special safety problems. The changes in the process could create a hazard where none before existed. A JSA should be made to determine the new accident potential.

Choose the demonstrator

If the observer has an opportunity to choose from among several people doing the job being analyzed, he will have to determine which one best meets the requirements. The person selected should be experienced, capable, cooperative, and willing to share ideas. Such a person will be easy to work with on an analysis.

If the one selected has never worked on a JSA, the supervisor should thoroughly explain the purpose of the analysis and show him a copy of a completed JSA. The demonstrator must be reassured that he is not being watched to see whether he works safely. He should understand (*a*) that the purpose is to study the job, not the person doing it, and (*b*) that he was selected for observation because of his experience and capability.

Break the job down

Before the search for hazards begins, the job should be broken down into basic steps. The steps should describe what is being done and should be given in the order of occurrence. Details should be omitted.

Here is an example of a step-by-step breakdown of a simple job—planting a tree:

1. Select the site.
2. Bring tools, equipment, and the tree to the site.
3. Dig the hole.
4. Prepare the hole.
5. Put the tree into the hole.
6. Backfill, tamp, and water.
7. Brace the tree.
8. Clean up and return the equipment.

There are two common errors made in breaking a job down into its basic steps. One is to make the breakdown too detailed. The result is an unnecessarily large number of job steps, many of which may not be basic. For example, the same tree planting job might be overloaded with these typical details:

1. Pick up the shovel.
2. Position the shovel so that it points down.
3. Place the right foot on the top edge of the shovel blade.
4. Press the shovel into the ground with the right foot.
5. Tilt the shovel handle backward and down to pick up the dirt.

The other common error is to make the job breakdown too general. The result is that important basic steps are not recorded, as in this two-step breakdown of the tree planting job:

1. Dig the hole.
2. Plant the tree.

In this case, all but one of the basic steps have been omitted. Obviously, the JSA will not show the hazards associated with all the basic steps and will be worthless.

Key points in breaking a job down into successive basic steps are:

1. Select the right person to demonstrate the job.
2. Explain the purpose.
3. Observe the job for breakdown by basic steps.
4. Record each step in the breakdown.
5. Check the breakdown with the person who is observed.

The job should be observed for breakdown by basic steps. The supervisor should ask, "What is the first basic step of the job; what starts the job? What is the next basic step?" and so on. The steps must not be either too general or too limited.

Check the breakdown for accuracy

After the supervisor has completed the breakdown, he should check it with the person he has observed. The supervisor should get agreement on what is done (not how it's done) and on the order in which the steps are taken. It should go without saying that the supervisor should thank the person when the breakdown has been completed.

List the steps on the JSA form

In recording the breakdown, the supervisor should number the job steps consecutively in the first column of the JSA work sheet. Each step should describe *what* is done, not *how* it is to be done. The wording for each step should begin with a verb or an "action" word, like "remove," "open," "weld." Description of the job step is completed by naming the item to which the action applies, for example, "remove *extinguisher,*" "open *valve,*" "weld seam."

Identify the hazards and potential accidents

After the job has been broken down into its basic steps, each step is analyzed for hazards and potential accidents. The purpose is to identify *all* the hazards, whether produced by the environment or connected with the job procedure, so that each step, and thus the entire job, can be made safer and more efficient.

The supervisor should look for specific types of potential accidents. For each basic step in the job breakdown, he should ask himself these questions:

1. Can the employee strike against, be struck by, or otherwise make injurious contact with an object?
2. Can he be caught in, on, or between objects?
3. Can he slip or trip? Can he fall on the same level or from one level to another?
4. Can he strain himself by pushing, pulling, or lifting?
5. Does the environment present a hazardous exposure (toxic gases, vapors, mists, fumes, dusts, heat, radiation, and so on)?

Observation plus knowledge of the job should supply the answers to these questions. The job observation should be repeated as often as necessary until *all* hazards and potential accidents have been identified.

While observing each step, the supervisor should record the hazards that might result in accidents. Only two items of information are required: the type of accident and the agent involved. For example, to record the idea that an employee might injure his legs or feet by dropping a fire extinguisher, all the supervisor needs to write down is "struck by extinguisher."

List the hazards

Each hazard or potential accident should be recorded on a separate line in the center column on the JSA work sheet. A hazard or potential accident pertaining to a particular job step should be kept parallel with that step. If a job step entails several hazards or potential accidents, they should be identified "(a)," "(b)," "(c)," and so on.

The supervisor should check with the employee observed after the hazards and the potential accidents have been recorded. The employee's experience with the job may suggest ideas that did not occur to the supervisor.

The supervisor should also check with others who have had experience with the job. By alternately observing the job and discussing its dangers with experienced people, the supervisor will soon develop a reliable list of hazards and potential accidents.

Develop solutions

When the hazards and potential accidents associated with each job step have been identified and their causes understood, the final step in the job safety analysis is to develop ways to eliminate the hazards and prevent occurrences of the potential accidents. The principal solutions are:

1. *Find* an entirely different way to do the job.
2. *Change* the physical conditions that create the hazards.
3. *Revise* the job procedure if changing the physical conditions does not eliminate all the hazards.
4. *Reduce* the frequency of the job by correcting the conditions that make it necessary.

Occasionally, it is possible to find or devise an entirely different way to do the job that will eliminate the hazards. Attention should be focused on the work goal of the job. The ways in which that work goal can be accomplished should be determined and then should be analyzed for hazards to see if any one way is entirely safe. When such a study is being made, work-saving tools and equipment should be considered.

If a different and safe way to do the job cannot be found, then for each hazard and each potential accident this question should be asked: "What change in physical condition, such as a change in tools, materials, equipment, or location, will eliminate the hazard or prevent the accident?"

When a physical change to make the job safe is in order, it should be carefully studied to determine what other benefits, such as greater production or a saving in time or effort required to do the job, will also result from the change. These other benefits should be pointed out when the proposed change is presented to higher management—they will make good selling points.

If the hazards cannot be eliminated either by doing the job in a different way or by changing the physical conditions, the next effort in effecting a solution should be to investigate the possibility of making changes in job procedures.

For each hazard and each potential accident recorded on the JSA work sheet, this question should be asked: "What should the employee do—or not do—to eliminate this particular hazard or prevent this particular potential accident?" Where appropriate, an additional question: "How should it be done?" should be asked. In most cases, the supervisor should be able to supply satisfactory answers to those questions from his own experiences.

The answers must be specific and concrete if a new recommended safe procedure is to be worthwhile. Such general instructions as "Be alert," "Use caution," or "Be careful," are useless. Answers should precisely state what to do and how to do it.

Here is an example of a *poor* recommendation for a safety procedure: "Make certain the wrench does not slip and cause loss of balance."

It is poor because it does not tell how to prevent the wrench from slipping.

Here, in contrast, is an example of a good recommended safe procedure that tells not only what to do but how to do it.

"Set the wrench securely. Test the grip of the wrench by exerting a slight pressure. Brace yourself against something immovable, or take a solid stance with feet wide apart before exerting full pressure, to prevent loss of balance if the wrench slips."

Often a repair or service job has to be done at frequent intervals because a condition needs to be corrected. For such repetitive jobs, this question should be asked: "What can be done to eliminate the *cause* of the condition that makes excessive repairs or service necessary?" If the cause cannot be eliminated, then the question "Can anything be done to minimize the effects of the condition?" should be asked.

For example, machine parts may become worn at a rapid rate and therefore require frequent replacement. Study of the problem may reveal that excessive vibration is the cause of this condition. When the vibration is eliminated or reduced substantially, the machine parts will have longer life and the job of replacement will need to be done less often.

Reducing the frequency of a job contributes to safety only that it limits the exposure. Every effort still should be made to eliminate hazards and to prevent potential accidents through changing physical conditions or revising job procedures or both.

The supervisor should check or test proposed changes by reobserving the job and by discussing the changes with the people who do the job. Their ideas about the hazards and proposed solutions may have considerable value. They can judge the practicality of proposed changes and perhaps suggest improvements.

Such discussions, however, are more than a way to check a JSA. They are safety contacts that promote awareness of job hazards and safe procedures.

Benefits and Uses of JSA

The major benefits of a job safety analysis come after its completion. However, benefits are also to be gained from the development work itself.

While making job safety analyses, supervisors learn more about the jobs they supervise. When employees are encouraged to participate in job safety analyses, their safety attitudes are improved and their safety knowledge is increased. As a JSA is worked out, safer and better job procedures and safer working conditions are developed.

But these important benefits are only a portion of the total benefits to be derived from the JSA program. The principal benefits come from use of the JSA in these phases of the supervisor's work:

1. Giving individual training to employees.
2. Making employee safety contacts.
3. Instructing the new person on the job.
4. Preparing for planned safety observations.
5. Giving prejob instructions on irregular jobs.
6. Reviewing job procedures after accidents or near-accidents occur.
7. Studying jobs for possible improvement in job methods.

When a JSA is distributed, the supervisor's first responsibility is to explain its contents to employees and, if necessary, to give them further individual training. The entire JSA must be reviewed with those people who are concerned so that they will know how the job is to be done—without accidents.

The JSA can furnish material for planned safety contacts. All steps of the JSA should be used for this purpose. The steps that present major hazards should be emphasized and reviewed again and again in safety contacts.

New workers on the job must be trained in the basic job steps. They must be taught to recognize the hazards associated with each job step and must learn the necessary precautions. There is no better guide for this training than a well-prepared JSA.

Occasionally, the supervisor should observe his people as they perform jobs for which job safety analyses have been developed. The purpose of these observations is to determine whether or not the workers are doing the jobs in accordance with the safe job procedures. Before making such observations, the supervisor should prepare himself by reviewing the JSA in question so that he will have firmly in mind the key points that should be part of his observations.

Many jobs, such as certain repair or service jobs, are done infrequently or on an irregular basis. The people who do them will benefit from prejob instruction that reminds them of the important hazards and the necessary precautions. Using the JSA for the particular job, the supervisor should give this instruction at the time he makes the job assignment.

Whenever an accident or near-accident occurs on a job covered by a job safety analysis, the JSA should be reviewed to determine whether or not it needs revision. If the JSA is revised, all employees concerned with the job should be informed of the changes and instructed in any new procedures.

When an accident or near accident results from failure to follow JSA procedures, the facts should be discussed with all the employees who do the job.

It should be made clear that the incident would not have occurred had the JSA procedures been followed.

All supervisors are concerned with improving job methods to increase safety, reduce costs, and step up production. The job safety analysis is an excellent starting point for questioning the established way of doing a job. And study of the JSA may well suggest definite ideas for improvement of job methods. The details of preparing a job safety analysis are available in audio-visual programs from the National Safety Council.

Chapter 15

Off-the-Job Safety Programs

The knowledge, experience, and credibility you have acquired because of your position as director of a fleet safety program can be used to positively influence the private lives of others. As serious and numerous as work-related accidents are, off-the-job (OTJ) accidents, injuries, and deaths are an even greater problem:

- The records show that employees are safer on the job than they are on the highway, the street, or in the home.
- According to the records of a large manufacturing corporation, the frequency of its OTJ injuries was 18 times that of on-the-job injuries, and fatalities were 35 times more likely to occur *off* the job.
- On the average, employees suffer about 94 OTJ accidental deaths and approximately 7,100 OTJ disabling injuries every day in the United States.

Everyone Benefits

Your community benefits

In the mid 1980s, it was estimated that motor vehicle accidents killed more people, over 46 thousand per year, than all other accident causes combined. With figures this high, there is hardly a person whose life has not been touched by a disabling or fatal motor vehicle accident to himself, a family member, or a friend. Undoubtedly, your community's residents would welcome leadership in the instituting of a safety program to reduce OTJ accidents, especially in the area of your specialty—motor vehicles.

Your company benefits

One of the basic reasons for a company to become involved in OTJ safety is to conserve employee power. While companies now have a legal responsibility to prevent injuries on the job, they have a moral responsibility to try to prevent injuries away from the job. All injuries are a waste of a valuable resource—people. Injuries and fatalities happen to people who call on customers, make a product, service equipment, keep the books, and do many other jobs involved in running a business.

A large part of OTJ accident cost is borne by employers. Some cost is paid directly in the form of wages to absent workers and the cost of hiring and training replacement workers. Some of the cost is hidden. For example, a skilled driver, a technician, or a salesperson injured off-the-job, may not be replaced immediately. Their absences may result in late deliveries, lost production, lost sales, and loss of customers.

Injury, illness, and death off the job are as emotionally and financially costly to employees and their families as injury, illness, and death on the job, and the impact on employers' profits is considerable. To offset even so small a loss as a $150 accident involving only minor emergency medical treatment, an organization must produce at least that much in profits. If a company makes a 10 cent profit on every dollar, it has to make sales of $1,500 just to cover that expense.

In a recent year, OTJ accidents cost the nation at least $25 billion. Approximately one-third of this cost was paid by employers. This figure includes all or part of the premiums for hospitalization, medical, accidental death, and wage continuation insurance.

Some of the cost is hidden even deeper, although it is still very real. As accidents in a community increase, so do insurance costs, taxes, and welfare contributions. Probably no company is fully aware of all the costs that result from OTJ accidents, and the impact they have on operations and profits. Enough experience has been accumulated, however, to develop a simplified plan for estimating such costs (discussed later in this chapter).

These facts and figures indicate the seriousness of OTJ accidents and the need for more to be done about reducing these accidents. An OTJ safety program is one effective solution. It can help to reduce or eliminate OTJ accidents in much the same way traditional safety programs reduce occupational accidents.

If your company is too small, or otherwise unable to promote an OTJ safety program, community safety programs are an alternate means of reducing accidents and injuries. Individuals or groups interested in starting a project should contact the Council for information on community safety resource materials and kits.

You benefit

Your involvement in an OTJ safety program places you in a position of higher visibility both within your company and within your community. This contribution of your valuable knowledge and time to the welfare of others can help speed your professional development and career movement.

You can enhance your public image as a safety expert by:

Becoming aware of your influence over others. There are people in your life who respect you and are influenced by what you say and what you do. You might not realize it, but because of your position, you can actually improve the way others behave behind the wheels of their vehicles.

Consciously exercising the role. The image you present must be of a person who is more than causally interested in better driving and who is, in fact, vitally concerned about promoting better driving both on and off your job.

Speaking about traffic safety. Accept opportunities to speak at community, company, or industry functions. Your public speaking skills can be increased by taking a class at your local college or university. Or, by joining one of the more than 5,000 Toastmaster International public speaking clubs. For further information contact the headquarters office, Toastmaster International, 2200 North Grand Avenue, Santa Ana, California 92711.

Traffic safety is a frequent subject of private conversations. Speak up and express positive attitudes, correct misconceptions. Show that you regard traffic safety as a serious matter that deserves the informed support and cooperation of every individual.

Your objective in speaking about traffic safety, both publicly and privately, is to encourage, not push, people's attitudes in the right direction.

Knowing your field. If you are to be a positive influence, you must know the facts. One of the easiest ways to increase your knowledge of the field is by educating yourself through reading. In addition to the books listed in the bibliography, a basic fact-source is the driver's handbook issued by your state driver licensing bureau.

Being a good driver. The example you set as a driver says more about your attitude toward traffic safety than anything else. Learn and put into practice good driving principles. Learn each basic driving maneuver; then perform it correctly every time.

Supporting other traffic safety efforts. If high school or adult education courses, or Driver Improvement Training are available in your area, you will be repaid for time and money spent in helping such courses by your effective influence on other drivers. Cooperation in giving the National Safety Council's "Defensive Driving Course" can help both the public and fleet drivers.

As you become more familiar with traffic safety, you will find more and more groups and agencies devoted to making driving safer. Among these are your local safety council, the safety committees of your church and service club, high school groups, and others. Each views the problem from a different angle. They can learn a lot from you and you can learn from them.

Taking part in your trade association safety activities. Most associations have committees or divisions working on safety matters. The Council of Safety Supervisors of the American Trucking Associations is an excellent example, since it is national but consists of local councils within each state trucking association. The Motor Transportation Division of the National Safety Council is another example; it has three sections (Commercial Vehicle, Transit, and School Bus) which meet nationally. The Private Truck Council of America, Inc. is a national organization representing private truck operators. Its safety and driver training programs offer excellent opportunities for professional growth to the safety director. These groups study, work, and learn to improve their abilities, and to educate others in the field of fleet safety. By investing time and effort you can gain knowledge and stature in the field of fleet safety, and can influence the laws that govern your company's operations.

Joining a professional safety organization. When you are working full time as a safety professional, you should join a professional association such as the American Society of Safety Engineers (see Appendix E for the address). Here you will be exposed to leaders in the tremendously broad field of general safety. You will learn how to handle yourself as a professional, and will immediately have the resources of an endless stream of fellow experts at your disposal. You will also have the chance to build your chosen field of motor fleet safety into a larger sphere of interest in these groups, where it can be recognized by them as a branch of safety engineering.

Implementing the OTJ Program

As your professional stature increases, through self-education and participation in group activities, your suggestions will become more highly respected by the management of your company.

Selling the OTJ safety program to management

As has been pointed out in earlier chapters, the first step is to sell your management on the idea that a safety program is good business—in the case of an OTJ program, this will be somewhat harder than with an on-the-job program because management often cannot at first see the tie-in. To enlist the support of your company's management, prepare a written proposal for a working OTJ safety program, and present it, in person, to the appropriate manager. The proposal should include:

1. **Published data** showing the high cost of OTJ accidents and the benefits to the company, for their reduction. Usable examples can be found throughout this chapter.

2. **An estimate of present OTJ accident costs** and projected cost savings. Although no one can fully estimate all the costs that result from OTJ accidents, and the full impact they have on operations and profits, enough experience has been accumulated to develop a simplified plan for estimating such costs:

Direct costs are wages and benefits paid to injured drivers and other employees while off the job. They include disability insurance payments, medical and hospital costs, plus medical and hospital costs for retirees and employees' families. Organizations that are insured by an outside carrier should use the premiums paid on that portion of health and accident policies that cover accident experience to determine cost. Organizations that are self-insured should take the amount of claims paid for the OTJ injuries plus the costs of administering their program to determine the cost.

Indirect costs of disabling injuries and nondisabling injuries. The indirect costs related to disabling injuries is an amount estimated to be equal to the direct costs, or the value of wage losses even if wages are not paid for all lost time. Indirect nondisabling cost is estimated as being about two-thirds of the indirect disabling cost. However, these are conservative estimates for determining indirect costs. Indirect costs can range from 1 to 10 times the direct costs, depending on the type of industry or organization involved. These costs may include such factors as:

- Personnel cost of hiring replacements.
- Wage cost of supervisors for time spent in training replacement drivers and other employee(s).
- Wage cost due to lower output of replacement drivers or employees during break-in period.
- Vehicles, products, materials, tools, and other items damaged by replacement worker(s) during break-in period.
- Wage costs of time lost by other employees who were delayed getting started because the injured employee was a member of a team, and his or her knowledgeable imput was needed.
- Wage cost due to absence of injured employees.
- Wage cost due to decreased output of injured employee after return to work.
- Wage cost of other employees who may be slowed down, either because the injured employee was slow, temporarily absent, or needed the help of other employees.
- Damage to vehicles and spoilage of products or materials due to less efficient work because of the injury, upon the driver's or employee's return to work.

Here's an example of how to estimate these costs:

Company X carries full accident and health insurance, as well as disability insurance, on all of its 1,000 employees (for purposes of this example, family coverage is excluded). Company X's insurance carrier stated that 20 percent, or $150,000, of the annual premium for both group insurance policies went to pay for employee OTJ injuries. Estimating the direct and indirect costs is done as follows:

Direct cost (insurance benefits paid for the OTJ injuries)	$150,000
Indirect disabling injury cost (1:1 ratio to direct cost)	150,000
Indirect nondisabling injury cost (2:3 ratio indirect disabling injury cost)	100,000
Total annual estimated direct and indirect OTJ employee injury cost	$400,000
Cost per employee (1,000)	$ 400

These costs will, of course, vary among companies, depending upon the insurance plans in force, scope of coverage, and plan provisions. For example, if a company's disability insurance plan requires a waiting period before paying, the disability costs will be less than for a plan paying disability from the first day of an absence due to an OTJ accident.

Projected costs savings. Set a target number and date for the reduction of OTJ accidents. This will provide a tangible indication to management as to where the program is headed. The reduction in accidents can be translated into a goal for dollar savings.

The program budget could be based on a percentage of the return on investment projected for a two-year period or less. For example, if your organization's OTJ injury cost is $250,000, and you project that with a budget of $7,500 you could save $37,500 (which is fifteen percent of the total OTJ injury cost), the estimated net return would be $30,000 or *four-hundred percent.*

If management can expect a reasonable return on its organization's investment, then it will be more likely to back the program. It is important to point out that because of the high costs of OTJ accidents, any reduction in accident rates will bring substantial savings to the organization.

3. Describe how your OTJ safety program will work in your fleet. Gear your program to your fleet's needs, and hold to a realistic budget. Be sure to tell (*a*) how accidents will be reported; (*b*) how much time and money the program will take; (*c*) how the program will be introduced (list specific activities and costs); and (*d*) how the program's effectiveness will be measured. Plans and methods for setting up an actual program will be described later in this chapter.

4. Discuss how the increase in safety awareness caused by an OTJ program can improve on-the-job safety records.

5. Explain how an OTJ safety program can be integrated with present on-the-job safety activities without involving heavy expenditures of money or time.

6. Present plans for measuring and evaluating the program's effectiveness following the guidelines to be found later in this chapter.

An OTJ safety program can easily be integrated with an on-the-job program—much of it does not require an increased expenditure, but rather wider, more realistic thinking. A little added discussion and broader emphasis will add OTJ effectiveness to on-the-job safety activities. Properly handled, this will provide a more consistent on-the-job safety program, because people should think safety all the time, not just while at work.

The actual program

What's involved? There is nothing particularly complicated about OTJ safety programming. In fact, it is similar in many respect to on-the-job safety programming. Management backing and an operating budget are just two requirements that both programs share in common. Also the program tools used in OTJ safety are, for the most part, the same ones used in safety awareness training on the job. They include: safety talks, in-house publications, films, videotapes, displays, posters, reference booklets, contests, defensive driving courses, and safety fairs.

Generally, the aim of the OTJ safety program is to train individuals in safe practices and to create safety awareness. To accomplish this objective, an OTJ safety program has to depend on education and motivation to get its message across. The reason for this is that once employees leave the garage, office, plant, or job site, they are on their own and supervision is no longer available.

There are, perhaps, three major reasons why people commit unsafe practice—whether off or on the job:

- Lack of knowledge
- Inattention or distraction
- Intentionally violating safe practices.

Lack of knowledge can be overcome through OTJ safety education and training. However, overcoming the latter two practices is more difficult. An example of inattention or distraction would be a person driving through a red light because his mind was on something else. An example of intentionally violating safe practices would be a driver who decides not to wear a safety belt even though he knows better and cannot offer a good reason for not doing so. In these two instances where a lack of knowledge is not necessarily the problem, more creative countermeasures are needed. OTJ safety awareness and motivational activities are required.

Influencing attitudes. Individuals cannot be forced to behave safely. Unless a person develops the attitude that this is the best thing to do, any safety motivation efforts will be futile. That is why the only practical approach to OTJ safety programs is to educate, motivate, and sell, and, in doing so, to influence the attitudes of employees and their families. The idea is to emphasize that most any activity can be performed safely if the individual uses the correct procedures and equipment or tools. It sounds simple, but keep in mind the following:

1. Don't preach or try to coerce. The facts should speak for themselves.

2. Be positive. Avoid negative phrases like: "Don't do this," or 'Don't

do that." Stress the *benefits* for the individual employee.

3. Don't scold or patronize; it will also be a sure turn off.

When employees and their families begin to be aware of unsafe conditions and acts in their daily lives, the organization will have accomplished a major objective in its OTJ safety program.

Success guidelines. On the basis of reports from companies that have conducted successful OTJ safety campaigns, the National Safety Council has concluded that the following factors are essential to an effective program:

- Management and employee participation must be vocal, visible, and continuous from management through all levels, including first line supervisors, to hourly employees. Conveying the feeling that management is concerned for its employees is essential. At the same time, employees must feel involved in the program by being allowed to participate in its development. Use employee-management safety committees as a basis to develop OTJ safety programs.
- It cannot be overemphasized that results are better when the safety message gets into the home. The family can be extremely influential in bringing about attitude changes. Some suggestions include: make the materials that are sent to the home attractive, well organized, and as informative as you can to capture the reader's attention. A letter from the fleet manager or other management official is always an attention getter.
- The interest of cooperating drivers and others should appear spontaneous, as much as possible. Play down that this is part of a systematic campaign.
- Make use of management authority when appropriate—but go easy. It is best that most of the activity be conducted by the drivers and other employees.
- Order all materials well in advance and have them on hand before beginning the campaign. Make sure all participants know their parts and will carry out their duties as scheduled. *Timing is important.*
- Keep the individual safety campaigns going at a good pace, but terminate them at definite, predetermined dates. There is such a thing as overdoing it!

The OTJ safety campaign. Broken down simply, the steps involved in implementing an OTJ safety campaign are as follows:

1. Determine how much ground should be covered in the campaign. This is directly related to the extent of the OTJ safety problems.

2. Itemize campaign objectives and establish a timetable for accomplishing them.

3. Estimate cost-benefit factors. Be realistic and include manpower hours, planning time, meeting time, work interruptions, and other inputs.

4. Obtain management commitment.

5. Organize the campaign strategy.

6. Order and receive materials.

7. Gather and prepare employee publication materials.

8. Organize and train campaign supervisors.

9. Announce the campaign to the employees.

10. Start the campaign.

11. Set up ways to monitor or track the success, or lack of success, of a campaign and to measure the results.

12. Plan for the future.

Now that the basic overview of what's involved has been presented, the next question will most likely be: *How does our organization get there from here?*

At this moment, you have four basic means available to communicate OTJ safety to drivers and their families. They are:

1. *Personal*—Those communications that reach employees through private and social channels.

2. *Public*—Those media-centered communications directed toward more general populations.

3. *Peer/Supervisor*—Those communications obtained at work.

4. *Corporate*—Those formal communications that reflect the corporate philosophy, policy, and other guidelines.

When these avenues of communication are maximized, your program can provide a variety of stimulating messages in order to gain the audience's attention and commitment. The formats for such messages may include the following program tools:

• *In-house publications.* The program will undoubtedly benefit from a means of publicity that is convenient, inexpensive, and effective.

• *Reference booklet or magazine.* A reference booklet can provide certain, distinct advantages to employees and their families' safety. It is permanent and can serve as a small directory for answering specific safety questions. The National Safety Council's *Family Safety and Health* magazine reaches more people than any other OTJ safety publication. It has a proven record of motivating its readers to take safety and health precautions.

- *Safety calendar:* A safety calendar offers ways to get across timely safety information. The National Safety Council publishes a popular one.
- *Posters.* A poster is often seen at a quick glance, but its message (which should be easy to comprehend) may be long remembered. A poster can summarize major safety messages, and thereby reinforce the more detailed "how-to" information. The National Safety Council publishes "POP" posters that can be placed in garage areas, or on the dashboard, or right at the "Point of Problem" (see Chapter 7).
- *Contests.* One of the most successful ways to promote information retention and/or a particular kind of behavior is to provide a competitive situation in which the winner receives something of value. Two of the most widely used contest ideas that involve drivers' families are essays or posters.
- *Films, slide shows, and videotapes.* A visual message communicates better than a spoken message. However, a combined visual and spoken message, such as a film, videotape, or slide show, is better yet.
- *Safety fair/company picnic/family night.* These events offer excellent opportunities to reach both the employees and their families.
- *Youth activities.* Sponsorship of activities like bicycle rallies can result in strong, positive community sentiment.
- *Recreational motor-vehicle program.* Company-sponsored clinics with registered or competent instructors that educate on the operation and inspection of motorcycles, bicycles, and other leisure-time vehicles are popular with employees and their families.
- *Vacation/holiday programs.* These are opportunities to offer safe-driving tips and promotional literature, especially regarding fatigue and driving too fast for conditions.
- *Safety talks.* Safety talks can cover both occupational and OTJ safety concerns at the same time.

Program topic ideas. Generally, individuals are more receptive to program topics or themes that coincide with their normal routines. Refer to Figure 15-1 for a chart that lists some of the major OTJ topics by season. Use this chart as the basis for developing OTJ safety program content.

The safety message also can be reinforced by offering drivers and

OTJ TRAFFIC SAFETY PROGRAM TOPICS BY SEASON		
SPRING	**FALL**	**YEAR-ROUND**
New signs, signals, pavement markings Motorcycles Recreational vehicles Vehicle maintenance Vacation safety	Back to school—young pedestrians Winter car maintenance—battery, snow tires, chains, defroster check	Railroad grade crossings Defensive driving Occupant protection—safety belts, child restraints Alcohol and other drug abuse Two-wheelers—bicycles mopeds, minibikes Roadside hazards
SUMMER	**WINTER**	
Trailer-towing Hot-weather vehicle maintenance—cooling system, tires	How to "jump start" a car Winter driving techniques—how to avoid getting stuck, how to handle a skid, etc. Snowmobiles	

Figure 15-1. *These off-the-job safety program topics all have a motor vehicle theme.*

other employees the chance to purchase safety equipment at wholesale prices. For instance, before summer and vacation time arrive, offer first aid kits and automotive restraints for children. A payroll deduction system can be set up to help make the purchase of these items more affordable. All the items sold should meet applicable quality control and safety standards.

Timing. Timing is important to the success of any program. Set an appropriate time interval between the initial announcement and each featured safety topic. Too-frequent change will not provide complete saturation. Leaving too much time between topic change can result in a loss of interest. The minimum time suggested for each topic is one month, or six months for the entire campaign. However, extending the campaign to nine or twelve months may be preferable in some cases.

Announcing the program

Before a new program is announced, several months of the program activities should already have been developed and be ready for use.

The different program phases can be covered several times in a year—when the overall OTJ safety program begins and at the start of each separate campaign within the program. Keep in mind during those times that support and participation can only be gained through awareness.

Advance publicity assures driver support by communicating the objectives, plans, and activities. An informal personalized letter from senior management sent to each employee's home emphasizes the organization's concern for the safety of the drivers and their families.

An initial introductory meeting for drivers can be followed by other meetings to which the members of the employee's family are also invited. The in-house publication can carry the word, too. Company bulletin boards, posters, and displays can reinforce the message. Also, a well-organized contest can promote involvement and generate enthusiasm.

Your company's ongoing job

Once an OTJ safety program has begun, continuing program responsibilities include:

- *Assess* previous and ongoing OTJ safety program activities.
- *Maintain* the wholehearted support and involvement of management, drivers, employees, and their families.
- *Survey* outside organizations to learn what programs worked and how well they worked.
- *Make changes* as necessary to revitalize individual programs.
- *Encourage* continuous programming ideas and feedback, possibly through a joint employee-management or OTJ committee, and an employee suggestion box.
- *Report periodically* the program's status to management.
- *Monitor, record, and publicize* your organization's progress in the eduction of OTJ fatalities, injuries, and illnesses. Let the drivers and their families know about the good job they're doing.

Recording and Classifying Data

Reporting OTJ accidents and injuries

In any OTJ safety program, accidents should be analyzed to find the most frequent causes of injury. This requires an effective accident-reporting procedure: the nature and primary causes must be obtained. How is this best done? By having uniform reports made through a predetermined channel. Reports should include:

- Name of employee involved in the accident.
- Date and time of day the accident took place.
- Brief description (such as "Painting 2nd-story window frame when ladder slipped").
- Nature of injury (such as "Broken right forearm, sprained back").
- Number of calendar days that employee was disabled. This can be an estimate. (When disability extends into more than one quarter of

the year, days in each quarter should be counted, but the accident should be counted only in the quarter in which it happened.)

A fleet has an absence and sickness reporting system which is used to operate the payroll. The OTJ accident reporting procedures can be added to this system.

Should submitting reports be voluntary or required? The system can be based upon voluntary employee cooperation or first-line supervisors can be made responsible for initiating the reports.

The voluntary approach is better than no system at all, and although it cannot give the complete picture, it gives leads and provides sufficient data to develop an effective prevention program. A sincerely conducted voluntary reporting program increases interest and cooperation.

When a required reporting system is used, sufficient information will be available in about six months to plan an effective program to combat the specific off-the-job accidents of fleet employees.

When either system is used, respect employees' privacy by keeping their names out of published materials: press releases, announcements, and company materials—unless given specific permission by the employees. Having had an accident can cause feelings of embarassment to the parties involved; the same code of privacy and confidentiality in regard to medical records would apply here.

Prior to finding specific accident information, concentrate on the major off-the-job accidents: slips, trips, falls, and automobile accidents.

Guidelines for measuring OTJ injury experience

Companies should use a uniform method for determining OTJ accident data. However, current methods of information gathering, recording, and measuring of employee accidental OTJ injuries may vary. Only when companies with OTJ safety programs record their accident data uniformly can the data necessary for computation of OTJ accidental injury frequency rates nationwide be determined.

When compiling OTJ accident data for computation of an overall OTJ accidental injury incidence rate, the following definitions should be considered:

EMPLOYEE—Any person on the company payroll, full or part time, at the time of injury. This excludes temporary or part-time agency persons who are paid directly by an outside agency.

EMPLOYEE'S FAMILY—Spouse or dependents of employee who live at home with employee and/or are covered under the employee's accident and health insurance plan.

RETIREE—Retired employee of employer who is covered under employer's accident and health insurance plan.

OTJ INJURY—An injury suffered by an employee or family member and retiree that does not arise out of an accident in the course of employment.

DAYS OF DISABILITY (employee OTJ injuries only)—A first day of disability is any full work shift or any full workday on which an employee is unable, because of OTJ injury, to perform the essential functions of his regularly established job.

In the case of permanent total disability, days of disability would be the number of days of inability to work between the date of the accident and the date that the company decides the employee will not be able to return to some form of gainful employment.

In the case of an OTJ fatality, the days of disability would be the number of days of inability to work between the date of the accident and the date of death. (If the death occurred on the day of the OTJ accident, there would be no days of disability recorded; however, the fatality is included in the total of OTJ accidents during the month in which the accident occurred.)

DEATH—Any OTJ injury which ultimately results in death regardless of the time intervening between the occurrence of the injury and death.

The exclusions under this definition include:

- Illness
- Suicide or attempted suicide
- Legal intervention—employee injuries experienced while resisting arrest, attempting to escape from, or disobeying the orders of a duly constituted officer of the law; a legal execution shall *not* be considered an OTJ injury.
- Military duty
- Moonlighting—any injury experienced while performing work for another employer for financial gain or while conducting personal business for profit shall *not* be counted. Any injury experienced while performing voluntary work for which there is no financial gain *shall* be counted.

Comparison of OTJ data

In 1973, the American National Standards Institute (ANSI) provided a statistical means of measuring OTJ injury experience—a standard known as ANSI Z16.3. This standard required the use of a 1,000,000 exposure-hour to determine OTJ injury incidence rates. This figure was chosen to agree with the then-current on-the-job work hour base (ANSI Z16.1). The 1,000,000 exposure-hour base is relatively simple to work with and can provide a basis for comparison with other on-the-job rates. Most companies now, however, follow the Occupational Safety and Health Administration's (OSHA) recordkeeping requirements for determining occupational injury incidence rates, which use a 200,000 work-hour base. An advantage to using this 200,000 exposure-hour base to determine the OTJ incidence rate is uniformity. This would allow meaningful comparison between occupational and off-the-job injury experiences.

For example, if your organization's OTJ disabling injury (loss of time from work) incidence rate was 5.0 for employees and your OSHA lost workday case incidence rate was 1.0, that would indicate that your organization was having 5 times more OTJ disabling injuries than job-related disabling injuries (per 200,000 hour unit of exposure). Therefore, the ANSI Z16.3 standard formula for measuring OTJ experience has been modified here so as to make OTJ and on-the-job injury comparisons possible. The modified formula for calculating OTJ injury incidence rates is:

$$\text{OTJ incidence rate} = \frac{\text{No. of OTJ disabling injuries} \times 200{,}000}{312 \times \text{Average number of employees} \times \text{Time period.}}$$

The "312" figure in the formula is based on the premise that an employee works 8 hours a day, 5 days a week. Excluding 8 hours for sleeping, this leaves 8 hours a day or 40 hours a work week OTJ exposure time. In addition, the employee has 2 days of 16 hours non-work exposure each week-end, making a total of (40 + 16 + 16) or 72 non-work exposure hours a week. The 72 hours multiplied by $4\frac{1}{3}$ weeks a month totals 312 hours of non-work exposure each month. Since overtime is considered to be offset by holidays, vacations, and other absences, no special allowance is provided for it.

There is an alternative way of estimating off-the-job exposure hours, but it has a higher percentage of error. This method is based on the assumption that there are 3,840 hours of active OTJ time per person per year. This figure is obtained as follows:

24 hours/day × 365 days	8,760 hours
Minus work time	−2,000 hours
	6,760 hours
Minus sleep 8 hours/day × 365 days	−2,920 hours
	3,840 hours

A simplified method of calculating off-the-job exposure hours is to multiply on-the-job exposure hours by 1.9. This factor (actually 1.92, a 1 percent difference) is the ratio of OTJ hours to work-hours (3,840 –

2,000 = 1.9 rounded to one decimal place). Therefore, by multiplying 1.9 times a location's occupational exposure hours, the off-the-job exposure hours for that location can easily be estimated.

Using this method; the incidence rate formula may be expressed as:

$$\text{OTJ incidence rate} = \frac{\text{No. of OTJ disabling injuries} \times 200{,}000}{1.9 \times \text{On-the-job exposure hours.}}$$

This rate relates the total number of OTJ injuries to the total hours of exposure during a specified period of time, and expresses them in terms of 200,000-hour exposure.

Example: The following calculation shows the OTJ disabling injury incidence rate for a group of 100 employees experiencing one OTJ injury for one month.

Note: Work hours for 100 employees equals 17,300; this × 1.9 = 32,870 OTJ exposure hours for the month.

$$\frac{1 \times 200{,}000}{32{,}870} = 6.08 \text{ Incidence rate}$$

These incidence rate formulas are an integral part of your company's measurement system. Over a period of months, evaluation of your findings can help to determine the progress being made in improving your organization's OTJ injury experience.

Rates are normally computed for employee exposures only. If spouse, dependent(s), and retiree OTJ injury experience are also being recorded, it would be difficult to calculate OTJ injury rates for them because their OTJ exposures vary tremendously. Usually, raw numbers and costs are reported and categorized separately from employee OTJ injury experience.

Evaluating results

Although it is difficult at times to measure how many accidents an OTJ safety program has actually *prevented,* "bottom-line results" *can* be measured. These results would include the reduction in overall OTJ injury rates and OTJ injury costs.

For instance, an overall reduction in motorcycle injuries following a special campaign to promote motorcycle safety would suggest a possible cause-and-effect relationship. However, other variables besides the motorcycle safety campaign may also have affected the reduction in injuries, such as little rain may have fallen during the spring and summer, thus reducing hazardous driving conditions. In the absence of exposure information and controlled studies, the assumption of the effectiveness of the safety campaign is about all that one has to go on.

Other factors that affect the results of an OTJ safety program are:

1. The employees' attitudes about themselves, their families, and their place of employment.
2. If your organization has both an occupational and an OTJ safety program, the success of one program cannot be divorced totally from the other. Both efforts should be coordinated.

Audits. Periodically, audits should be made of the OTJ safety program in order to measure the quantity and quality of your organization's efforts to prevent OTJ accidents. An audit may include the following questions:

- Is there appropriate OTJ accident information on both employees and their families?
- What is the OTJ performance record in this area?
- How many OTJ safety meetings with employees are there?
- What is the quality of those OTJ safety meetings with employees?
- Are the OTJ safety meetings being monitored or audited by management?
- Are there performance critiques of the speaker?
- What type of OTJ material is being distributed to employees and their families?
- Are families of employees being exposed to OTJ safety through print media, community meetings, television, radio, films, videotapes, slide shows, or a combination of these?
- Have readership and viewer surveys been done to determine the quality and use of these OTJ materials?
- Are there reports from employees on lives saved and serious accidents prevented?

Monitor and record your organization's OTJ injury experience (see Figure 15-2) and change or modify your program as necessary. Keep management informed of the progress.

Successful OTJ Safety Programs

Safety belt campaign

When the safety task force at Kodak in Rochester, N.Y., set out to do an OTJ safety program to encourage the use of safety restraints, they wanted to appeal to each employee's "common sense" concern for safety. The program consisted of timed distributions of brochures, stickers, posters, and greeting cards.

EMPLOYEE OTJ INJURY REPORT FORM

DIV. ________ LOCATION ________ MONTH ________ YEAR ________

Total No. of Off-Job Injuries This Month: ________
Year-To-Date ________

Transportation	1 No. Cases	2 No. Fatal-ities	3 Days Lost	4 Days Old Cases	5 Tot. Cal. Days Lost This Month
Motor Vehicle:					
Auto. Truck					
a) Collision					
b) Repair work					
c) Pedestrian					
d) Miscellaneous					
Bus Streetcar					
Bicycle					
Motorcycle, Moped					
Railroad					
Aircraft					
Watercraft					
Other					
TOTAL					

Total Calendar Days Lost This Month: ________
Year-To-Date ________

Home	1 No. Cases	2 No. Fatal-ities	3 Days Lost	4 Days Old Cases	5 Tot. Cal. Days Lost This Month
Fall, Slip					
Fire, Explosion					
Firearm					
Animals, Insects					
Exposure: Heat, Cold					
Lifting					
Pushing, Pulling					
Struck By Object					
Struck Against Object					
Toxic Material					
Electricity					
Machinery, Tools					
Sharp Object					
Other					
TOTAL					

Total No. of Fatalities This Month: ________
Year-To-Date ________

Public	1 No. Cases	2 No. Fatal-ities	3 Days Lost	4 Days Old Cases	5 Tot. Cal. Days Lost This Month
Fall, Slip					
Fire, Explosion					
Firearm					
Animals, Insects					
Exposure: Heat, Cold					
Lifting					
Pushing, Pulling					
Struck by Object					
Struck Against Object					
Toxic Material					
Fight, Assault					
Sports					
Recreation					
Other					
TOTAL					

Col. 1. **Number Cases.** Include all off-the-job **Injuries** occurring this month when one or more working days are lost.
Col. 2. **Number Fatalities.** Include all fatalities occurring this month.
Col. 3. **Days Lost.** Total calendar days lost on injuries occuring this month.
Col 4. **Days Old Cases.** Records **additional days** lost this month due to injuries previously reported.
Col 5. Total calendar days lost this month (Cols. 3 + 4).
Total Number of Off-Job Injuries This Month (Cols. 1 + 2—Include Fatalities).

Fatal Injuries: Give brief description of accident below. If death results from injury reported previously, refer to month and classification of original reporting.

Remarks: ________

________ ________
Report Prepared By **Date**

Figure 15-2. *Employee off-the-job injury report form.*
From "OTJ Safety Program Manual."

Response to the safety restraint campaign was both enthusiastic and effective, as shown in before-and-after surveys of safety belt use conducted by Kodak's safety task force.

One month before the campaign started, the traffic that entered the plant parking lot was recorded according to the number of people who arrived at work with their safety belts fastened. The lot held up to 4,000 vehicles and provided a sampling of Kodak Park's total employee population of 30,000 (at the time), according to Kodak's statistics. The first survey established a benchmark before the campaign started. It showed 13.8 percent of the drivers entering the lot were wearing their safety belts. At the time of the survey, this percentage of safety belt use was close to the national average.

The second survey, taken two months after the program began, showed belt usage had increased to 16.4 percent. This was 2.6 percent higher than before and slightly above the statistical margin of error of two percent.

The real proof of success for Kodak came on the third survey, held five months later, in which 19.5 percent of the drivers observed were wearing their safety belts. This was an increase of 3.1 percent over the second survey, and 5.7 percent over the pre-campaign survey.

OTJ injuries reduced by 47 percent

Armco, Inc., a diversified metals fabricator, had a most convincing reason for starting its OTJ safety program in 1979—the discovery that eight times as many of its people were being hurt off the job as were being hurt at work. Armco put some of its on-the-job safety know-how to work in preventing accidents and injuries off the job and began a program called "Safety for the Family."

Armco's OTJ statistical evidence is striking. Recent reports showed the total number of Armco people killed in OTJ accidents was down from sixteen to only one in four years. And the total number of OTJ injuries to Armco employees was down forty-seven percent in five years. Days lost from work because of OTJ injuries was down thirty-six percent. And the OTJ injury frequency rate had been reduced by twenty-three percent.

Although Armco statistics point to success at preventing OTJ accidents, Armco admits that it is not possible to determine exactly how or why people change their behavior. The bottom line, however, is that Armco employees are having fewer accidents off the job.

Hazards corrected

A cement company conducted a home fire safety campaign over a period of several weeks. It used departmental meetings, bulletin board notices, and posters.

Although it was impossible to estimate how many home fires, if any, were prevented by the company's effort, the feedback from the employees indicated the material was well received and that it did result in a number of hazards being corrected.

No serious accidents

A mining company, located in a small community, used several programming tools to prevent injuries to employees and their families over the vacation period. The in-house publication, the local news media, posters, and reference booklets were used.

Was the campaign a success? The company believes it was. Not one employee was injured or involved in a serious accident during the vacation period. The year before when there was no extensive campaign, there were 23 serious accidents of which two were fatal.

OTJ and community safety programs *do* work, and their importance cannot be overemphasized. The integration of an OTJ safety program with a fleet safety program can increase the cost-effectiveness of your company's operation, because the safe way is, usually, the most efficient way.

Appendices

Appendix A

Getting Publicity from 'Safe Driver Awards'

Many times company publications and local newspapers, radio, and TV will carry a story based on presentation of "Safe Driver Awards" (also of "Safe Worker Awards," see Chapter 7). But to carry a story, they must know in advance that these awards are going to be presented.

The news media are alert to the public's interest in the street and highway accident problem. With over 46,000 persons killed in the U.S. each year, and more than 1.7 million persons injured in motor vehicle accidents every year, hardly a family in our nation has been left unaffected. Moreover, virtually everyone either operates or frequently rides in a motor vehicle and should therefore be interested in safe driving.

Pictures and personality sketches of the drivers being recognized at the award presentation or a story about the accident prevention program are certain to attract reader interest and result in goodwill for your company, as well as promote interest in better driving. The award presentation itself can build goodwill. Community knowledge that your company has many award-winning safe drivers can result in sales being directed your way.

How To Prepare for Publicity

Advance planning counts. Plan the program and set the date at least a month ahead for daily and weekly media, three months for monthly magazines and newsletters. This permits the story to be printed about the same time the award is made. Some media will cover the presentation itself. Your company publication will probably do both.

The amount of publicity will usually be in proportion to the importance you place upon the awards, the number of awards, and the length of time between awards. You can't make a big event over one or two awards given each month, but you can over 15 or 20 awards given once a year. Company officers can be present—city and state officials can be invited. Some firms invite a representative of the police department, usually the traffic captain. Inviting a representative of the local safety organization is also a good idea.

What to expect

Each edition of a newspaper or a magazine needs fresh news. Community papers and regional editions of larger papers feature local people, companies, and events. Editors know this increases readership.

However, since the space is limited and the competition for coverage is strong, there is no assurance that every editor contacted will allot space to the story. Chances for media coverage are greatly increased when the information is sent well in advance of the event, and is presented in a short, clear, and interesting manner. A widely accepted method is to mail a news release (see Figure A-1) with photo, if available, and some background information on the company to the attention of the community affairs editor.

When preparing a news release, remember that editors are trained to ask these questions about all stories—who? why? what? when? where? and how? So tell them—*who* is getting the awards and *who* will be there to give them; *why* this event is important to the editor and to the readers he serves; *what* the award means; *when* the event will take place; *where* it will be held; and *how* the editors can get more details if they want them

Give them the facts. Let them determine their relative importance. Of course, try to present the facts in such a way that they will interest the editor. The editor usually tries to find some "angle," some approach to handling the story that will appeal to his readers and be different from the stories other news media carry. Work with him if he asks you to.

The news release will not only contain details of the ceremonies, but also tell about the award winners themselves. Some editors may send over a photographer. Others may ask you to get photographs for them. Usually, you'll want to take your own pictures whether they take them or not.

Three to four persons in a photograph are usually tops. Photos should have some action—even a nice smile gives some variety to the "present plaque—give handshake" routine.

A company official and the award recipients can be photographed ahead of the event, in a simulated ceremony, when photos are needed to accompany an advance news release. A simple method of preparing the news release follows:

Fast Delivery Service, a company operating a fleet of 50 delivery trucks, has just received "Safe Driver" awards from the National Safety Council. Fifteen of its drivers have operated their vehicles for at least a year without a preventable accident. The safety director lists the following facts as help in preparing a story for the local newspapers.

Who? Fast Delivery Service, Evansville, Indiana.
What? Presentation of National Safety Council Safe Driver awards.

National recognition for safe driving to 15 of 55 drivers.

List the winners as follows:

4 Years	3 Years	2 Years	1 Year
______	______	______	______
______	______	______	______
______	______	______	______
______	______	______	______

When? The awards are to be presented by the company president, Craig Wilson, to the qualifying drivers on Thursday, June 15, at 7:00 p.m. A list of the guests expected to be present would follow; it would give their names, titles, their company names and addresses.

Where? The awards are to be made at a dinner meeting at the Johnson Inn.

Why? Awards are given in recognition of 15 drivers having driven a total of 100,000 miles, four times the distance around the earth, during the past year without having a preventable accident.

Other Highlights. Other outstanding figures or facts pertaining to the fleet as a whole, the drivers as a group, or their safety program would be mentioned here.

Statements. Quotes from the president's presentation speech, the National Safety Council statement, and guest speakers are listed.

The safety director then writes the story in a news release format (See Figure A-1). The news release should be typed on company stationery with the words "NEWS RELEASE" typed in bold lettering near the top of the page. It is important that the name and phone number of the safety director, or other contact person, be given in the release.

Company Name
Address
Phone Number

For Your Information:
Name and Title
Phone Number
For release by June 15

NEWS RELEASE

Four times around the earth, 100,000 miles, driven this year without a preventable accident.

JUNE 15, 19--. That's the record 15 drivers for the Fast Delivery Service set during the past year on the streets of Evansville and its suburbs. In recognition of their accomplishments, the drivers were presented with National Safety Council Safe Driver awards. The presentations were made at a dinner held tonight at the Johnson Inn that was attended by all drivers in the Fast Delivery Service fleet.

27,000 Safe Miles

Those drivers honored: John Smith, 1608 Maple Avenue, 1st year award; Vicki Brown, 458 E. Second Street, 2nd year award; and Harold Klien, 103 Fifth Avenue, 3rd year award.

Smith had the best safety record, operating his truck 27,000 safe miles during the past year.

Klien compiled his safety record despite volunteering to drive under almost impossible conditions during the recent floods near Evansville. He transported drinking water around the clock to needy families, often with part of his truck submerged in the flood waters.

Green Praises Drivers

In the winter, the drivers provide a real public service by keeping the roads open, clearing their routes with a huge, specially built snow plow-equipped tractor.

Figure A-1. *This news release presents the facts in a clear and interesting manner; it would have a good chance of obtaining media coverage of the safety awards ceremony.*

Traffic Captain Henry Green, speaking briefly at the dinner, gave tribute to the winners' fine records. He said, "You have proved safe driving is a good investment. I hope your example will be followed by every driver in the city. It goes to show what caution and good sense behind the wheel can do."

Green pointed out that five persons had met death in our city in automobile accidents since New Year's Day. "Everyone of these accidents could have been prevented had the drivers shown the courtesy and care exercised by you award winners," he asserted.

Accidents Down by 30 Percent

Craig Wilson, President of the Fast Delivery Service, cited official figures from the National Safety Council in his presentation talk, and noted that the overall company safety program had reduced the fleet's accident rate by more than 30 percent in the past year. He thanked the award winners and also voiced his appreciation to the entire group of drivers and other employees for their cooperation.

MEMBERS OF THE MEDIA. Photos of the award winners, biographical sketches of them and a company brochure are enclosed. For further information, or to arrange personal interviews, please contact: Name of safety director, and phone number.

Figure A-1*—concluded.*

Advertising Possibilities

Many companies—especially operators of passenger-carrying vehicles—stress safety in their advertising. Newspaper display advertising can be purchased to announce awards and to play up fleet safety records. Be sure to keep clear the distinction between advertising and publicity—advertising you pay for. Publicity is "free" (sometimes you work awfully hard to get it, though), and it is entirely up to the editor how much space you are going to get, if any. Although the editorial departments of the news media are friendly to advertisers, the editor must judge news on its merits.

Appendix B

Safety Meetings For Commercial Drivers

Safety meetings for drivers are an important part of any balanced motor fleet program. Management's reasons for holding safety meetings should be to arouse and maintain interest in accident and injury prevention, develop attitudes sympathetic to the safety program, and educate and train drivers and supervisory personnel in all facets of safe vehicle and equipment operation.

Group safety meetings can further the efficiency of all operations. They can cause a common bond of interest and a closer feeling of identity between coworkers that results in stronger company loyalties.

Classifications of Safety Meetings

There are numerous ways of classifying safety meetings, but the simplest and most direct groupings are: (*a*) motivational meetings, (*b*) recognition of accomplishments in accident prevention, (*c*) group instruction and training.

Motivational meetings

The purpose behind motivational meetings is to spark interest and encourage participation in the safety program. Current safety problems should be mentioned, along with management's proposals on how to minimize or eliminate the risks to drivers, employees, and company property. The supervisory personnel in charge of ongoing accident and injury prevention projects should give progress reports, stressing positive results, and ask for continuing and increased support of their efforts.

Management could mention any operating costs savings that have been realized because of a successful safety program. This should definitely be done when the costs reductions have caused additional benefits to be given to the drivers, such as, greater job security, higher wages, or a better employee benefit package.

The mood of the motivational meeting should be positive and encouraging; any favorable effect or by-product of the safety program would be an appropriate topic for discussion. Because safe driving is also courteous driving, an effective safety program will probably give management the opportunity to talk about an elevated company image within the community, and local media coverage of safety award ceremonies.

Recognition of accomplishments in accident prevention

These meetings are called as the occasion demands. This may be at the close of a contest or for presentation of bonuses or awards; or at any time for the express purpose of recognizing good records. The theme closely parallels that of the motivational gathering. The talks are positive and there is little opportunity for training. When practical it is desirable to hold a ceremony of this kind in conjunction with a meal function as this helps to give it the significance of an important event. These recognition meetings can be scheduled at times convenient for family and friends to attend. How to get maximum publicity from these awards meetings is discussed in Appendix A.

Group instruction and training

Drivers must understand the operating policies of the company and all the factors that enter into the safe and efficient handling of the business. They should be instructed in the elements of safe, courteous, and efficient driving and be informed about accidents that have occurred and how they could have been prevented. Group instruction and training affords the most practical medium for accident and injury prevention education and is indispensible to an effective safety program. Driver training is the subject of Chapter 9.

Factors to Consider

Scheduling

The first step in planning the program should be to arrange a schedule of meetings extending over a designated period such as six or 12 months. This schedule should be considered as a course of safety education and each meeting planned to cover a desired objective. Safety meetings are far too important to call on short notice without (*a*) careful consideration of the field to be covered and (*b*) intelligent selection of the discussion subjects. The topics and outline for each meeting can be put into a booklet sent out at the beginning of the year, and furnished to each location where meetings are required.

Type of meeting

Specialized meetings. Most meetings can be planned to be of interest to all drivers. In large fleets, however, where the operations include several distinct types of driving it may be advantageous to schedule separate meetings for different groups. Even when this practice is followed it is advisable to hold several meetings during the year for all personnel. The program for these gatherings can be planned accordingly. Employees should not be required to attend meetings where the instruction and training is irrelevant to their particular work.

Small meetings. The size and nature of the fleet will determine arrangement of meeting schedules. Operations in scattered locations or including more than one shift may necessitate smaller groups. Regardless of how small the meetings may be, they should be scheduled and planned in advance. Even in fleets of no more than three to five vehicles, regular meetings should be held where drivers and the owner or manager get together to discuss safety. In small meetings of this kind, more emphasis can be placed on group discussion, and dinner meetings can often be held.

Short meetings. Many of the firms that do not hold regular meetings of an hour or more conduct brief meetings lasting 10 to 15 minutes. The general practice is to hold these meetings at least once a week and, in some instances, they are made a part of each workday. Because of their brevity, in many cases they can be held during the day or at close of work.

At the end of the day, however, drivers are tired and anxious to get home and by the next morning the safety message is forgotten. For this reason the early morning meeting is far superior; the employees are receptive and receive the safety message at a time when it will do the most good—just before they set out for the day's work. Some fleets have been successful in holding "safety breakfasts."

It is not necessary to accomplish actual training or to enter into detailed discussion at short meetings. Their purpose is more for inspection or issuance of warnings about current, daily hazards. Usually, one subject is treated at each meeting. Some firms using this plan prepare special bulletins which are read to the group and then posted on the bulletin board for future reference. Such bulletins can be used to caution drivers about seasonal hazards.

Full-length meetings. Extensive educational meetings require more time. It is the general opinion, however, that with the exception of dinner meetings and other special events, full-length meetings should not exceed one hour. A one-hour (or less) program each month is preferable to longer sessions every two or three months.

During the full-length meeting, instructions should be given to improve driving techniques. This training should be supplemented by a thorough analysis of the accident experience as well as a discussion of recent accidents. Continuous training is necessary for both new and old drivers.

Generally, it is not advisable to attempt to cover more than two subjects at any one meeting, even if it is a long one.

Meeting times

Conditions peculiar to each fleet govern the hour at which meetings are held. In many operations, it is practically impossible to hold meetings during working hours because not all drivers can be present at the same time. Dinner meetings are held during non-working hours.

Regardless of the hour at which meetings are held it is important that they be scheduled at regular intervals such as the second Tuesday of every month. Select a time when most employees are able to attend. In most operations, the second week of the month is good because summaries of the accident experience for the preceding month will have been prepared and can be discussed at the meeting.

Some fleets do not schedule full-length meetings during the summer months but substitute early morning sessions so the routine will not be disrupted. Many fleets have more accidents during November, December, January, and February, and find it to their advantage to schedule full-length meetings beginning in fall.

Meeting places

The meeting place should be free from noise or other distractions. Short 10 or 15 minute meetings may be held in the garage, if suitable facilities are available. But longer sessions require a room with adequate heat, light, and acoustics. Some transportation companies use a mobile trailer as a classroom. This can be either a large travel trailer or a truck semi-trailer. The unit is equipped with heat and air conditioning, light-proof windows, audiovisual equipment, and chalkboards. It might have mockups of mechanical systems. Usually it can be plugged into a building's electric supply and parked conveniently. Such a training unit can be easily shuttled between terminals.

Teaching rooms are described under "Where to teach" in Chapter 9, "Driver Training."

Subjects To Cover

Although the major emphasis should be placed on instruction and training, provision should also be made for the motivational theme. The proportion of time allocated to each phase is largely determined by the accident experience of the fleet, the interest of the employees and the tone of their morale. Some of the more important subjects which should be covered are listed below. They need not be taken in the order given but those that are pertinent to the most serious problems of the particular operation should receive attention first.

Thorough explanation of operating and public relations policies of the firm.

Instruction in driving practices, courtesy, and safety in general.

Traffic rules and regulations: Explanation of the purpose, intent, and language of the regulations.

Mechanics of the vehicle, its care and maintenance. Whenever possible, these demonstrations should be conducted by expert mechanics or specialists.

Explanation of the physical problems involved in driving such as reaction time, stopping distance, skidding, passing distance, centrifugal force, and force or impact.

Accidents: A thorough coverage of past accidents, common situations, unusual accidents, seasonal hazards, what to do in case of an accident, and how to report an accident. An analysis of the major types of accidents, from frequency and severity standpoints. Drivers participate in discussions of their causes and prevention. Mention costs, trends, prevalent types, and accident repeaters.

First aid and general health: The importance of first aid; value of regular physical examinations; discussion of fatigue, illness, and general health; and explanation of company policy with respect to these subjects.

Loading and unloading. How to lift large and small articles, proper storage of cargo, and handling of passengers are three examples.

Necessity for and proper use of special equipment such as emergency warning equipment, flags, chains, standards, foglights, spot lights, tarpaulins, ropes, tailgates, the fifth wheel, air brake equipment and connections, lighting equipment and connections.

Special safety topics such as hazardous materials handling, and treatment of passenger problems.

Open forum with questions to be asked and answered.

A full discussion of "What to Teach" is given in Chapter 9, "Driver Training."

Planning the Program

Just as the meetings should be scheduled in advance, each program should be planned sufficiently ahead of time to assure its success. Variety and unique methods are needed to maintain interest and ensure attendance; drivers must look forward to each meeting. Strive to make the program interesting, entertaining, and educational. Do not become discouraged if the first meetings fall short of this goal. Continued poor attendance by employees calls for a review of planning and handling techniques.

The chairman should prepare a training plan (or it may be done for all locations by a central safety department). The plan shows the key discussion points on the right side of the sheet, with the trainer's actions on the left (such as, "write accident rate on chalkboard"). The plan should include a list of materials needed for the meeting. (See sample plan in Figure B-1.)

Type of Speakers

Specialists and instructors. The selection of the specialists who will be instructing is very important. They should be able to talk authoritatively, instill confidence, and convince listeners of the benefits of safety. Unqualified speakers or teachers cause employees to lose confidence and interest. Outside speakers add variety but should not be

SAMPLE TRAINING SESSION PLAN

Meeting date: October 15th
Topic: Forklift Safety
Meeting times: 0630-0730-0830 (30 minute meeting)
Location: Terminal Conference Room
Group: Dock and Local Drivers

Materials needed:
15 copies of company forklift rules for each session (total 45)
List of forklift injuries this year.
NSC poster showing forklift accident
Chalkboard Eraser
Chalk 3 Sign in sheets

What To Do	What To Say
PUT *14* ON BLACKBOARD. HAND OUT SIGN IN SHEET.	1. Open meeting: a) Greetings b) Intro Terminal Manager-*brief remarks* by him.
WRITE "**FORKLIFT INJURIES**" AFTER 14.	2. There have been 14 forklift injuries in the company this year; compared to 9 a year ago.
	3. (Read descriptions of forklift injuries. Don't allow comment yet).
WRITE *3* ON BOARD.	4. Three of the injuries were here. (Discuss result of John Brown case).
HOLD UP POSTER. WRITE POINTS ON BOARD.	5. How can you keep this from happening to you? a) Pretrip your lift before using it b) Look where you are driving c) Hold your speed down d) Keep forks down when empty e) *Never* enter trailer unless wheels are blocked f) Don't run forklift into a bobtail unless supervisor approves g) Use horn or pause at blind aisles h) Fuel lifts only in Bay 2 and put gas can back in proper place i) No horseplay j) Be extra careful for other workers when moving in a trailer k) No riding on forks or loads l) No pulling with chains to mast m) Never raise forks above six feet. Watch mast height in trailer
HAND OUT FORKLIFT RULES.	6. Here is your copy of the posted company forklift rules. Sign the attached slip and turn it in as you leave. Keep the rules and refer to them.
COLLECT SIGN IN LIST.	7. There will be a brief test on these rules next meeting.
WRITE "**NOVEMBER 12TH**" ON BOARD.	8. Thanks for attending. The next safety meeting is November 12th.

AFTER THE MEETING, PREPARE MEETING REPORT FORM 23 AND SUBMIT IT TO THE SAFETY DEPARTMENT.

Figure B-1. *Sample training session plan.*

used for a major share of the program. Persons not familiar with the details peculiar to each fleet may make conflicting statements if required to cover too broad a subject. A company's policies and procedures manual should be furnished to all employees engaged in a supervisory capacity. It will guide those who act as instructors in presenting recommended practices correctly and uniformly.

Company officials. The fleet safety director or other persons responsible for safety should preside over the meeting. In addition, at least one official of the firm should participate in every meeting. This is of utmost importance in demonstrating management's interest and support. If possible, this assignment should be rotated throughout the year among different executives. By scheduling subjects in advance, impromptu talks can be discouraged. A well-directed 10-minute talk by the management representative is usually sufficient. Courtesy, company plans for the future, employees' welfare, plant deliveries, progress, and financial condition are suggested subjects.

Insurance company representatives. The insurance company representative can help by taking part in the meeting program. It must be remembered, however, that he services other fleets and cannot be expected to know every detail of operation peculiar to each fleet.

Training aids and quizzes

Training aids and quizzes are discussed in Chapter 9.

Door prizes

Many fleets introduce some sort of a door prize to stimulate attendance. The expense involved is small and the results exceptionally good. One plan is for the employees who attend to place their names in a box at the beginning of the meeting. At the close of the meeting, the winning card is drawn from the box. One fleet uses a $10 bill as a prize at every meeting. Other prizes which may be used are parts of uniforms, safety shoes, tools, goggles, pen and pencil sets, gloves, and household and personal items. This plan reduces tardiness because the cards must be deposited before the meeting begins.

As a refinement, the card can carry a safety message and be given out at one meeting, to be collected at the next for a drawing. Drivers with accidents that month would not be eligible. If everyone goes accident-free, the pot might be doubled.

Program arrangement

The character of the program and the sequence in which the various parts should be presented depends, of course, on the type of meeting.

An essential requisite of every safety meeting is stimulating interest. There must be no lag in the discussions, no lull in the proceedings, and no tiresome or aimless digressions from the subjects. Quickly moving meetings bring the best results. Typical program features are listed below:

Motivational program where good records are recognized:

1. Dinner (often with music)
2. Entertainment (if desired)
3. Introduction of visitors (by chairman)
4. Address of welcome and preliminary remarks
5. Principal speaker
6. Presentation of awards (by the firm president or manager)
7. Closing remarks (by chairman).

Group instruction and training type of meeting:

1. Roll call (or pass sign in sheet)
2. Introduction of visitors (by chairman)
3. Preliminary remarks with emphasis on high frequency types of accidents to be discussed at this meeting (by the person responsible for safety)
4. Films or other visual aids on the subject
5. Discussion by person responsible for safety, followed by an open forum
6. Summary and conclusion (by chairman).

A buffet lunch is appropriate to this type of meeting. Some firms feel that if the lunch precedes the meeting the employees are in a more receptive mood for the meeting which follows. Others are of the opinion that there is a decided value in the good fellowship and discussions which result from the mingling of the employees in the meeting room when food is served at the close of the meeting.

Conducting the Meeting

Chairman. The person responsible for the safety program, the drivers' immediate supervisor, or some selected representative of management should preside.

Relevancy. The chairman must be sensitive to digressions from the essential purpose and tactfully guide the meeting along the course.

Criticism. Criticism evokes resentment rather than willing cooperation and has no place in the meeting. Individuals should not be corrected or reprimanded during group gatherings; discipline should be handled by private conference at other times. Of course, the correction of individual faults is covered indirectly during general discussions of bad practices.

Formality. The meetings should be conducted in an orderly manner with sufficient formality to lend the program dignity and respect but not be overdone to the extent of making it stiff and boring. It should be started, carried through, and adjourned according to schedule. Humor should not be injected where it will detract from emphasis on serious points.

Personal touch. Collection of invitation cards at the door by an official of the firm affords an opportunity for a personal handshake or greeting and tends to stimulate attendance. Also it serves to express management's interest and to add credibility to the proceedings.

Attendance. A record should be kept of all those in attendance at each meeting. One safety director sends a personal note to the home of each absent driver to tell him that he was missed at the meeting, and expresses the hope that he will be present at the next one.

Notification of Meeting and Publicity

Announce the meeting well in advance, giving details such as time, place, and the nature of the program. Notices are more impressive when signed by the person in charge of safety or other official. They should be posted on all bulletin boards and published in employee publications. Some firms inform drivers of meetings by letter. Others issue invitation cards or tickets. Those are collected at the meeting and often must be signed by the person attending.

Of course, attendance at meetings held during working hours can be mandatory; this is the rule in many companies. The expenditures involved usually return big dividends to the companies, because the biggest weakness of voluntary safety meetings is that those who need the message most are the least likely to show up.

Develop interest in the meeting by building it up through publicity channels. Report regularly in company publications interesting developments in connection with each meeting. Keep employees informed of the purpose of each meeting and the subjects that will be discussed.

Importance of Details

Many meetings fail because seemingly insignificant matters are not taken care of beforehand. An ample number of chairs, for instance, should be placed in an orderly arrangement before the meeting begins. The room must be kept at a comfortable temperature and be well ventilated. Provision should be made for a place to put hats and coats. Drinking water should be furnished for speakers. If films or slides are used, windows must have shades which will keep out light, and a screen of adequate size must be provided. Spare projector light bulbs should be available, as well as necessary extension cords.

Appendix C

Skill Drills and Test Courses

Skill drills and test courses are used to train new drivers as well as to test the skills of trained drivers.

This course is based on the National Truck Driving Championship of the American Trucking Associations, Inc., 2200 Mill Road, Alexandria, Va. 22314. Copies of the book, *The National Truck Driving Championship,* may be ordered from its Department of Safety.

The National Truck Driving Championship, formerly called the Roadeo, is designed to determine, through a series of challenging competitive events, the contestant's knowledge of safety, courtesy, efficiency, first aid, and driving skill. In addition to being a testing and training device, the Roadeo serves as a community goodwill project and promotes better employee relations.

To be eligible to take the entrance tests, a contestant must have had at least one year's service as a professional truck driver, and a minimum of one year of accident-free driving. Preliminary tests consist of a written examination on the trucking industry, safe driving rules, first aid, and firefighting. The contestant is then given a personal interview to judge his attitude, general appearance and self-expression.

Following the interview, an equipment defects test is administered to grade his ability to properly conduct a pretrip inspection of his vehicle. Lastly, he competes in the field test course, which is a series of driving problems simulating everyday operating conditions.

Some of these skill tests in a typical Roadeo are described below. They can be changed to suit the training situation, and additional problems may be added.

A general layout of a test course is shown in Figure C-1. Dimensions can be adjusted to fit the size and type of vehicle that is being driven.

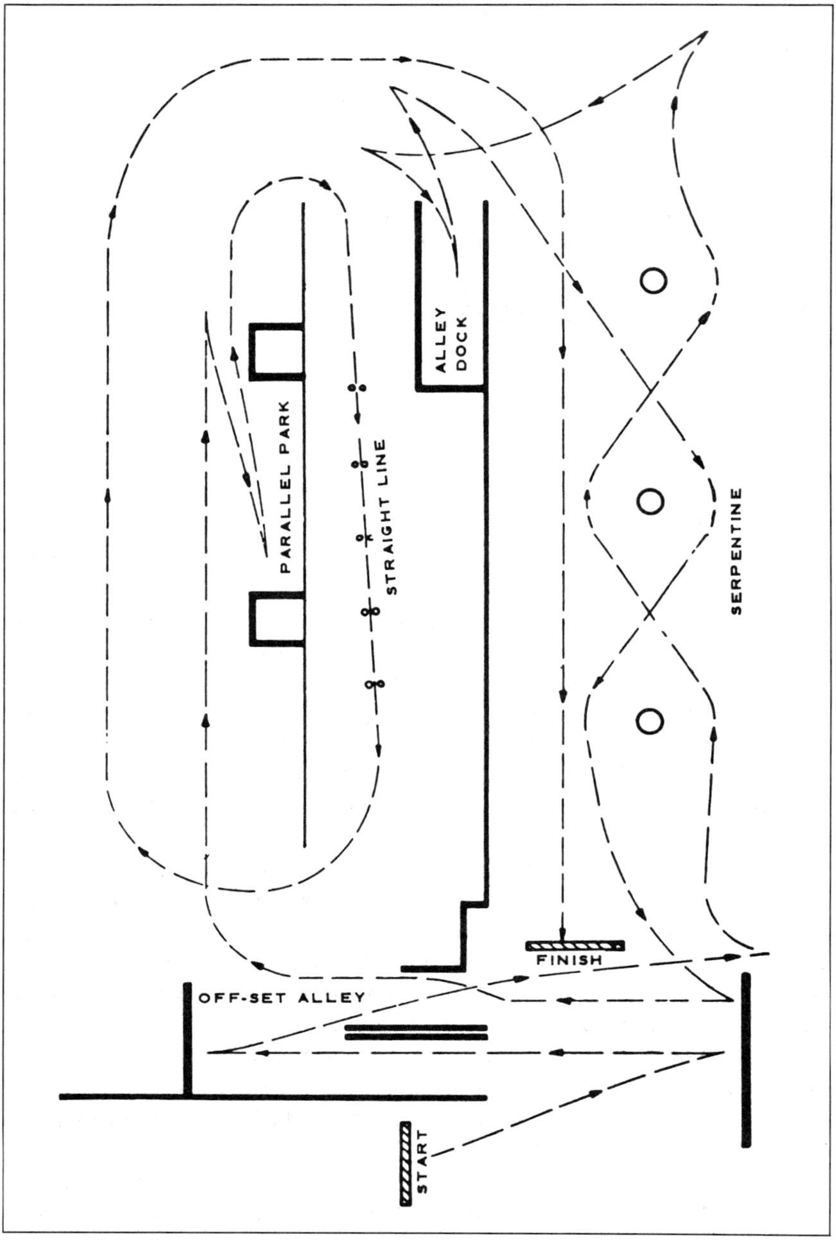

Figure C-1. *General design of the field test course used for the National Truck Driving Championship.*

American Trucking Associations, Inc., Alexandria, Va.

Parallel parking

The object of this test is to determine the driver's ability to park parallel to a simulated curb as in making a curbside street delivery, or in moving the unit off to the side of the road.

Alley dock

This test determines the driver's ability to back his vehicle into a narrow space. He is expected to back through a restricted area without hitting either side, and must stop close to, but not touching, the dock.

Offset alley

Here, the driver is judged on his skill in making a right turn, in a continuous movement, through a confined space. He is expected to properly control his speed while avoiding touching the two pairs of barricades.

Forward serpentine

In this test, the driver's ability to maneuver the vehicle in and out of tight places in forward movement is tested. It is designed to simulate conditions that might be encountered: when disabled or wrecked vehicles partially block a highway; in negotiating detours; moving in heavy traffic; when unusual situations require expert skill and control of the vehicle. In the skill drill, the driver must drive around drums or barrels arranged somewhat like a slalom run for skiers.

Backward serpentine

This test is similar to the above, except that vehicle movement is backward. It is designed to test the driver's ability to back his vehicle into narrow places.

Straight line

This test challenges the ability of the driver to accurately judge the position of the right wheels of his vehicle and to steer the vehicle in a straight line. It simulates conditions in which the driver must keep as far to the right as possible as on narrow streets and highways when meeting oncoming traffic. It helps him to gage distances on the righthand side of the pavement to avoid running off onto a highway shoulder with the resultant danger of loss of control, tire abuse, and "dusting" of the following traffic.

Stop line

Here the driver's ability to judge the position of his front bumper with respect to a fixed line is challenged. This problem simulates the conditions encountered in stopping at a marked crosswalk, or a situation in which it is advantageous for the driver to pull as far forward as possible in close quarters without hitting a stationary object or vehicle.

Drivers successfully negotiating the test courses are sometimes awarded certificates or trophies as proof of their expert driving abilities.

Watching a truck driving championship can be exciting for company employees and the general public. Companies planning these events should send press releases to their local media to receive advance publicity and press coverage (see Appendix A).

Appendix D

Work-Related Motor Vehicle Injuries

According to preliminary estimates by Alan Hoskin, manager of the Statistics Department of the National Safety Council, work-related motor vehicle accidents caused about 4,100 fatalities and 200,000 disabling injuries in 1985. Motor vehicle accidents are the leading cause of occupational fatalities, accounting for about 35 percent of the total.

Detailed data on this significant problem is rare. Police reports of motor vehicle accidents do not record whether or not those persons involved were traveling in the course of employment. Workers' compensation case reports could be used, but until recently it was very difficult to combine data from two or more states to get a picture of the national experience. That has changed with the development of the Supplementary Data System (SDS) by the Bureau of Labor Statistics (BLS). The SDS combines the workers' compensation reports of several states into a single file and makes the data available on computer tapes and in standard tabulations on microfiche.

The results summarized here are based on the standard tabulations published by BLS for the 1981 data year.

Occupant vs. nonoccupant

The SDS tabulations use the term "motor vehicle accident" to apply only to cases in which in injured person was an occupant of a highway-type vehicle. These cases accounted for 2.6 percent of all reported cases. However, in looking at motor vehicles as a source of injury, 8.0 percent of all work-related injuries were motor vehicle involvements. The other types of accident in which a motor vehicle was the source of injury were "struck by or against" (most likely pedestrian-motor vehicle collisions), 2.2 percent; "overexertion," 1.5 percent; "caught in or between," 1.0 percent; "falls," 0.5 percent; and all other types, 0.2 percent.

TABLE D-1

COMPARISON OF MOTOR VEHICLE RELATED INJURIES
TO ALL INJURIES
Major Industry Groups, 1981

Major Industry Group	Percent Distribution		
	All Injuries	MV Injuries	Employment
Private Sector	100.0%	100.0%	100.0%
Agriculture, forestry, and fishing	3.3	3.8	3.6
Mining and quarrying	2.5	2.7	1.2
Construction	10.4	7.8	6.3
Manufacturing	37.3	15.4	23.0
durable goods	24.4	8.4	13.9
nondurable goods	12.9	7.0	9.1
Transportation and public utilities	7.8	29.2	7.0
Wholesale trade	7.0	10.9	4.2
Retail trade	15.8	9.9	17.3
Finance, insurance, and real estate	1.8	4.0	6.4
Services	14.1	16.2	31.0

Source: Bureau of Labor Statistics, Supplementary Data System, 1981, cases involving disability, data from 17 states.
Bureau of Labor Statistics, *Employment and Earnings, 29* (1), p. 167, "Employed persons by industry and occupation," household data, annual averages.

The remainder of this analysis deals only with cases where the type of accident was reported as "motor vehicle accident;" i.e., with motor vehicle occupants only.

Industry

Table D-1 shows the distribution across major industry groups of all injuries, motor vehicle-related injuries and employment. As expected, the most common industry for motor vehicle accident is transportation and public utilities. Motor vehicle-related injuries, however, also occur more frequently than expected, in agriculture, forestry and fishing, mining and quarrying, wholesale trade, finance, insurance and real estate, and service.

Occupation

Looking at occupational data gives an understanding of who sustains the greatest risk of motor vehicle-related injury. Table D-2 shows, for selected occupations, the percent of the total work injuries for each occupation that were motor vehicle-related. The total number of workers in each occupation is also shown so as to assess the relative importance of each occupation as a contributor to the motor vehicle-related problem. The examples listed in Table D-2 show more than ten percent of the injuries in those occupations were due to motor vehicle accidents.

TABLE D-2

PERCENT OF WORK INJURIES DUE TO MOTOR VEHICLE ACCIDENTS AND EMPLOYMENT
Selected Occupations, 1981

Occupation	Percent of Injuries due to Motor Vehicles	Employment
Total	2.5	98,313,000
Professional, technical and kindred workers	3.5	16,055,000
Accountants	10.8	1,096,000
Electrical engineers	10.5	370,000
Lawyers	20.0	548,000
Geologists	15.2	n.a.
Operations and systems researchers	10.7	196,000
Clergy	10.5	277,000
Social workers	10.7	383,000
Editors and reporters	25.9	202,000
Public relations and publicity writers	14.9	121,000
Managers and administrators, except farm	5.1	11,315,000
Assessors, controllers, treasurers, local public administrators	22.1	n.a.
Bank officers, financial managers	10.1	680,000
Construction inspectors, public administrators	13.2	n.a.
Inspectors, except construction, public administrators	14.7	108,000
Officials and administrators, public administrators	11.5	469,000
Officials of lodges, societies, unions	16.5	116,000
Sales managers, except retail trade	18.7	367,000
Salesworkers	6.8	6,291,000
Advertising agents, salespersons	20.6	126,000
Insurance agents, brokers, underwriters	20.6	584,000
Newspaper carriers and vendors	17.0	111,000
Real estate agents and brokers	17.1	546,000
Sales representatives, manufacturing industries	25.9	410,000
Sales representatives, wholesale trade	23.0	951,000
Sales persons (except clerks), retail trade	12.9	514,000
Sales persons of services and construction	17.6	237,000
Clerical and kindred workers	2.5	18,187,000
Insurance adjusters, examiners, and investigators	19.1	186,000
Messengers, office helpers	24.5	94,000
Craftsmen and kindred workers	1.3	12,397,000
Data processing machine repair personnel	13.7	97,000
Office machine repair personnel	13.0	73,000
Operatives, except transport	0.4	10,316,000
Transport equipment operatives	12.4	3,411,000
Bus drivers	23.2	355,000
Taxi drivers, chauffeurs	36.1	161,000
Truck drivers	13.0	1,843,000
Laborers, except farm	1.1	4,469,000
Farmers and farm managers	6.1	1,477,000
Farm laborers and foremen	2.2	1,235,000

(Listing continues on page 270.)

TABLE D-2—concluded

PERCENT OF WORK INJURIES DUE TO MOTOR VEHICLE ACCIDENTS AND EMPLOYMENT
Selected Occupations, 1981

Occupation	Percent of Injuries due to Motor Vehicles	Employment
Service workers, except private household . . .	2.1	12,136,000
Policemen and detectives	14.6	503,000
Sheriffs and bailiffs	11.7	69,000
Private household workers	3.9	1,024,000

Source: Bureau of Labor Statistics, Supplementary Data System, 1981, cases involving disability, data from 16 states. Bureau of Labor Statistics, *Employment and Earnings, 29* (1), p. 165-166, "Employed persons by detailed occupation, sex, and race," Household data, annual averages.
n.a. = not available

For all occupations together in the 16 states reporting these data, 2.5 percent of the injuries were motor vehicle-related. The greatest percentage was for taxi drivers and chauffeurs, 36.1 percent, followed by editors and reporters and sales representatives in manufacturing industries, both at 25.9 percent.

As a group, sales workers are second only to transport equipment operatives in the importance of motor vehicle accidents as a producer of work injuries, and the number of workers at risk just in the eight sales occupations listed in Table D-2 (3,479,000) exceeds the total number of transport equipment operatives.

Type of motor vehicle accident

Two-fifths of the work-related motor vehicle accidents were noncollision, or single-vehicle, accidents as shown in Table D-3. Two-vehicle collisions were mostly with both vehicles in motion, usually at intersections.

Unfortunately, the way the collision-type categories are defined in the SDS follows ANSI Z16.2, Appendix A1.4, which does not allow valid comparisons with statistics compiled from police accident reports because the latter are classified in accordance with ANSI D16.1.

Source of injury

The vehicle was the source of injury in 99.0 percent of the injuries due to motor vehicle accidents.

TABLE D-3

TYPE OF MOTOR VEHICLE ACCIDENT

Accident Type	Percent of Injuries
All types	100.0
Both vehicles in motion, collision or sideswipe	37.4
Oncoming vehicle	6.2
Vehicles moving in same direction	14.9
Vehicles moving in intersection	16.4
Standing vehicle or stationary object, collision or sideswipe	21.8
Standing vehicle or object in roadway	3.9
Standing vehicle or object at side of road	5.1
Struck by another vehicle while standing in roadway	11.5
Struck by another vehicle while standing off roadway	1.3
Noncollision accidents	40.8
Overturned	13.5
Ran off roadway	11.0
Sudden start or stop	4.7
Other noncollision	11.6

Source: Bureau of Labor Statistics, Supplementary Data System, 1981, cases involving disability, data from 17 states.

Nature of injury

The most common kinds of injuries resulting from work-related motor vehicle accidents were sprains and strains (34.5 percent of the total), fractures (14.9 percent), contusions, crushings, bruises (13.6 percent), multiple injuries (21.0 percent), and cuts, lacerations, punctures (8.3 percent). Together these five categories account for 92.3 percent of all motor vehicle-related injuries. For comparison sprains and strains make up 43.2 percent of *all* work injuries reported, but multiple injuries account for only 2.2 percent of the total.

Costs

The average cost of a work injury in 10 states reporting closed cases in the SDS was $4,494 (in 1985 dollars). This was composed of $3,490 in indemnity compensation and $1,004 in medical expenses. Motor vehicle accidents, on the other hand, resulted in $7,231 in indemnity payments and $1,943 in medical expenses for a total of $9,174—more than twice the average. By comparison, the most costly type of accident was aircraft accidents at $36,895; $22,779 in indemnity and $14,116 in medical expenses.

For these 10 states, motor vehicle-accident-related injuries accounted for 2.5 percent of the total cases but 5.2 percent of the total payments.

Appendix E

Bibliography and Additional References

No single book or reference source can provide all the information that someone involved in motor fleet safety requires, especially in an individual's area of specialization where more in-depth information is needed. Therefore, the following bibliography has been carefully selected to provide a balanced resource.

Because available information in this field is expanding rapidly, agencies, organizations, and societies that promulgate regulations and publish standards, as well as those that collect and share their specialized knowledge, are listed and described.

Books, Manuals, and Standards

American National Standards Institute, 1430 Broadway, New York, N.Y. 10018.

Method of Recording Basic Facts Relating to Nature and Occurrence of Work Injuries, ANSI Z16.2-1962(R1969).

Method of Recording and Measuring the Off-the-Job Disabling Accidental Injury Experience of Employees, ANSI Z16.3 1973.

Method of Recording and Measuring Work Injury Experience, ANSI Z16.1-1967(R1973).

Motor Vehicle Traffic Accidents, Manual on Classification of, ANSI D16.1-1983.

Recordkeeping for Occupational Injuries and Illnesses, Uniform, ANSI Z16.4-1977.

Powered Industrial Trucks, ANSI/NFPA 505-1981.

Powered Industrial Trucks—Low Lift and High Lift Trucks, Safety Standard for, ANSI/ASME B56.1-1983.

Recording and Measuring Motor Vehicle Fleet Accident Experience and Passenger Accident Experience, Method, ANSI D15.1-1976.

American National Red Cross. *Standard First Aid and Personal Safety Manual,* 2nd ed. Washington, D.C.: American National Red Cross, 1979.

American Society of Safety Engineers, 1800 E. Oakton, Des Plaines, Ill. 60018.

Dictionary of Terms Used in the Safety Profession.
Photographic Techniques for Accident Investigation.
Profitable Risk Control.
Safety Law—A Legal Reference for the Safety Professional.

American Trucking Associations, Inc., 2200 Mill Road, Alexandria, Va. 22314.

ATA Hazardous Materials Tariff, 1983.
Bulletin Advisory Service (3 vols.), 1983.
Effective Truck Terminal Planning and Operations, 1980.
Fundamentals of Transporting Hazardous Materials, 1982.
Fundamentals of Transporting Hazardous Waste, 1980.
National Truck Driving Championship, 1986.

Association of American Railroads. *Loading, Blocking and Bracing of Freight in Closed Trailers for Trailer or Flat Bed Service, Suggested Methods for.* Washington, D.C.: Association of American Railroads.

Baker, J. S. *Traffic Accident Investigation Manual.* Chicago: Traffic Institute, 1975.

Kirk-Othmer Encyclopedia of Chemical Technology, 3rd ed. New York: Wiley Interscience, 1984.

National Committee for Motor Fleet Supervisor Training, *Motor Fleet Safety Supervision, Principles and Practices.* East Lansing, Mich.: National Committee for Motor Fleet Supervisor Training, 1983.

National Fire Protection Association, Batterymarch Park, Quincy, Mass. 02269.

Flammable and Combustible Liquids Code, NFPA 30.
Fire Prevention Code, NFPA 1.
Fire Protection Handbook, 15th ed., 1981.

Hazardous Chemical Data, NFPA 49.
Hazardous Materials Transportation Accidents, 1978.
Life Safety Code Handbook, 1981.
National Electrical Code Handbook, 1984.

National Safety Council, 444 N. Michigan Ave., Chicago, Ill. 60611.

Accident Facts. (Published annually.)
Accident Investigation . . . A New Approach.
Accident Prevention Manual for Industrial Operations, 8th ed.,
Administration and Programs volume.
Engineering and Technology volume.
Annual Directory of Safety Posters.
Chemical Hazard Fact Finder.
Driver and Home Safety Manual.
Fleet Accident Rates. (Published annually.)
Fundamentals of Industrial Hygiene, 2nd ed.
Industrial Noise and Hearing Conservation.
Introduction to Occupational Health and Safety.
Million Mile Club.
National Directory of Safety Films.
National Fleet Safety Contest.
Off-the-Job Safety Manual.
101 More Ideas That Worked.
Professional Way—Defensive Driving.
Safe Driver Award Program.
School Buses and Operations, Standards for.
Small Business Safety and Health Manual.
Small Fleet Guide.
Supervisors Guide to Human Relations.
Supervisors Safety Manual, 6th ed.
Talking About Safety.
Traffic and Transportation Catalog.

Olishifski, J. B., ed. *Fundamentals of Industrial Hygiene,* 2nd ed. Chicago: National Safety Council, 1979.

Peterson, Dan. *Techniques of Safety Management,* 2nd ed. New York: McGraw-Hill, 1978.

Private Truck Council of America. *Driver Trainer Manual.* Washington, D.C.: Private Truck Council of America, 1981.

Sax, N. Irving, and Benjamin Feiner. *Dangerous Properties of Industrial Materials,* 6th ed. New York: Van Nostrand-Reinhold Publishing Co., 1984.

U.S. Department of Labor, 200 Constitution Avenue NW., Washington, D.C. 20210.

Occupational Safety and Health Standards.
OSHA Compliance Guide, Volume 3.
OSHA Compliance Operations Manual.
OSHA Recordkeeping Requirements.
OSHA Job Hazard Analysis.

U.S. Department of Transportation, 400 Seventh Street SW., Washington, D.C. 20590.

Bureau of Motor Carrier Safety Regulations.
Hazardous Materials Emergency Response Guidebook.

U.S. Government Printing Office, North Capitol and H Streets NW., Washington, D.C. 20402.

Code of Federal Regulations:
Title 29—"Labor"
Title 40—"Protection of the Environment"
Title 49—"Transportation"

Periodicals and Newsletters

Commerce Clearing House. *Employment Safety and Health Guide.* Chicago: Commerce Clearing House, updated weekly.

National Safety Council, 444 N. Michigan Ave., Chicago, Ill. 60611.

Driver Letter. Bimonthly.
Family Safety and Health. Bimonthly.
Fleet Safety Newsletter—Motor Transportation. Bimonthly.
National Safety and Health News. Monthly.
OSHA Up To Date. Monthly.
Today's Supervisor. Monthly.
Traffic Safety. Bimonthly.
Safe Driver. Monthly.

Agencies, Organizations, and Societies

American Society of Safety Engineers (ASSE)
1800 E. Oakton St.
Des Plaines, Ill. 60018

The American Society of Safety Engineers is the only organization of individual safety professionals dedicated to the advancement of the safety profession and to the fostering of the well-being and professional development of its members.

American Society of Mechanical Engineers (ASME)
345 East 47th St.
New York, N.Y. 10017

This society, a professional mechanical engineers' organization, encourages research, prepares papers and publications, sponsors meetings for the dissemination of information, and develops standards and codes under the supervision of its policy board.

American Trucking Associations, Inc. (ATA)
2200 Mill Rd.
Alexandria, Va. 22314

The American Trucking Associations, Inc., offers guidance to the state trucking associations, and their councils of safety supervisors. They publish and distribute timely information to the motor fleet industry, and are responsible for rules and procedures used in state and national truck driving championships.

Department of Transportation (DOT)
400 Seventh Street SW.
Washington, D.C. 20590

The Department of Transportation establishes the nation's overall transportation policy. Under its umbrella, there are nine administrations, (including the Bureau of Motor Carrier Safety) whose jurisdiction includes highway planning, development, and construction; urban mass transit; railroads; aviation; and the safety of waterways, ports, highways, and oil and gas pipelines.

National Association of Fleet Administrators (NAFA)
120 Wood Avenue South
Iselin, N.J. 08830

The National Association of Fleet Administrators is an organization committed to helping expand the educational and professional horizons of the motor fleet industry. Its members are managers of fleets of cars and light trucks in both the public and private sectors.

National Committee for Fleet Supervisor Training (NCFST)
70 Kellogg Center
Michigan State University
East Lansing, Mich. 48824-1022

The membership of the National Committee for Motor Fleet Supervisor Training has for many years contributed immeasurably to the education of motor fleet supervisory management personnel.

National Institute for Occupational Safety and Health (NIOSH)
4676 Columbia Parkway
Cincinnati, Ohio 45226

The National Institute for Occupational Safety and Health (NIOSH) was established within the Department of Health and Human Services under the provisions of the OSHAct. NIOSH is the principal federal agency engaged in research, education, and training related to occupational safety and health.

Occupational Safety and Health Administration (OSHA)
200 Constitution Avenue NW.
Washington, D.C. 20210

The Occupational Safety and Health Administration (OSHA) came into existence officially on April 28, 1971, the date the William-Steiger Occupational Safety and Health Act became effective. This agency was created in the Department of Labor to discharge the Department's responsibilities under the Act.

Private Truck Council of America, Inc. (PTCA)
2022 P Street NW.
Washington, D.C. 20036

The Private Truck Council of America, Inc. (PTCA), is the only independent organization representing exclusively the interests of private truck operators.

Contests and Awards

The Golden Shoe Club
2001 Walton Rd.
P.O. Box 36
St. Louis, Mo. 63166

Awards are made to employees who have avoided serious injury because they were wearing safety shoes.

Million Mile Club
National Safety Council
444 N. Michigan Ave.
Chicago, Ill. 60611

Membership in the Million Mile is exclusive. Enrollment is open only to professional drivers who have achieved 1,000,000 miles (or 25,000 hours) of accident-free driving. Applications are accepted only from those firms that are members of the National Safety Council, Division of State and Local Safety Organizations, American Trucking Associations, Inc., or cosponsoring organizations of the National Fleet Safety Contest.

National Fleet Safety Contest
National Safety Council
444 N. Michigan Ave.
Chicago, Ill. 60611

An exciting nationwide competition, the National Fleet Safety Contest gives recognition to motor vehicle fleets with outstanding safety records. Fleets compete with other fleets of comparable size and operations. Only Council members (with fleet operations), government agencies, and military units are eligible to participate.

Safe Driver Award Program
National Safety Council
444 N. Michigan Ave.
Chicago, Ill. 60611

The Safe Driver Award Program is the recognized trademark of professional drivers who have proven their skill in avoiding traffic accidents. The more than six million drivers who have earned this award since 1930 have made it the preeminent award for professional safe driving performance.

Wise Owl Club
National Society to Prevent Blindness
79 Madison Ave.
New York, N.Y. 10016

Founded in 1947, this is the oldest of all such clubs. Membership is restricted to industrial employees and students who have saved their eyesight by wearing eye protection.

Index